Ox_____es

Oxford Paperback Reference

The most authoritative and up-to-date reference books for both students and the general reader.

*forthcoming

Oxford Dictionary of

Nicknames

ANDREW DELAHUNTY

OXFORD
UNIVERSITY PRESS

Great Clarendon Street, Oxford OX2 6DP

Oxford University Press is a department of the University of Oxford.
It furthers the University's objective of excellence in research, scholarship,
and education by publishing worldwide in

Oxford New York

Auckland Cape Town Dar es Salaam Hong Kong Karachi
Kuala Lumpur Madrid Melbourne Mexico City Nairobi
New Delhi Shanghai Taipei Toronto

With offices in

Argentina Austria Brazil Chile Czech Republic France Greece
Guatemala Hungary Italy Japan Poland Portugal Singapore
South Korea Switzerland Thailand Turkey Ukraine Vietnam

Oxford is a registered trade mark of Oxford University Press
in the UK and in certain other countries

Published in the United States
by Oxford University Press Inc., New York

British Library Cataloguing in Publication Data

Data available

Library of Congress Cataloging in Publication Data

Data available

Typeset in Minion and Argo
by SPI Publisher Services, Pondicherry, India
Printed in Great Britain by Clays Ltd, St Ives plc
Bungay, Suffolk

ISBN 0-19-860948-5 978-0-19-860948-3

1

Contents

Introduction

The *Oxford Dictionary of Nicknames* aims to identify and explain the origins of a wide range of nicknames applied to individual historical figures, politicians, sports people, actors, entertainers, and so on. Nicknames associated with many organizations and places are also included. It is hoped that this book will serve as a useful source of reference for those wanting to know more about particular nicknames and an enjoyably browsable read for anyone with a general interest in the who, what, and why of nicknaming.

The word *nickname* is recorded from late Middle English, and comes from *an eke name* (*eke* meaning 'addition') misinterpreted, by wrong division, as *a neke name*. A similar acquisition of an initial *n* occurred with *an ewt*, which became *a newt*. A nickname is a familiar or humorous, sometimes derogatory, name given to a specific person, place, or thing instead of or as well as the proper name. It commonly reflects some key aspect of an individual's physical appearance, personality, or achievement.

A nickname often pithily encapsulates some quality or attribute thought of as characteristic of a particular person. Names such as the MERRY MONARCH or TUMBLEDOWN DICK or the IRON DUKE may be thought of as capsule biographies, both summarizing an individual's reputation and personalizing a public or historical figure who might otherwise seem rather remote. While personal names are themselves neutral, many nicknames express some value judgement on the part of those who bestow or use them, sometimes even serving some propagandist function. The tone of a nickname may vary enormously: it may, for example, be affectionate, approbatory, respectful, scornful, scurrilous, derogatory, or vitriolic. The following pairs of nicknames illustrate this variety: BONNIE PRINCE CHARLIE and the YOUNG PRETENDER; GOOD QUEEN BESS and BLOODY MARY; the COMEBACK KID and SLICK WILLY; TRICKY DICK and HONEST ABE; the THUNDERER and the NEWS OF THE SCREWS; SUPERBRAT and the DON.

Nicknames also vary in their level of formality. There is clearly more of a sense of familiarity and approachability expressed in calling the British footballer Paul Gascoigne GAZZA than there is in referring to his celebrated predecessor Stanley Matthews as the WIZARD OF THE DRIBBLE. While the core of this dictionary is made up of such informal designations as KAISER BILL, TRICKY DICK, SATCHMO, and EDDIE THE EAGLE, they are to be found alongside those more formal-sounding epithets and sobriquets, such as the ATHENS OF THE NORTH, the FATHER OF MEDICINE, and the EMPRESS OF THE BLUES. Other honorifics of the *Catherine the Great* variety are also included, as are descriptive titles that have come to be used as legitimate historical designations, such as *Edward the Confessor*, the VENERABLE BEDE, and the BLACK PRINCE. A selection of names that originated as nicknames but have become fully established is included. Some figures are best known to us now by such adopted names, including BOTTICELLI, TINTORETTO, EL GRECO, CALIGULA, and EL CID.

A brief word on what the *Oxford Dictionary of Nicknames* does not include may be useful. The dictionary does not cover generic nicknames such as *Four-Eyes*, *Lofty*, and *Ginger*, nor racial or regional epithets such as *Kraut*, *Taffy*, and *Geordie*. Those inseparable surname-inspired nicknames of the *'Chalky' White* and *'Dusty' Miller* variety are similarly excluded. Nor are occupational nicknames such as *Chips*, *Sparks*, *Sawbones*, or *Bobby* dealt with here. Stage-names such as *Sting*, *Little Tich*, and *Big Daddy*, though some of these may have originated as nicknames, are generally excluded, as are pseudonyms such as *Saki* and *Boz*.

Various principles of nickname-coining may be identified from the entries in this dictionary. Punning nicknames are popular. So there are many nicknames that play on an individual's real name, such as the THORPEDO (Ian Thorpe), BATHING TOWEL (Lord Baden-Powell), and JESSYENORMOUS (Jessye Norman). Other nicknames, especially common in sport, cleverly depend on the person's surname being added in order to complete a punning phrase: TUGGA Waugh, CHARIOTS Offiah, SINGING Indurain. Some nicknames are slight alterations of a familiar phrase or title: ATTILA THE HEN, the PRINCE OF WAILS (and indeed the PRINCE OF WHALES), the LIZARD OF OZ.

Another common form of nickname incorporates some rhyming element. Some of the more memorable nicknames fall into this category: ELVIS THE PELVIS, HUNT THE SHUNT, YIFTER THE SHIFTER, the MUSCLES FROM BRUSSELS, FAMOUS SEAMUS, CLOCKWORK OCWIRK, STORMIN' NORMAN, ALLY PALLY, the NEWS OF THE SCREWS. Many nicknames have an alliterative form, which is likely to account for the ease with which they catch on. Among the many examples covered in this book are: the CRAFTY COCKNEY, DUGOUT DOUG, EDDIE THE EAGLE, the FORDHAM FLASH, FUM THE FOURTH, JOLLY JACK, LUCKY LINDY, the MERRY MONARCH, PADDY PANTSDOWN, PISTOL PETE, SOAPY SAM, the SULTAN OF SWAT, the WELSH WIZARD.

Nicknames often allude to some physical characteristic, especially stature. There are numerous *Bigs* and *Littles* to be found: the BIG FELLOW, BIG TRAIN, BIG JACK, the LITTLE GIANT, the LITTLE WONDER, LITTLE MO. Variations on this theme include LONG TOM, the AMBLING ALP, and MIGHTY MOUSE. Other references to physical appearance are evident in such sobriquets as the SCHNOZZOLA, OLD CONKY, YELLOW HAIR, the GOLDEN BEAR, FIERY FACE, the GREAT PROFILE, and THREE-FINGERED BROWN.

Many nicknames make reference to a placename. There is a long-established tradition of boxers' nicknames combining their birthplace with a suitably alliterative epithet: among these are the BROCKTON BLOCKBUSTER, the CLONES CYCLONE, the LIVERMORE LARRUPER, the MANASSA MAULER, and the TONYPANDY TERROR. Writers' sobriquets typically have a slightly different form: the BARD OF AVON, the NUN OF AMHERST, and (alluding not to their native town but to the place with which they are most closely associated), the SAGE OF CHELSEA, the WASP OF TWICKENHAM, the CURATE OF MEUDON. One of the most straightforward types of nickname is where a single word, referring to some accomplishment, issue, or expression for which an individual is most famous, is simply attached to the person's surname. Nicknames on this model include AUSTERITY CRIPPS, CAPABILITY BROWN, DICTIONARY JOHNSON, HELL BRUEGEL, HUDIBRAS BUTLER, MONK LEWIS, PROSPERITY ROBINSON, and STARVATION DUNDAS.

A nickname is often coined to express disapproval or derision, or sometimes real animosity. Among the many such derogatory sobriquets may be listed BLOODY BALFOUR and BLOODY MARY, the BUTCHER, SLICK WILLY, SUPERBRAT, HANOI

JANE. According to William Hazlitt, 'A nickname is the heaviest stone that the devil can throw at a man.' Occasionally a label that was first applied as an insult has been subsequently adopted by the person so described. Margaret Thatcher was happy to accept the title IRON LADY bestowed on her by the Soviet press. In the British army, the OLD CONTEMPTIBLES and the CHEESEMONGERS proudly embraced epithets that were originally intended as slurs.

As mentioned above, nicknames are widely variable in tone and formality. Many of the sobriquets included in these pages are rather formal titles expressing respect and admiration, celebrating some accomplishment, or honouring a person's legacy. Examples are: the APOSTLE OF FREE TRADE, the FATHER OF THE CONSTITUTION (along with many other 'Fathers' of such-and-such), the LION OF THE NORTH, the WIZARD OF THE DRIBBLE, the ACHILLES OF ENGLAND, the EMPRESS OF THE BLUES, the ANGELIC DOCTOR, the SHEPHERD OF THE OCEAN, the GREAT EMANCIPATOR. Some of these elaborate titles were originally coined as publicity billings: the MAN OF A THOUSAND FACES, the PRIME MINISTER OF MIRTH, the LAST OF THE RED HOT MOMMAS. Compare these with the following selection, which are much less formal, whether affectionate or derogatory: BEEFY, BOZZY, BRANDY NAN, DORIS KARLOFF, GAZZA, GORBY, IKE, OUR 'ENERY, SHAGGER NORRIS, TUM-TUM, WOODBINE WILLIE.

Sometimes the same nickname has come to be shared by more than one referent. In some cases this is simply a matter of there being two or more rival claimants to a title, such as the FATHER OF THE SKYSCRAPER or the QUEEN OF CRIME. More intriguing is when the identical sobriquet has been applied to figures from completely different spheres. The QUEEN OF THE BLUES was both Elizabeth Montagu, who in the 18th century hosted a series of literary gatherings known as 'Blue Stocking' circles, and Dinah Washington, the blues singer. The British politician Peter Mandelson shares one nickname, the PRINCE OF DARKNESS, with the US late-night chat-show host Johnny Carson, and another, the SULTAN OF SPIN, with the Australian cricketer Shane Warne. The Irish statesman Eamon de Valera was known as the LONG FELLOW, as was the British champion jockey Lester Piggott. BUBBLES can be identified either as William James, British Admiral of the Fleet, or as Beverly Sills, the US operatic soprano.

Finally, there are some notable instances of one nickname begetting another. Once the Parliamentarians had derisively accorded Charles I the title the LAST MAN, that is, the last king of England, it was perhaps inevitable that the Royalists would defiantly dub his son Charles II the SON OF THE LAST MAN. Amelia Earhart, the US aviator, was acclaimed as LADY LINDY, linking her feats in the public imagination with those of her contemporary Charles Lindbergh, known as LUCKY LINDY. Eric Moussambani, the hopeless Equatorial Guinean swimmer at the 2000 Sydney Olympic Games, was instantly nicknamed ERIC THE EEL in the media. This was a deliberate echo of EDDIE THE EAGLE, Eddie Edwards, the similarly hopeless British ski-jumper at the 1988 Winter Olympics in Calgary.

To end this introduction to this book on names there are a few more names that need to be mentioned. I would like to express my thanks to Alysoun Owen, Jesse Ingham, Judy Pearsall, and Judith Wilson of Oxford University Press for seeing this book through from conception to publication. I am particularly grateful to Elizabeth Knowles for her many helpful comments on early drafts of much of the text. My thanks are also due to the copy editor Justine Cornish and the proofreader Sarah Couper for their careful attention to the text.

AD June 2003

Aa

The Accidental President   The title the *Accidental President*, or *His Accidency*, has been applied to those US vice presidents who have assumed the presidency on the the death in office of the incumbent. The first such president was John Tyler (1790–1862), who replaced William Henry Harrison. Others include Millard Fillmore (1800–74), who succeeded Zachary Taylor, and Andrew Johnson (1808–75), successor to Abraham Lincoln.

The Achilles of England   Arthur Wellesley, 1st Duke of Wellington (1769–1852), British soldier and Tory statesman, Prime Minister 1828–30 and 1834. He commanded the British forces in the Peninsular War (1808–14) and in 1815 defeated Napoleon at the Battle of Waterloo, finally ending the Napoleonic Wars. His success on the battlefield earned him the title the *Achilles of England*. In 1822 a colossal bronze statue of Achilles by Richard Westmacott (cast from captured French cannon) was erected in Hyde Park to commemorate Wellington's victories. It was the first public nude statue in England. ➤ See also *The* IRON *Duke*, OLD *Conky.*

Action Man   Charles, Prince of Wales (b.1948), eldest son of Elizabeth II and heir apparent. Before his marriage in 1981, Charles was widely referred to as *Action Man* in the newspapers. The prince, who had served in the Royal Navy from 1971 to 1976, was known for his pursuit of a variety of adventurous and sporting activities. Action Man is the tradename of a toy soldier figure. ➤ See also BRIAN.

The Addicks   Charlton Athletic football club. There are several theories that have been put forward to explain the London club's nickname *Addicks*. Most plausible is that *Addicks* is a corruption of *Athletic*. It has also been suggested that it refers to haddock, from a tradition that the fish used to be served as a supper to visiting teams.

The Addison of the North   Henry Mackenzie (1745–1831), Scottish lawyer and author. His writings were held to resemble those of the essayist Joseph Addison (1672–1719). In particular, Mackenzie's *The Man of Feeling* (1771), in which the quixotic hero is presented in a series of sentimental sketches, was thought to be reminiscent of Addison's de Coverley papers in the *Spectator*. The title was bestowed on Mackenzie by his compatriot Walter Scott.

The Admirable Crichton   James Crichton (1560–c.85), Scottish adventurer, swordsman, and scholar. A man of many accomplishments, he had mastered ten foreign languages by the age of 15, went on to serve with distinction in the French army, and later spent time at the Universities of Genoa, Venice, and Padua. The epithet traditionally applied to him can be traced back to Johnstone's *Heroes Scoti* (1603): '*Iacobus Critonius Clunius, Musarum pariter ac Martis alumnus, omnibus in studiis, ipsis etiam Italis admirabilis*'. It first appeared in English in Thomas

Urquhart's *Jewel* (1652) 'The admirable Crichton...did...present himself to epilogate this his almost extemporanean Comedie.' *The Admirable Crichton* was also the title of a play by James Barrie (1914), in which the model butler Crichton, shipwrecked on a desert island with the aristocratic family he serves, becomes the party's natural leader through his innate authority and ingenuity.

The Admirable Doctor   Roger Bacon (*c.*1214–94), English philosopher, scientist, and Franciscan friar. He was greatly interested in natural science, which he did not regard as contradicting his faith, and emphasized the need for an empirical approach to scientific study. Bacon also wrote on alchemy and has been credited with the discovery of the magnifying lens and, by some authorities, of gunpowder. Called the *Admirable Doctor* (also DOCTOR MIRABILIS and the WONDERFUL DOCTOR) because of his great learning, his *Opus Majus* (1266) is a compendium of all branches of knowledge.

The Adonis of Fifty   George, Prince Regent 1811–20 and later George IV (1762–1830). In March 1812 the *Morning Post* described the Prince Regent as 'an Adonis in Loveliness'. This prompted Leigh Hunt to write in the *Examiner*, 'This Adonis in loveliness is a corpulent man of fifty'. Hunt was prosecuted and sent to prison for two years. ➤ See also *The* FIRST *Gentleman in Europe*, FLORIZEL, FUM *the Fourth*, *The* PRINCE *of Whales*, PRINNY.

Afghan   Mark Edward Waugh (b.1965), Australian cricketer. Although his twin brother Steve made his Test debut in 1985–86, it was not until 1990–91 that Mark Waugh eventually played his first Test match for Australia, scoring 138 against England at Adelaide. During the period before he made his international debut, he acquired the nickname *Afghan* (or *Afghanistan*), 'the forgotten Waugh', in punning allusion to the Afghan War of the 1980s, when Soviet forces occupied Afghanistan. This conflict was sometimes dubbed 'the Forgotten War'. Waugh's other nickname is *Junior*, since he is the younger twin. ➤ See also TUGGA.

Air Jordan   Michael (Jeffrey) Jordan (b.1963), US basketball player. His nickname *Air Jordan* refers to his gravity-defying jumping ability and is the brand name of a Nike sports shoe which he endorses. He was also known as *His Airness*.

The Alexander of the North   Charles XII (also Karl XII) (1682–1718), king of Sweden (1697–1718). He embarked on the Great Northern War against Denmark, Poland, and Russia, in which he won a succession of victories, earning himself the title *Alexander of the North*. His attempt to invade Russia in 1709, however, ended in the crushing defeat of his army at Poltava. James Thomson in *The Seasons* (1744) refers to 'The frantic Alexander of the North'.

Alligator Alley   The west-east section of the Tamiami Trail (US 41) in the US state of Florida, which runs from Tampa to Miami. It takes its nickname *Alligator Alley* from the abundance of alligators that inhabit the Everglades.

All Souls' Parish Magazine   *The Times* newspaper. It was known as *All Souls' Parish Magazine* during the 1920s and 30s, because the editor G. G. Dawson, a fellow of All Souls College, Oxford, and some of his associates, also fellows of the college, would often meet there to discuss editorial policy. ➤ See also *The* THUNDERER.

Ally Pally   Alexandra Palace, in Muswell Hill, North London. Built in 1873 and originally designed as an exhibition centre, Alexandra Palace was used from 1936 on as the first headquarters of BBC television. The familiar nickname *Ally Pally* dates from around this time. ➤ See also *The* TRIPE *Shop*.

The Almighty Nose   Oliver Cromwell (1599–1658), English general and statesman. He was the driving force in the revolutionary opposition to Charles I in the English Civil War, and led the Parliamentary army. He became Lord Protector of the Commonwealth 1653–58. A number of contemporary epithets allude to Cromwell's large nose, including the *Almighty Nose*, the *Nose Almighty*, and NOSEY. ➤ See also COPPER *Nose*, CRUM-HELL, IRONSIDES, KING *Oliver*, OLD *Noll*.

The Aloha State   The US state of Hawaii. *Aloha* (meaning 'love') is a Hawaiian word used in greeting or parting from someone.

The Ambling Alp   Primo Carnera (1906–67), Italian boxer. A man-mountain at 6ft 5in tall and weighing 260lb, Carnera rose from circus strongman to world heavy-weight champion 1933–34. Usually nicknamed the *Ambling Alp*, he was also known as the *Italian Alp* and *Da Preem*. He later gave up boxing to become a professional wrestler.

The American Caesar   Two US generals have been called the *American Caesar*, Ulysses S. Grant (1822–85) and Douglas MacArthur (1880–1964). Grant was Supreme Commander of the Unionist armies during the American Civil War. As the 18th President of the US 1869–77, he presided over an administration marked by corruption, financial scandal, and partisan politics. The nickname derived not from his military prowess, but from his political opponents' concerns that he was con-sidering running for a third term. During the Second World War, MacArthur was in command of the US forces in the Far East and subsequently of the Allied Forces in the south-west Pacific. He was later put in charge of UN military forces during the Korean War but clashed with President Truman, who relieved him of his command in 1951. MacArthur's reputation as a military commander won him the sobriquet the American Caesar from his admirers. ➤ See also *The* BUTCHER, DUGOUT *Doug*, UNCONDITIONAL *Surrender Grant*.

The American Cincinnatus   George Washington (1732–99), US soldier and statesman, 1st President of the US 1789–97. ➤ See *The* CINCINNATUS *of the West*.

The American Fabius   George Washington (1732–99), US soldier and statesman, 1st President of the US 1789–97. During the American War of Independence (1775–83), Washington, as Commander-in-Chief, adopted delaying tactics against the British and avoided direct conflict in pitched battle. Similar tactics were employed by the Roman general Fabius (d.203 BC), known as Fabius Cunctator (meaning 'delayer'). After Hannibal's defeat of the Roman army at Cannae in 216 BC, Fabius successfully pursued a strategy of harassing the Carthaginian invaders in order to wear them down. ➤ See also *The* CINCINNATUS *of the West*, *The* FATHER *of his Country*.

The American Louis-Philippe   Millard Fillmore (1800–74), US Whig statesman, 13th President of the US 1850–53. Fillmore was said to resemble Louis Philippe (1773–1850), king of France 1830–48, both in his physical appearance and in his aristocratic manner. ➤ See also *The* ACCIDENTAL *President*.

The American Workhouse   Park Lane Hotel, London. The hotel was dubbed the *American Workhouse* by London taxi drivers, ironically referring to the palatial luxury enjoyed by wealthy American tourists staying there. The term dates from the early 20th century.

America's Boyfriend   Buddy Rogers (Charles Rogers) (1904–99), US film actor. He was a matinée idol in the 1920s and dubbed *America's Boyfriend*, so it was appropriate that in 1937 he married the actress Mary Pickford, known as *America's Sweetheart*.

America's Sweetheart   Mary Pickford (born Gladys Mary Smith) (1893–1979), Canadian-born film actress. She was one of the first stars of silent films, usually playing the innocent but plucky young heroine in such films as *Rebecca of Sunnybrook Farm* (1917), *Pollyanna* (1920), and *Tess of the Storm Country* (1932). For two decades she was the most popular screen star in the world, earning the sobriquet *America's Sweetheart* and later THE WORLD'S SWEETHEART. In 1919 she co-founded the film production company United Artists with Charlie Chaplin, D. W. Griffith, and her husband Douglas Fairbanks. An astute businesswoman, she became one of America's richest women. According to Sam Goldwyn: 'It took longer to make one of Mary's contracts than it did to make one of Mary's pictures'.

Anacreon Moore   Thomas Moore (1779–1852), Irish poet and musician who wrote patriotic and nostalgic Irish songs including 'The Harp that once through Tara's Halls' and 'The Minstrel Boy'. In 1800 he published a translation of the 'Odes of Anacreon' into English verse. The Greek lyric poet Anacreon (*c.*570–478 BC) is most famous for his poems written in celebration of love and wine. Moore also wrote poems of his own in the style of the Greek poet. His friend Byron (whose biography Moore wrote) refers to him as *Anacreon Moore*.

The Anatomic Bomb   Silvana Pampanini (b.1927), a voluptuous Italian film actress of the 1950s, who was a former Miss Italy. She was promoted as the *Anatomic Bomb*, an ingenious conflation of *anatomy* and *atomic bomb*.

The Angelic Doctor   St Thomas Aquinas (1225–74), Italian philosopher, theologian, and Dominican friar, regarded as the greatest figure of scholasticism. His achievements include introducing the work of Aristotle to Christian western Europe, and the influence of his teachings on the doctrines of the Roman Catholic Church was enormous. His major work *Summa Theologiae* (1267–73) is a systematic exposition of Christian theology. He was known as the *Angelic Doctor* (or *Doctor Angelicus*) because of the sublime quality of his teaching. ➤ See also *The* DUMB *Ox*.

The Angel of Death   Josef Mengele (1911–79), Nazi doctor who worked at the Auschwitz concentration camp (1943–45). He was known as the *Angel of Death* because of the barbaric 'medical experiments' he conducted and the power over life and death he wielded. It is thought that he was responsible for the deaths of 400 000 people.

The Animated Meringue   (Mary) Barbara (Hamilton) Cartland (1901–2000), English writer. She was a prolific author of light romantic fiction, whose popular romances include *Bride to a Brigand* (1983) and *A Secret Passage to Love* (1992). She habitually wore full, pink chiffon dresses and heavy make-up, earning the nickname the *Animated Meringue* from the journalist Arthur Marshall.

Anne of the Thousand Days   Anne Boleyn (1507–36), second wife of Henry VIII and mother of Elizabeth I. It was Henry's determination to divorce Catherine of Aragon in order to marry Anne Boleyn that led to England's break with the Roman Catholic Church and brought about the English Reformation. Anne's failure to produce a male heir caused her to fall from favour and she was eventually executed for alleged adultery and incest. She became known as *Anne of the Thousand Days* because of the length of time she was Henry's queen. This is the title of a film about her, made in 1969. ➤ See also *The* GREAT *Whore*.

The Apache State   The US state of Arizona. The Apache are an American Indian people living chiefly in Arizona and New Mexico. ➤ See also *The* AZTEC *State*, *The* GRAND *Canyon State*, *The* VALENTINE *State*.

The Apostle of Free Trade   Richard Cobden (1804–65), English political reformer, one of the leading spokesmen of the free-trade movement in Britain. A co-founder with John Bright of the Anti-Corn Law League in 1838, he campaigned for the repeal of the Corn Laws.

The Apostle of the Indies   St Francis Xavier (1506–52), Spanish Catholic missionary. He was one of the founders of the Jesuit order (1534). Known as the *Apostle of the Indies*, he spent the last eleven years of his life travelling to southern India, Ceylon (now Sri Lanka), Malacca, the Moluccas, and Japan, making thousands of converts. He died while on his way to China.

The Apostle of the Scottish Reformers   John Knox (*c*.1505–72), Scottish Protestant reformer. After studying under Calvin in Geneva, Knox returned to Scotland in 1559 to lead the Reformation there. He established the Presbyterian Church of Scotland (1560) and led opposition to the Catholic Mary, Queen of Scots when she returned to rule in her own right in 1561.

Apple Isle   Tasmania. Australians sometimes refer to the island as *Apple Isle* or *Apple Island*, because it is noted as an apple-growing region. ➤ See also *The* SPECK, TASSIE.

The Ariosto of the North   Walter Scott (1771–1832), Scottish novelist and poet. This nickname relates to Scott's early career as poet. His poetry was partly influenced by medieval Italian poetry, such as Ludovico Ariosto's *Orlando Furioso* (final version 1532), the greatest of the Italian romantic epics. In a stanza of Byron's *Childe Harold's Pilgrimage* (1812–18), the poet first describes the Italian poet Ariosto (1474–1533) as 'the southern Scott', going on to refer to Scott as 'the Ariosto of the North'. Both Ariosto and Scott 'sang ladye-love and war, romance and knightly worth'. ➤ See also *The* GREAT *Magician*, *The* GREAT *Unknown*.

Arkle   Derek William Randall (b.1951), English cricketer. Randall was an outstanding fielder, noted for the speed with which he covered the ground and the accuracy of his throwing. His Nottinghamshire teammates called him *Arkle*, after the famous racehorse, winner of the Cheltenham Gold Cup three years in a row (1964–66).

The Artful Dodger   Jack Dawkins, a character in Charles Dickens's novel *Oliver Twist* (1837–38), a senior member of Fagin's gang of child pickpockets: 'as he had a rather flighty and dissolute mode of conversing, and furthermore avowed that among his intimate friends he was better known by the *sobriquet* of "The artful Dodger", Oliver concluded that, being of a dissipated and careless turn, the moral precepts of his benefactor had hitherto been thrown away upon him.' In the novel he is generally referred to as the *Dodger*.

The Athens of America The US city of Boston, Massachusetts. In the 19th century the city gained the title the *Athens of America* because of its blossoming as a centre of cultural, literary, and educational activity. Boston's cultural institutions include the Museum of Fine Arts, the Symphony Orchestra, the Public Library, and the Athenaeum. Its educational institutions include Boston University and Harvard Medical School. The Greek city of Athens was an important cultural centre in the 5th century BC. ➤ See also *The* CRADLE *of Liberty*.

The Athens of the North The city of Edinburgh, Scotland, a flourishing cultural centre in the 18th and 19th centuries. The city was nicknamed the *Athens of the North* because of its academic and intellectual traditions, and the predominantly neoclassical style of architecture in its city centre. Prominent Edinburgh-based intellectual and literary figures included Adam Smith, David Hume, Robert Burns, Walter Scott, and Thomas Carlyle. ➤ See also AULD *Reekie*.

Attila the Hen Margaret (Hilda) Thatcher (b.1925), British Conservative stateswoman, Prime Minister 1979–90. Among her many nicknames was *Attila the Hen*. This humorous sobriquet, punning on Attila the Hun (406–53), alludes to Thatcher's authoritarian style of leadership. ➤ See also *The* BLESSED *Margaret*, *The* GROCER'S *Daughter*, *The* IRON *Lady*, *The* LEADERENE, MAGGIE, *The* MILK *Snatcher*, TINA.

The Auk Claude (John Eyre) Auchinleck (1884–1981), British Commander in the Second World War. He won the First Battle of El Alamein in 1942 and the following year he became Commander-in-Chief in India. Auchinleck was made a field marshal in 1946. He was universally known as the *Auk*, an army nickname that he had acquired before the war. Suggesting the name of the seabird, it is based on his surname.

Auld Reekie The city of Edinburgh, Scotland. Dating back to the late 18th century, the nickname originally applied only to the old-town part of Edinburgh, but later came to refer to the whole city. *Auld Reekie* literally means 'Old Smoky' and describes the smoky atmosphere produced by the city's many chimneys. It thus corresponds to terms such as the *Smoke* and the *Big Smoke* denoting other large cities. ➤ See also *The* ATHENS *of the North*.

Auntie The BBC (British Broadcasting Corporation). The nickname *Auntie*, dating from the advent of British commercial television in the 1950s, initially reflected the BBC's image as a somewhat prim, staid, and cosy institution in comparison with its new rival. ➤ See also *The* BEEB.

Austerity Cripps (Richard) Stafford Cripps (1889–1952), British Labour politician, Chancellor of the Exchequer 1947–50. As Chancellor, Cripps presided over Britain's postwar austerity programme, involving such measures as rationing and voluntary wage freezes. Together with his rather puritanical demeanour, these measures led him to become known as *Austerity Cripps*.

The Austrian Oak Arnold (Alois) Schwarzenegger (b.1947), Austrian-born US film actor. A former bodybuilder and Mr Universe, he became a huge star of the 1980s and 90s in such action films as *Terminator* (1984), *Total Recall* (1990), *Terminator 2* (1991), and *True Lies* (1994). His nickname the *Austrian Oak* alludes to his Austrian descent, his muscular physique, and his alleged woodenness as an actor. An Austrian pine is a species of tall European pine tree.

The Auto State The US state of Michigan. This state is where the city of Detroit, the centre of the US automobile industry, is situated. ➤ See also *The* GREAT *Lake State*, MOTOWN, *The* WOLVERINE *State*.

Avonian Willy William Shakespeare (1564–1616), English dramatist and poet, born in Stratford-upon-Avon in Warwickshire. This affectionate sobriquet for Shakespeare was coined by David Garrick (1717–79), the great Shakespearean actor. ➤ See also *The* BARD *of Avon*, *The* SWAN *of Avon*.

Awfully Weirdly Aubrey (Vincent) Beardsley (1872–98), English artist and illustrator, associated with art nouveau and the Aesthetic movement. He is chiefly known for his stylized black-and-white illustrations on grotesque, macabre, and erotic themes, such as those for Oscar Wilde's *Salome* (1894) and Pope's *The Rape of the Lock* (1896). His controversial work earned him the nicknames *Awfully Weirdly* and DAUBAWAY WEIRDSLEY, both plays on the artist's name.

The Aztec State The US state of Arizona. It is so called because the remains of old Indian cultures were once believed to have been built by the Aztecs. ➤ See also *The* APACHE *State*, *The* GRAND *Canyon State*, *The* VALENTINE *State*.

Bb

Babe Oliver Norvell Hardy (1892–1957), US film actor, remembered for his successful comedy partnership with Stan Laurel (1890–1965). They made their screen debut together in *A Lucky Dog* (1917) and the duo went on to appear in 100 shorts and feature films, including *Sons of the Desert* (1933) and *A Chump at Oxford* (1940). The rotund Hardy acquired his nickname while working for the Florida-based Lubin studio. According to his own account, he used to get his hair cut by a local Italian barber: 'Well, he took a great fancy to me and every time after he'd finish shaving me, he'd rub powder into my face and pat my cheeks and say, "Nice-a bab-ee, Nice-a bab-ee"'. His friends teased him about this and started to call him *Baby*, later shortened to *Babe*.

The Babe Babe (George Herman) Ruth (1895–1948), US baseball player. Often regarded as the greatest player of all time, he played for the Boston Red Sox (1914–19) and the New York Yankees (1919–35). A prodigious hitter, he set a record of 714 home runs which remained unbroken until 1974. He attracted huge numbers of baseball fans to the newly-built Yankee Stadium, which became known as 'The House that Ruth Built'. His famous nickname *Babe* was bestowed on him by teammates when he was 19. ➤ See also *The* BAMBINO, *The* SULTAN *of Swat*.

Baby Doc Jean-Claude Duvalier (b.1951), President of Haiti 1971–86. At the age of 19 he became dictator of Haiti on the death of his father François Duvalier (known as *Papa Doc*). The son's inevitable nickname was *Baby Doc*. He presided over a slightly more enlightened regime than his father but still refused to tolerate any political opposition. In 1986 a mass uprising forced Jean-Claude to flee the country. ➤ See also PAPA *Doc*.

Baby Face Nelson Lester Nelson Gillis (1908–34), US bank robber and gangland killer who worked with both Al Capone and John Dillinger. Although he adopted the name George Nelson, his youthful looks, which belied his violent personality, led to him being known as *Baby Face Nelson*, a nickname he intensely disliked. He was killed in a shoot-out with FBI agents in 1934. ➤ See also PRETTY *Boy Floyd*.

The Bachelor President James Buchanan (1791–1868), US Democratic statesman, 15th President of the US 1857–61. Buchanan is the only president who remained a bachelor all his life. ➤ See also *The* SAGE *of Wheatland*.

The Backbone of England The Pennines, a range of hills in northern England, extending approximately 240 km (150 miles) from the Cheviot Hills near the Scottish border southwards to the Peak District in Derbyshire.

The Backbone of Italy The Apennines, a mountain range running 1 400 km (880 miles) down the entire length of Italy, from the north-west to the southern tip of the peninsula.

The Backbone of North America The Rocky Mountains (or Rockies), the chief mountain system of North America, extending more than 4 800 km (3 000 miles) from the US–Mexico border to the Yukon Territory of northern Canada. It separates the Great Plains from the Pacific coast and forms the Continental Divide.

The Badger State The US state of Wisconsin. Inhabitants of Wisconsin are known as Badgers, perhaps because early 19th-century lead miners lived in caves in the hillside that were thought to resemble badger burrows. Wisconsin's nickname is thus the *Badger State* and the badger is its official state animal.

The Baggies West Bromwich Albion football club. The Midlands club's nickname the *Baggies* derives from the baggy working clothes worn by supporters from the local ironworks in the early years of the club. ➤ See also *The* THROSTLES.

Baillie Vass Alec Douglas-Home (1903–95), British Conservative statesman, Prime Minister 1963–64. Douglas-Home was dubbed *Baillie Vass* (or the *Baillie*) by the satirical magazine *Private Eye*, after the *Aberdeen Evening Express* had printed photographs of the Prime Minister and a local official with the picture captions transposed. The magazine ironically pledged support for the Conservatives with the slogan 'The Baillie will no fail ye!'

The Baker Louis XVI (1754–93), grandson and successor of Louis XV, king of France 1774–93. He acquired the nickname the *Baker* after he and his wife Marie Antoinette (the *Baker's Wife*) gave bread to the starving mob at Versailles on 6 October 1789.

The Baker's Wife Marie Antoinette (1755–93), French queen, wife of Louis XVI. ➤ See *The* BAKER. ➤ See also MADAME *Veto*.

Le Balafré François, Duc de Guise (1519–63), French soldier and politician. He became known as *Le Balafré* (meaning 'the Scarred') after the Siege of Boulogne (1545) during which he received a wound from a sword that left a scar on his face.

The Bald Eagle Jim Smith (b.1940), English football manager. Affectionately known as the *Bald Eagle* because of his lack of hair, Smith has managed a succession of clubs including Oxford United, Queen's Park Rangers, Newcastle United, and Derby County.

Baldilocks Gerald (Bernard) Kaufman (b.1930), British Labour politician. The nickname *Baldilocks*, a mocking variation on Goldilocks, was coined for the bald politician by the satirical magazine *Private Eye*.

Bambi Tony Blair (b.1953), British Labour politician, Prime Minister from 1997. When he became leader of the Labour Party in 1994, his relative youth and inexperience led the British press initially to give him the nickname *Bambi*, after the young deer in Felix Salten's story for children (1923). Blair was soon being criticized for an authoritarian style of leadership, causing him to remark to a party conference that he seemed to have gone from Bambi to Stalin in one leap. ➤ See also THUMPER.

The Bambino Babe (George Herman) Ruth (1895–1948), US baseball player. Based on his famous nickname *Babe*, the alternative *Bambino* was conferred on him by Italian-American baseball fans. ➤ See also *The* BABE, *The* SULTAN *of Swat*.

Barbarossa Frederick I (*c*.1123–90), king of Germany and Holy Roman emperor 1152–90. On his accession, he made a sustained attempt to subdue Italy and the papacy, but was eventually defeated at the Battle of Legnano in 1176. He was known as *Barbarossa* which means 'Redbeard'.

The Barbary Coast The Tenderloin waterfront district of San Francisco, regarded as the main centre for vice, gambling, and corruption. It was notorious in the 1850s. The original *Barbary Coast* was the Mediterranean coast of North Africa from Morocco to Egypt, noted between the 16th and 18th centuries as a haunt of pirates. The word *Barbary* derives from the Berbers, a term applied by ancient Arab geographers to the natives of north Africa west and south of Egypt. It is related to the word *barbarian*, from the Greek *barbaros*, 'foreign'.

The Bard of Avon William Shakespeare (1564–1616), English dramatist and poet, born in Stratford-upon-Avon in Warwickshire. This name for Shakespeare is recorded from the late 19th century. ➤ See also AVONIAN *Willy, The* SWAN *of Avon.*

The Bard of Ayrshire Robert Burns (1759–96), Scottish poet, born at Alloway in Ayrshire, the son of a cottar and himself a farm labourer until the age of 27. In 1786 he published his *Poems, Chiefly in the Scottish Dialect*, a collection of narrative poems and songs written in the Scottish vernacular, which launched his career as a poet. Given that Burns is regarded as Scotland's national poet, this nickname appears to be a direct echo of Shakespeare's *Bard of Avon*.

The Bard of Twickenham Alexander Pope (1688–1744), English poet and satirist, a major figure of Augustan literature, famous for his caustic wit and metrical skill, in particular his use of the heroic couplet. He gained financial independence following the success of his translations of the *Iliad* (1715–20), and later the *Odyssey* (1725–26); after the publication of the first parts of the former Pope was able to buy in 1719 the lease of a house at Twickenham, where he spent the remainder of his life. Keenly interested in horticulture and landscape gardening, he devoted a good deal of his time to his garden and the shell-lined grotto he built for himself there. Pope is buried in Twickenham church. The acerbic poet was also known as the *Wasp of Twickenham*.

Barnacle Trevor Edward Bailey (b.1923), English cricketer, who played for Essex and England. An outstanding all-rounder of the 1950s, he was known for his obdurate deployment of the forward defensive stroke. His tenacious refusal as a batsman to be removed from the crease, no matter how slowly he was scoring runs, earned him the nickname *Barnacle*. ➤ See also *The* BOIL.

Bart's St Bartholomew's Hospital, the oldest hospital in London on its original site (founded in 1123), whose famous medical college was founded in 1662. It is familiarly known as *Bart's*.

Basil the Bulgar-Slayer Basil II (*c*.958–1025), Byzantine emperor (963–1025). A formidable military commander, he inflicted heavy defeats on the Bulgarians, hence his nickname *Bulgaroctonos* or *Bulgar-Slayer*. In 1014, after a victory in the Belasica Mountains, he ordered 14 000 prisoners to be blinded.

The Bastard William I (*c*.1027–87), the first Norman king of England, reigned 1066–87. William was the illegitimate son of Robert, Duke of Normandy (noted for his cruelty and bravery and known as *Robert the Devil*) by Arlette, daughter of a tanner of Falaise. He succeeded to the dukedom in 1035. He was known by contemporary writers as *William the Bastard* because of his parentage. ➤ See also *The* CONQUEROR.

Bathing Towel Robert (Stephenson Smyth) Baden-Powell (1857–1941), 1st Baron Baden-Powell, English soldier and founder of the Boy Scout movement. Having become a national hero after his successful defence of Mafeking (1899–1900) in the Boer War, he founded the Boy Scout movement (later called the Scout Association) in 1908. His nickname *Bathing Towel*, playing on his double-barrelled surname, can be traced back to his Charterhouse schooldays.

The Battle-born State The US state of Nevada. On 31 October 1864 Nevada was admitted to the Union, at the height of the Civil War, hence its nickname the *Battle-born State*. ➤ See also *The* SAGEBRUSH *State*, *The* SILVER *State*.

The Bayou State The US state of Mississippi. The state has an abundance of bayous, marshy outlets of lakes or rivers. ➤ See also *The* MAGNOLIA *State*.

The Bays The 2nd Dragoon Guards, or Queen's Bays (now incorporated in the 1st Queen's Dragoon Guards), a regiment of the British army. The regiment originally rode only bay horses, a custom begun in 1767. Other cavalry regiments had black horses. ➤ See also *The* RUSTY *Buckles*.

The Bay State The US state of Massachusetts. Its nickname the *Bay State* is a reference to the early colony of Massachusetts Bay. After the Pilgrim Fathers founded Plymouth Colony in Massachusetts in 1620, another settlement—Massachusetts Bay Colony—was founded in Salem in 1628. ➤ See also *The* OLD *Colony*.

Bean Coleman Randolph Hawkins (1904–69), US jazz saxophonist. He played with the Fletcher Henderson band in the 1920s and 1930s and his huge-toned sound was influential in establishing the tenor saxophone as a jazz instrument. Although he came to be more generally known as HAWK, he was earlier given the nickname *Bean*, apparently in reference to his alleged meanness, as justified by his frequent remark 'I haven't a bean'. It has also been suggested that the name conveys the idea of Hawkins as a fertile source of musical creativity.

The Bear H. Norman Schwarzkopf (b.1935), US general. A large man with a volatile temper, Schwarzkopf was sometimes known in the army before the Gulf War as the *Bear*. ➤ See also STORMIN' *Norman*.

The Beard Monty Woolley (Edgar Montillion Woolley) (1888–1963), US film actor. A former Yale professor, the bearded Woolley became a film star in his fifties with his performance as the acerbic wit and radio celebrity Sheridan Whiteside in *The Man Who Came to Dinner* (1941).

The Beast of Belsen Josef Kramer (1906–45), German commandant of the Belsen concentration camp from December 1944, notorious for his cruelty. At the end of the Second World War he was tried before a British military tribunal and executed in November 1945.

The Beast of Bolsover Dennis Skinner (b.1932), Labour politician, MP for Bolsover in Derbyshire since 1970. Skinner is noted for his forthright left-wing views and abrasive manner. In the House of Commons he has a reputation for heckling other MPs and interrupting their speeches. His long-standing nickname the *Beast of Bolsover* was originally conferred on Skinner by parliamentary correspondents.

The Beast of Buchenwald   Ilse Koch (d.1967), wife of the commandant of the Nazi concentration camp at Buchenwald, in eastern Germany. Infamous for the atrocities she committed there, she was known as the *Beast of Buchenwald* or the *Bitch of Buchenwald.*

Beast 666   Aleister (Edward Alexander) Crowley (1875–1947), British occultist. He became a member of the Order of the Golden Dawn, a group of theosophists involved in black magic. Crowley himself claimed to be the Beast from the Book of Revelation, whose name is said to be numerologically represented by the number 666: 'Let him that hath understanding count the number of the beast: for it is the number of a man; and his number is Six hundred threescore and six' (Revelation 13:18). As well as *Beast 666* Crowley boasted the sobriquet the WICKEDEST MAN IN THE WORLD.

Beau Brummell   George Bryan Brummell (1778–1840), English dandy and socialite, known as *Beau Brummell.* A close friend of the Prince Regent (later George IV), Brummell was the arbiter of fashion in London society for the first decade and a half of the 19th century. He introduced a sense of moderation to male attire, with simply-cut clothes and trousers instead of breeches. The term *beau,* denoting a rich, fashionable young man, is recorded from the late 17th century and derives from French (literally 'handsome').

Beauclerc   Henry I (1068–1135), king of England, reigned 1100–35. The youngest son of William I, Henry was better educated than his brothers and able to read and write in Latin and English. He was posthumously given the sobriquet *Beauclerc* or *Beauclerk,* meaning 'fine scholar'. His scholarly abilities helped to make him an accomplished administrator. ➤ See also *The* LION *of Justice.*

Beau Geste   Michael Geste, a character in P. C. Wren's romantic adventure novel *Beau Geste* (1924). Geste is a young Englishman who runs away to join the French Foreign Legion to spare his family the distress of his being wrongfully accused of the theft of a priceless sapphire. His nickname *Beau Geste* is a pun on the French phrase *beau geste,* 'noble and generous act'.

Beau Nash   Richard Nash (1674–1761), Welsh dandy and gambler. As Master of Ceremonies in Bath from 1705, he established the city as the centre of fashionable society and was an arbiter of etiquette and dress in the early Georgian age. Nash brought an end to the custom of wearing swords and boots in public places. He was known as *Beau Nash* and the KING OF BATH. ➤ See also BEAU *Brummell.*

The Beaver   William Maxwell Aitken, Lord Beaverbrook (1879–1964), Canadian-born newspaper magnate. His staff on the British newspaper the *Daily Express* bestowed on him the nickname the *Beaver,* partly from his title (itself taken from the New Brunswick town in Canada where he had a home) and partly from his industriousness.

The Beaver State The US state of Oregon. Its nickname the *Beaver State* reflects the widespread identification between the timber-producing state and the tree-gnawing rodent, the official state animal.

Beckingham Palace The home of David and Victoria Beckham, a £2.5 million neo-Georgian mansion in Sawbridgeworth, Hertfordshire, noted for its extravagance. The humorous newspaper nickname *Beckingham Palace* is a blend of their surname and *Buckingham Palace*, the London residence of the British sovereign. ➤ See also BECKS.

Becks David Beckham (b.1975), English footballer. He has played for Manchester United, Real Madrid, and England, having been appointed captain of the national team in 2000. Outside the world of football, Beckham is famous as one half of the celebrity couple *Posh 'n' Becks*. He is married to Victoria Adams, formerly known as Posh Spice, in the pop group the Spice Girls. ➤ See also POSH.

The Beeb The BBC (British Broadcasting Corporation). The term *Beeb* dates from the 1960s and derives from the first part of the initials BBC, spoken aloud. ➤ See also AUNTIE.

Beefy Ian (Terence) Botham (b.1955), English cricketer, who played for Somerset, Worcestershire, Durham, and England. An outstanding all-rounder, he was the first player to complete a Test double of over 5 000 runs and 300 wickets. In 1978 he became the first player to score 100 runs and take eight wickets in one innings of a Test match. His nickname *Beefy* refers to his powerful build. ➤ See also GUY *the Gorilla*.

The Beehive State The US state of Utah. A conical beehive, surrounded by a swarm of bees, appears on the state flag. This is intended to symbolize the industriousness of the Mormon inhabitants of Utah. ➤ See also The LAND *of the Saints*.

Le Bègue Lambert, 12th-century priest of Liège. Nicknamed *Lambert le Bègue* ('Lambert the Stammerer'), he founded the Beguine order, a lay sisterhood in the Low Countries.

Bell-the-Cat Archibald Douglas, 5th Earl of Angus (*c.*1449–1514), Scottish nobleman. He earned his nickname *Bell-the-Cat* by using the phrase to indicate to the other Scottish nobles that he was ready to lead them in a revolt against King James III's low-born favourites, including the mason Richard Cochrane who had been created Earl of Mar. The expression, meaning 'to take the danger of a shared enterprise upon oneself', comes from the fable in which mice proposed hanging a bell around a cat's neck so as to be warned of its approach. 'But who will bell the cat?', said one of the mice.

Bendigo William Thompson (1811–80), English prizefighter. He was one of triplets who were nicknamed Shadrach, Mesach, and (in William's case) Abednego. The names were taken from those of three Jews in the Bible who survive being thrown into a 'fiery furnace'. Thompson's first name became corrupted to *Bendigo*. Thompson retired from the ring in 1851 to become an evangelist, earning the nickname the REFORMED PUGILIST. Bendigo is also the name of a former gold-mining town in the state of Victoria, Australia, named after a local boxer who had adopted Thompson's nickname.

Bend Or Hugh Richard Arthur Grosvenor, 2nd Duke of Westminster (1879–1958). His nickname *Bend Or* derives from the *azure à bend or* (blue shield with a diagonal gold bar) in the Grosvenor coat-of-arms. Bend Or was the name of a racehorse his grandfather owned which won the 1880 Derby.

The Bengal Tigers The 17th Foot (later the Royal Leicestershire Regiment), a regiment of the British army. The nickname derives from the tiger badge worn in recognition of the regiment's service in India (1804–23).

Bertie Edward VII (1841–1910), king of Great Britain and Ireland 1901–10. He was christened Albert Edward (after his father), and his mother Queen Victoria called him *Bertie*. ➤ See also EDWARD *the Caresser*, EDWARD *the Peacemaker*, TUM-TUM, *The* UNCLE *of Europe*.

Bess of Hardwick Elizabeth Talbot, Countess of Shrewsbury (1518–1608). She was responsible for the building of several great Elizabethan houses in Derbyshire and Nottinghamshire, notably Hardwick Hall, designed by the architect Robert Smythson. Accordingly she earned the sobriquets *Bess of Hardwick* and BUILDING BESS.

The Bhoys Celtic football club. The Glasgow club was formed from a group of Catholic Boys' Club sides, hence their nickname the *Bhoys*. The unusual spelling of the word is thought to have been intended to represent the Irish pronunciation.

The Bible Belt Those areas of the southern and middle western United States and western Canada where Protestant fundamentalism is widely practised. The term the *Bible Belt*, alluding to the abundance of itinerant Bible salesmen in the region, was coined by H. L. Mencken, about 1925.

The Big Apple New York City. Numerous suggestions have been put forward as to the origin of the epithet the *Big Apple*. It seems to have been first used in the 1920s, perhaps after the name of a Harlem night club used by jazz musicians. Another possible explanation is that the Spanish word for a block of buildings is *manzana*, which is also the word for an apple. Alternatively, the expression may be an allusion to the apple in the Garden of Eden, characterizing the city as a den of temptation and sin. Whatever its origin, the term was revived in the 1970s as part of a publicity campaign designed to improve the city's image, with the slogan 'New York City – the Big Apple'. ➤ See also *The* EMPIRE *City*, GOTHAM.

Big Bill[1] William Hale Thompson (1867–1944), US Republican politician, mayor of Chicago three times 1915–23. Known as *Big Bill*, or sometimes as *Bill the Builder*, Thompson was responsible for a major building and construction programme in the city. Less admirably, under his tenure Chicago also acquired a reputation for corruption, gangsterism, and lawlessness. The nickname Big Bill is also sometimes applied to William Howard Taft (1857–1930), US Republican statesman, 27th President of the US (1909–13).

Big Bill[2] William Tatem Tilden (1893–1953), US tennis player. Tilden dominated tennis in the 1920s, winning Wimbledon three times (1920–21, 1930) and the US Open seven times (1920–25, 1929). A tall man of 6ft 2ins, he was known as *Big Bill*, partly to distinguish him from his great rival Bill Johnston (1894–1946), 5ft 8½ ins tall and accordingly known as *Little Bill*.

Big Bird Joel Garner (b.1952), West Indian cricketer. A fast bowler, Garner was, at 6ft 8in, one of the tallest Test cricketers ever. His long arms meant that the ball would be hurtling towards the batsman from well over 8ft. His nickname *Big Bird* was borrowed from the character of the same name, an enormous yellow bird, in the US children's television programme *Sesame Street*.

Big Blue The computer company IBM (in full International Business Machines), founded in the the US in 1911 as the Computing-Tabulating-Recording Company. It was known as *Big Blue* at the time of its market dominance, from its blue and white logo and the blue covers on much of its early hardware.

Big Cat Clive Hubert Lloyd (b.1944), West Indian cricketer. His nickname *Big Cat* (or *Big C* or *Supercat*) referred to the lightning speed of his fielding and explosive power of his batting, both belied by his relaxed manner and loping walk. Lloyd played in 110 Test matches, captaining the West Indies in 74 of them. He scored 19 Test centuries, including ones in his debuts against both England and Australia.

Big Daddy Idi Amin (full name Idi Amin Dada) (1925–2003), Ugandan soldier and head of state 1971–79. His regime was notorious for its brutality and repression, during which Uganda's Asian population was expelled and thousands of his political opponents murdered. He gave himself the nickname *Big Daddy*. Amin was overthrown in 1979 and forced to flee the country.

The Big Easy[1] The US city of New Orleans, Louisiana. The epithet the *Big Easy* refers to the relaxed pace of life. ➤ See also CRESCENT *City*.

The Big Easy[2] Ernie (Theodore Ernest) Els (b.1969), South African golfer. Els won the US Open in 1994 and 1997 and the British Open in 2002. He took three successive World Match Play titles 1994–96. His nickname derives from his 6ft 3ins frame, his natural, apparently effortless swing, and his easygoing demeanour.

The Big Fellow Michael Collins (1890–1922), Irish nationalist leader and politician. A member of Parliament for Sinn Fein, he was one of the negotiators of the Anglo-Irish Treaty of 1921. He commanded the Irish Free State forces in the civil war and became Head of State but was assassinated ten days later. Collins, a powerfully built man, was affectionately known as the *Big Fellow* by his supporters.

Big-Hearted Arthur Arthur Askey (1900–82), British comedian. Askey applied the nickname *Big-Hearted Arthur* to himself in the first edition of his radio show *Band Waggon* in 1938. From then on the label was used as part of his billing.

Big Jack Jack Charlton (b.1935), English football player and manager. A robust defender, he played for Leeds United (1952–73) and England. Charlton managed a number of league clubs before becoming manager of the Republic of Ireland national team (1986–95), whom he took to the quarter-finals of the World Cup in 1990. In his playing days he was also known as the *Giraffe* because of his long neck.

Big Mac Mark McGwire (b.1963), US baseball player. In 1998, playing for the St Louis Cardinals, he hit 70 home runs in the season, setting a new record. His great rival Sammy Sosa hit 66 home runs for the Chicago Cubs in the same season.

Big O Roy Orbison (1936–88), US singer and composer. Initially a writer of country-music songs for other artists, Orbison established himself as a singer with the ballad 'Only the Lonely' (1960). His subsequent hits include 'Crying' (1961) and 'Oh, Pretty Woman' (1964), one of the best-selling singles of the 1960s.

Big Ron Ron Atkinson (b.1939), English football player and manager. As a player he made over 600 appearances for Oxford United. Known for his extrovert and flashy image, Atkinson has managed many clubs including West Bromwich Albion, Atlético Madrid, Manchester United, Sheffield Wednesday, and Aston Villa. Many other football managers have acquired the *Big* tag, including *Big Mal*, Malcolm Allison (b.1927) and *Big Joe*, Joe Royle (b.1949).

The Big Ship Warwick Windridge Armstrong (1879–1947), Australian cricketer. An accomplished all-rounder, he captained Australia in the 1920s, leading his team to eight successive wins against England (1920–21). Armstrong weighed 22 stone at the end of his career, hence his nickname the *Big Ship*.

Big Sky Joe Montana (b.1956), US American football player, one of the game's greatest quarterbacks. He played for the San Francisco 49ers in four of the team's winning Super Bowls (1982, 1985, 1989, 1990). He was inevitably known as *Big Sky* since one of the nicknames of the US state of Montana is the *Big Sky State*. Another of his nicknames was *Cool Joe*.

The Big Smoke The city of London, England, and other cities. Before clean-air legislation, a large city was characterized by the smoky, sooty atmosphere produced by its many chimneys. In Britain the terms *Smoke* or the *Big Smoke* are usually applied to London. In Australia, the terms can refer to any large city or town, but chiefly to Sydney or Melbourne. ➤ See also AULD *Reekie*, The CITY *of Masts*, The GREAT *Wen*.

Big T Jack Teagarden (born Weldon Leo Teagarden) (1905–64), US jazz trombonist and bandleader. The T stood not only for Teagarden but also for Texas, where he was born. His younger brother Charles, who played the trumpet, was known as *Little T*.

Big Train Walter (Perry) Johnson (1887–1946), US baseball player. A pitcher for the Washington Senators, he was one of the fastest throwers in the history of the game. Early in his 21-year career, he was given the name *Big Train* because of the velocity of his deliveries and his stature (6ft 1in (1.85m); 200lb (91kg)).

The Big Yin Billy Connolly (b.1942), Scottish comedian and actor. When performing as a stand-up comedian and singer in the 1980s, the former shipyard welder was affectionately known as the *Big Yin*, Scottish dialect for 'the Big One'. The term was used by Connolly himself in one of his routines to refer to Jesus Christ. In 1997 Connolly starred in the film *Mrs Brown*.

Billy Blue William Cornwallis (1744–1819), British admiral. The Blue Peter is a blue flag with a white square in the centre, raised on board a ship as a signal that it is ready to set sail, and Cornwallis habitually kept it flying when bad weather forced him to take shelter. He was accordingly known in the Royal Navy as *Billy Blue* or BLUE BILLY.

Billy the Kid William H. Bonney (born Henry McCarty) (1859–81), notorious US robber and murderer, who was involved in the Lincoln County Cattle War in New

Mexico. He is alleged to have committed his first murder at the age of 12, hence his nickname *Billy the Kid*. He was captured by Sheriff Pat Garrett in 1880, and was shot and killed by Garrett after he escaped.

The Biograph Girl Florence Lawrence (1886–1938), US film actress, a leading lady of early silent films. In the days when screen actors were largely anonymous, Lawrence became highly popular with audiences and was given the promotional title the *Biograph Girl*. She became one of Hollywood's first major stars. 'Biograph' was an early term for a cinema. It was also the name of D. W. Griffith's New York Studios (1903–10).

Bird Charlie Parker (1920–55), US jazz musician and composer, a brilliant improviser on the alto saxophone. With the trumpeter Dizzy Gillespie, Parker pioneered the bebop movement. The nickname *Bird* is itself an abbreviation of YARDBIRD, an earlier nickname. There seem to be several versions of the story of how Parker acquired his nickname, usually associated in some way with his fondness for eating chicken. According to one account, in the early 1940s his band were driving to a gig in Lincoln, Nebraska when one of their cars ran over a stray chicken in the road. Parker was keen to pick up the 'yardbird' so that they could cook it later for dinner. The name stuck and was later shortened to *Bird*. Another version offers YARDBIRD as a convoluted derivative of the name Charlie, via Yarlie, Yarl, and Yard. In 1988 Clint Eastwood directed a film biography of Parker with the title *Bird*.

The Birdman of Alcatraz Robert Franklin Stroud (1890–1963), US murderer and ornithologist. He served 54 years in prison for two murders, 28 of them at Alcatraz, a top-security federal prison on a rocky island in San Francisco Bay, California. In his prison cell he turned himself into a noted ornithologist, earning himself the sobriquet the *Birdman of Alcatraz*. A 1961 film of this title starred Burt Lancaster as Stroud.

The Birthplace of Aviation The US city of Dayton, Ohio. It was the home of the US aviation pioneers Wilbur (1867–1912) and Orville (1871–1948) Wright. Dayton remains a centre of aerospace research.

The Biscuitmen Reading football club. Their ground Elm Park was at one time owned by the biscuit manufacturer Huntley and Palmer. The *Biscuitmen* became the club's nickname until the company left Reading in 1974. A new nickname the *Royals* was then adopted, though the old one has not been forgotten by the fans. The factory was next door to Reading Gaol, which was itself informally known as the *Biscuit Factory*.

Biscuit Pants Lou Gehrig (1903–41), US baseball player. ➤ See *The* IRON *Horse*.

The Bishop Jess Yates (1918–93), British TV presenter and producer, and former cinema organist. In the 1970s he presented the long-running TV programme *Stars on Sunday*, in which guests from the world of show business sang hymns and read passages from the Bible. Yates was known as the *Bishop* because of the programme's religious perspective.

Bites Yer Legs Norman Hunter (b.1943), English footballer. A central defender with Leeds United and England in the 1960s and 1970s, Hunter had a reputation as a 'hard man', earning his intimidating nickname *Bites Yer Legs* from his ferocious tackling.

The Black Boy Charles II (1630–85), son of Charles I, king of England, Scotland, and Ireland 1660–85. Before coming to the throne he was sometimes known as the *Black Boy* because of his swarthy complexion. ➤ See also *The* MERRY *Monarch*, OLD *Rowley*, *The* SON *of the Last Man*.

The Black Cats Sunderland football club. When in 1997 the club moved from its Roker Park stadium to the Stadium of Light, a new nickname was sought to replace the club's former nickname the *Rokerites* (or *Rokermen*). In 2000, following a poll of fans, the *Black Cats* was chosen, with 48% of the votes cast. The name refers to a battery of guns positioned at the mouth of the River Wear in the 18th century. The runner-up was the *Mackems* (a local word for inhabitants of Sunderland), with 37% of the votes.

The Black Diamond Tom Cribb (1781–1848), English prizefighter, who enjoyed a long and popular reign as the champion of England. He fought two famous bouts with the American Tom Molineaux (1784–1818) in 1810 and 1811, both of which Cribb won. His nickname derived from his earlier career as a coal porter. 'Black diamond' is an informal term for coal, dating from the mid-19th century; coal consists of carbon, like diamonds, and is valuable as a fuel.

Black Dick Richard, Earl Howe (1726–99), British admiral of the fleet. He commanded the victorious British navy against the French revolutionary forces off Ushant at the Battle of the Glorious First of June (1 June 1794). His nickname *Black Dick* derives from his swarthy complexion.

The Black Douglas James Douglas (1286–1330), Scottish champion and supporter of Robert Bruce. He plundered many towns and villages in the north of England, becoming known by the English as the *Black Douglas*. According to Walter Scott in his *History of Scotland* (1829–30), 'It was said that the name of this indefatigable and successful chief had become so formidable that women used in the northern counties to still their froward children by threatening them with the Black Douglas'. After King Robert's death, Douglas set out on a pilgimage to take the Bruce's heart to the Holy Land to fulfil a vow made by the king to go on crusade. He was killed in battle on the way, fighting the Moors in Andalusia.

Black Jack[1] John Philip Kemble (1757–1823), English actor-manager, noted for his appearances in Shakespearean tragedy. He was manager of Drury Lane (1788–1803) and Covent Garden (1803–17) theatres. Kemble had long black hair and a swarthy complexion.

Black Jack[2] John Joseph Pershing (1860–1948), US general who was Commander-in-Chief of the American forces in Europe in the First World War. Before the war, Pershing commanded a black cavalry unit, hence his army nickname at the time, *Nigger Jack*. When he later became better known, this was modified to the more generally acceptable *Black Jack*. The name had previously been applied to John Alexander Logan (1826–86), a general in the American Civil War with a dark complexion and long black hair.

The Black Octopus Lev Yashin (1929–91), Russian footballer. Between 1954 and 1967 Yashin was the Soviet Union's first-choice goalkeeper. He was dubbed the *Black Octopus* (or sometimes the *Black Spider*) because he always wore an all-black strip and his astonishing agility and reflexes gave the impression that he had more than the usual number of limbs.

The Black Panther[1] Donald Neilson (b.1936), English murderer and kidnapper, who killed four people between 1974 and 1975. He disguised himself by wearing a black hood, hence the press nickname the *Black Panther*.

The Black Panther[2] Eusébio (Eusébio Ferreira da Silva) (b.1942), Mozambique-born Portuguese footballer. He signed for the Lisbon club Benfica in 1961, going on to score 316 goals in 294 league appearances. Eusébio won 64 international caps for Portugal, scoring 41 goals. In the 1966 World Cup he was the top scorer with nine goals. He was known as the *Black Panther* and also as the *New Pelé*.

The Black Pearl Pelé (born Edson Arantes do Nascimento) (b.1940), Brazilian footballer, regarded by many as the greatest player of all time. For most of his playing career his club side was Santos (1955–74). He made his debut for Brazil at the age of 17 and went on to appear for his country 111 times, scoring 97 goals. Pelé took part in four World Cup competitions, three of which Brazil won (1958, 1962, and 1970). Admired around the world, he was nicknamed the *Black Pearl*.

The Black Prince Edward, Prince of Wales and Duke of Cornwall (1330–76), eldest son of Edward III of England. He was a soldier of considerable ability, and was responsible for a number of English victories during the early years of the Hundred Years War, most notably that at Poitiers in 1356. The designation *Black Prince* appears to date from the mid-16th century. It is thought to refer either to the colour of the armour he wore (though there is no clear evidence that he did wear black armour) or to the savagery of some of his deeds.

Black Tom Thomas Wentworth, Lord Strafford (1593–1641), English statesman. He was known as *Black Tom* or *Black Tom Tyrant* from his despotic rule as Lord Lieutenant of Ireland and in particular from the belief that he was prepared in 1640 to bring Irish troops over to England for the use of Charles I. The nickname Black Tom was also given to the English Parliamentary general Thomas Fairfax (1612–71), in this case from his dark complexion.

The Black Watch The Royal Highland Regiment (an amalgamation of the 42nd and 73rd Foot), a regiment of the British army. In the early 18th century the term *Watch* was given to certain companies of irregular troops in the Highlands. *Black Watch* referred to some of these companies raised *c.*1729–30 to keep watch over the Scottish rebels. They wore a distinctive dark-coloured tartan. Its usage as a nickname continued until 1861, when the term became part of the official regimental title.

The Blades Sheffield United football club. Their nickname the *Blades* derives from Sheffield's traditional steel industry, especially cutlery.

The Blessed Margaret Margaret (Hilda) Thatcher (b.1925), British Conservative stateswoman, Prime Minister 1979–90. The nickname the *Blessed Margaret* was coined by the Conservative politician Norman St John Stevas (b.1929), Leader of the House of Commons (1979–81). ➤ See also ATTILA *the Hen*, *The* GROCER′S *Daughter*, *The* IRON *Lady*, *The* LEADERENE, MAGGIE, *The* MILK *Snatcher*, TINA.

Blighty England or Britain, thought of as home. The informal and often affectionate term *Blighty* was chiefly used by soldiers serving abroad in the First and Second World Wars. During the First World War, a wound which was serious enough for a soldier to be sent back home to Britain was itself known as a Blighty. The term originated among British soldiers serving in India, and is an Anglo-Indian alteration of Urdu *bilāyatī* 'foreign, European', from Arabic *wilāyat, wilāya* 'dominion, district'. ➤ See also *The* OLD *Dart*, PERFIDIOUS *Albion*.

The Blind Half-hundred The 50th Foot (later the 1st Battalion Royal West Kent), a regiment of the British army. During the regiment's service in the Egyptian campaign of 1801, many of its troops suffered from ophthalmia, inflammation of the eye which can cause blindness. ➤ See also *The* DIRTY *Half-hundred*.

The Blind Harper John Parry (d.1782), blind Welsh musician. His playing caused the poet Thomas Gray to say that his 'tunes of a thousand years old' had helped Gray to finish his poem 'The Bard' (1757). Parry published some of the earliest collections of Welsh music.

The Blind Poet John Milton (1608–74), English poet. Milton's eyes had been weak from childhood and from about 1644 his sight began to deteriorate markedly. By 1650 he had almost lost the use of one eye. He became completely blind in the winter of 1651–52, when he was 43. Milton's famous sonnet on the subject of his blindness, probably written about this time, begins: 'When I consider how my light is spent,/ Ere half my days, in this dark world and wide'. His three major poems *Paradise Lost* (1667, revised 1674), *Paradise Regained* (1671), and *Samson Agonistes* (1671), were all written after he had gone blind. Milton has also been called the *British Homer*, in allusion to another celebrated blind epic poet.

The Blonde Bombshell Jean Harlow (born Harlean Carpenter) (1911–37), US film actress. She was a wisecracking platinum blonde and sex symbol of the 1930s. Her films include *Hell's Angels* (1930), *Platinum Blonde* (1931), *Red Dust* (1932), *Dinner at Eight* (1933), and *Bombshell* (1933). Although originally applied to Harlow, the term 'blonde bombshell' can be used to describe any startlingly attractive blonde woman. ➤ See also PLATINUM *Blonde*.

Blood and Guts George Smith Patton (1885–1945), US general. In the Second World War, he commanded the 7th Army during the Sicilian campaign (1943) and the 3rd Army in the Normandy invasion (1944), advancing rapidly across France and into Germany. Patton was noted for his unpredictable temper and his arrogant, outspoken, and dominant personality. His soldiers called him *Blood and Guts* or *Old Blood and Guts*. ➤ See also TWO-GUN *Patton*.

Bloody Balfour Arthur James Balfour (1848–1930), British Conservative statesman, Prime Minister 1902–5. Earlier in his career Balfour was appointed Irish Chief Secretary. In 1887 the nationalist leader William O'Brien was prosecuted for conspiracy. Two protesting rioters were shot and killed by police at Mitchelstown, County Cork. Balfour was accordingly given the nickname *Bloody Balfour* by Irish nationalists.

The Bloody Butcher William Augustus, Duke of Cumberland (1721–65), English military commander and third son of George II. Cumberland gained great notoriety,

and his sobriquets the *Bloody Butcher* or the *Butcher of Culloden* or simply the
BUTCHER, for the severity of his suppression of the Jacobite clans in the aftermath of
his victory at the Battle of Culloden (1746). He supervised the systematic search for
and pursuit of Jacobite sympathizers, who were ruthlessly slaughtered by Cumberland's men. According to a letter Horace Walpole wrote at the time, when it was
proposed to make Cumberland a freeman of a city company, an alderman said,
'Then let it be of the Butchers.' ➤ See also *The* BUTCHER.

The Bloody Eleventh The 11th Foot, later the Devonshire Regiment, a regiment of
the British army. The name was given after the heavy casualties sustained by the
regiment in the Battle of Salamanca in the Peninsular Wars, 22 July 1812.

Bloody Mary Mary I, also known as Mary Tudor (1516–58), the daughter of Henry
VIII and Catherine of Aragon. She reigned as queen of England 1553–58. A devout
Roman Catholic, Mary set out to reverse the country's move towards Protestantism
which had occurred during the reign of her brother, Edward VI. She married Philip
II of Spain and restored papal supremacy in England. Her subsequent sanctioning of
the religious persecution of Protestants earned her the nickname *Bloody Mary*, a
term used during her lifetime. Under her reign heresy laws were re-introduced and
around 300 Protestants were burnt at the stake as heretics, including the bishops
Cranmer, Ridley, and Latimer.

Bluebeard Henri Desire Landru (1869–1922), French murderer who killed ten
women over a five-year period, having first proposed marriage to them. The French
press dubbed him *Bluebeard*, after the character in a tale by Charles Perrault in the
collection *Histoires et Contes du Temps Passé* (1697). In Perrault's story, Bluebeard
kills several wives in turn and keeps their remains in a locked room. The term has
subsequently been applied to various murderous husbands or mass killers of
women.

Blue Billy William Cornwallis (1744–1819), British admiral. ➤ See BILLY *Blue*.

The Bluebirds Cardiff City football club, who play in blue and white. Their
nickname the *Bluebirds* dates back to 1911–12 when Maeterlinck's play *The Blue Bird*
was performed in Cardiff.

The Bluegrass State The US state of Kentucky. Bluegrass is a term for any grass
with bluish flowers, especially *Poa pratensis*, found abundantly in the central region
of Kentucky. This grass provides rich pasture for horses and has led to the state
becoming a centre of racehorse breeding in the US. ➤ See also *The* DARK *and
Bloody Ground*.

The Blue Hen State The US state of Delaware. The inhabitants of the state are
known as Blue Hen's Chickens. The term dates from the early 1800s and is said to
have come from a company in the American War of Independence, led by a Captain
Caldwell of Delaware. He owned two gamecocks, the offspring of a blue hen, that
fought fiercely and courageously, just like his men. The company became known in
Carolina as 'Caldwell's gamecocks', and later as 'the blue hen's chickens' and the
'blue chickens'. Accordingly, Delaware became known as the *Blue Hen State*. ➤ See
also *The* DIAMOND *State, The* FIRST *State,* NEW *Sweden*.

The Blues and Royals A regiment of the Household Cavalry, formed from an amalgamation (1969) of the Royal Horse Guards (also known as the *Blues*) and the Royal Dragoons. The nickname the *Blues* derives from the blue coats worn by the regiment from 1661. ➤ See also *The* OXFORD *Blues*.

Bluff King Hal Henry VIII (1491–1547), son of Henry VII, king of England 1509–47. His nickname derives from the king's cocksure and somewhat hearty manner.

Bluidie Clavers John Graham of Claverhouse, Viscount Dundee (1649–89), Scottish royalist soldier and Jacobite leader. During the reigns of Charles II and James II, he undertook the ruthless repression of the Covenanters (Scottish Presbyterians). A hated figure in Scotland, he became known as *Bluidie Clavers* (that is, 'Bloody Clavers'). He was killed in 1689 at the battle of Killiecrankie. ➤ See also BONNIE *Dundee*.

The Boar Richard III (1452–85), brother of Edward IV, king of England 1483–85. His emblem was a white boar. He is referred to in Shakespeare's *Richard III* as 'the wretched, bloody, and usurping boar'. ➤ See also CROOKBACK.

Bobbing John John Erskine, Earl of Mar (1675–1732), leader of the Jacobite rebellion of 1715. He had previously vacillated in his allegiance to the exiled Stuarts and had initially supported the Hanoverians, a contemporary account judging him to be 'a man of good sense but bad morals'. A Jacobite song of 1715 runs, 'Hey for Bobbing John, and his Highland quorum!'

Bob de Bilde Gilles (Roger Gerard) de Bilde (b.1971), Belgian footballer, a forward with Anderlecht, Sheffield Wednesday, and Aston Villa. When de Bilde played for Sheffield Wednesday, his teammates called him *Bob*, a pun on the British children's television character Bob the Builder.

Bobs Frederick Sleigh Roberts, 1st Earl Roberts (1832–1914), British field marshal. During the war between Britain and the Afghans, he marched from Kabul to relieve the British garrison at Kandahar (1880). Now acclaimed as a hero, he became well known throughout the Empire and was appointed to command the Madras army. Roberts was widely known by his soldier nickname *Bobs*, a familiar contraction of his surname. He was also known as *Bobs Bahadur*, from a Hindi word meaning 'gallant' and used as a title of respect. He was Commander-in-Chief of the British army during the second Boer War (1899–1902).

The Bod The Bodleian Library, the library of Oxford University. The first library was established in the 14th century, but it was refounded by Thomas Bodley (1545–1613), greatly expanded, and renamed the Bodleian in 1604. Informally the library is known as the *Bod*.

The Body[1] Marie McDonald (Marie Frye) (1923–65), US film actress. A former model, she was promoted as the *Body*.

The Body[2] Elle MacPherson (born Eleanor Gow) (b.1963), Australian model. Born in Sydney, she developed her modelling career in the US, where she became known as the *Body*. She acted in the film *Sirens* (1994).

Bogie Humphrey (DeForest) Bogart (1899–1957), US film actor. He made his name as a gangster in *The Petrified Forest* (1936). In the 1940s and 1950s he appeared in the role of the tough, cynical, yet soft-hearted hero in such films as *The Maltese Falcon* (1941), *Casablanca* (1942), *The Big Sleep* (1946), and *The African Queen* (1951). He was widely known as *Bogie*, sometimes spelt *Bogey*.

The Boil Trevor Edward Bailey (b.1923), English cricketer. His nickname derives from the apparent shouts of 'Come on, Boiley' from Cockney spectators at a football match he was playing in. This subsequently became abbreviated to the *Boil*. ➤ See also BARNACLE.

Bomba Ferdinand II (1810–59), king of the Two Sicilies (the former kingdom of Naples and Sicily) from 1830. He gained the nickname *King Bomba* after his heavy bombardment of Messina and other Sicilian towns while quelling a rebellion in 1848. His son Francis II was dubbed *Bomba II*, or *Bombalino* ('Little Bomba'), after his bombardment of Palermo in 1860.

Bomber Harris Arthur Travers Harris (1892–1984), British Marshal of the RAF. As Commander-in-Chief of Bomber Command (1942–45) in the Second World War, *Bomber* Harris organized mass bombing raids against Dresden and other German cities which resulted in large-scale civilian casualties. This strategy of heavy area bombing proved controversial and adversely affected Harris's postwar reputation.

Bones[1] Frank Sinatra (1915–98), US singer and film actor. This was one of Sinatra's early nicknames, on account of his skinny frame. ➤ See also *The* CHAIRMAN *of the Board*, OL' *Blue Eyes*, *The* VOICE.

Bones[2] Dr Leonard McCoy, a character in the original series of the long-running TV science-fiction series *Star Trek* (1966–69) and in several films. McCoy, played by DeForest Kelley, is the irascible doctor on board the USS *Enterprise*. The nickname *Bones* comes from *Sawbones*, both being 19th-century slang for a surgeon or doctor.

Boney Napoleon I (known as Napoleon; full name Napoleon Bonaparte) (1769–1821), emperor of France 1804–14 and 1815. The informal name *Boney* was used derisively by the English during the Napoleonic Wars. ➤ See also *The* CORSICAN *Ogre*, *The* LITTLE *Corporal*, *The* MAN *of Destiny*, *The* VIOLET *Corporal*.

Bonking Boris Boris Becker (b.1967), German tennis player. He became the youngest man to win the men's singles championship at Wimbledon in 1985 (at the age of 17), the first time that the title had been won by an unseeded player. Having retained the Wimbledon title the following year, Becker lost to the Australian Peter Doohan in the second round in 1987. According to the British tabloids, his unexpected loss of form was because he had been having too much sex and they accordingly dubbed him *Bonking Boris*.

Bonnie Dundee John Graham of Claverhouse, Viscount Dundee (1649–89), Scottish royalist soldier and Jacobite leader, killed at Killiecrankie. Among the Jacobites he was a romantic figure, celebrated in songs and ballads and affectionately known as *Bonnie Dundee*. ➤ See also BLUIDIE *Clavers*.

Bonnie Prince Charlie Charles Edward Stuart (1720–88), the grandson of James II and elder son of James Edward Stuart (the Old Pretender), on behalf of whose claim to the British throne he led the Jacobite uprising of 1745–46. Charles was known as *Bonnie Prince Charlie* to his supporters. He subsequently became a romantic folk hero in Scotland. ➤ See also *The* KING *over the Water, The* YOUNG *Chevalier, The* YOUNG *Pretender.*

Bosie Lord Alfred (Bruce) Douglas (1870–1945), poet and lover of Oscar Wilde, whose *Salomé* he translated from French into English (1894). Douglas's relationship with Oscar Wilde ultimately resulted in Wilde's imprisonment for homosexual offences. Wilde's essay *De Profundis* (1905), written in Reading Gaol, is addressed to Douglas. The affectionate nickname *Bosie* comes from 'Boysie', which is what his mother called him.

The Boss Bruce Springsteen (b.1949), US rock singer, songwriter, and guitarist. Born in New Jersey, Springsteen writes songs about blue-collar life and is known for his energetic stage performances. His albums include *Born to Run* (1975), *Born in the USA* (1984), and *The Rising* (2002).

The Boston Strangler Albert H. DeSalvo (1933–73), US murderer. Between June 1962 and January 1964 he killed at least eleven elderly women in Boston, all of whom he strangled. The *Boston Strangler*, as the press called the killer, was later identified as DeSalvo, who had already been arrested for a large number of sexual assaults, for which he was given a life sentence in 1967. He was later stabbed to death in prison by one or more fellow inmates.

The Boston Strong Boy John L(awrence) Sullivan (1858–1918), Irish-American boxer. Born in Boston of Irish parents, Sullivan gained the nickname the *Boston Strong Boy* when as a youth he demonstrated his prodigious strength by lifting full barrels of beer over his head. He was the last world heavyweight champion of the bare-knuckled era, losing the title to James J. Corbett in 1892, the first championship match fought with gloves under the Marquess of Queensbury Rules.

Botticelli Alessandro di Mariano Filipepi (1445–1510), Italian painter, generally known by the name Sandro Botticelli. His elder brother's nickname *Botticelli*, meaning 'little barrel', was passed on to him as a child. A Florentine painter of religious and mythological subjects, Botticelli is best known for such paintings as *Primavera* (*c.*1478) and *The Birth of Venus* (*c.*1480).

The Bottomless Pitt William Pitt (1759–1806), known as Pitt the Younger, Prime Minister 1783–1801 and 1804–6, the son of Pitt the Elder. The youngest-ever Prime Minister, he introduced financial reforms to reduce the national debt. The phrase 'the bottomless pit' is used in the Book of Revelation to denote Hell. It was punningly applied to Pitt on account of his thinness. Contemporary caricatures, particularly those drawn by James Gillray, show him as an extremely thin figure with no bottom, even on occasion as a darning needle.

The Bouncing Czech (Ian) Robert Maxwell (born Jan Ludvik Hoch) (1923–91), Czech-born British publisher and media entrepreneur. A former Labour MP (1964–70), he built up a considerable publishing empire during the 1980s. After his mysterious death while yachting off Tenerife, it emerged that he had misappropriated the pension funds of some of his companies. He was known as the *Bouncing Czech* and *Captain Bob.*

Boycs Geoffrey Boycott (b.1940), English cricketer. He began his career with Yorkshire in 1962 and first played for England two years later. Boycott was an outstanding opening batsman and prolific run-maker who had scored more than 150 centuries by the time he retired from first-class cricket in 1986. He scored 8 114 runs in Test cricket (1964–82). Although usually referred to informally as *Boycs*, to his many admirers at Yorkshire CC he was SIR GEOFFREY.

The Boy David   David (Martin Scott) Steel (b.1938), British politician, leader of the Liberal Party 1976–88 and briefly joint leader with David Owen of the Social and Liberal Democrats. In 1999 he was elected speaker of the new Scottish parliament. Steel entered Parliament as an MP in 1965. During the late 70s and 80s the sobriquet the *Boy David* fitted his youthful looks and his perceived role as the junior partner both in the Lib–Lab pact, a temporary political alliance with Labour (1977–78), and in his relationship with David Owen.

The Boy Orator of the Platte   William Jennings Bryan (1860–1925), US Democratic politician. Bryan was the Democratic candidate for president three times, never winning. He first contested the presidency in 1896 at the age of 36, which was only a year older than the minimum age for a presidential candidate. Having delivered a memorable speech at the Democratic party convention to secure his nomination, Bryan went on the stump during the election campaign (something no candidate had done before), making dozens of speeches a day. The press dubbed him the *Boy Orator of the Platte*, after the Platte River region in Nebraska that Bryan represented as a Congressman.

The Boy Wonder[1]   Irving Grant Thalberg (1899–1936), US film producer. Known as Hollywood's *Boy Wonder*, he was appointed head of production at Universal Pictures at the age of 20, then made head of the newly formed MGM studio at 25. He produced such MGM films as *Grand Hotel* (1932), *The Barretts of Wimpole Street* (1934), and *Mutiny on the Bounty* (1935).

The Boy Wonder[2]   Robin, a US comic-book superhero, the young crime-fighting partner of Batman, first appearing in a 1939 comic strip by Bob Kane and Bill Finger. Robin's real name is Dick Grayson. The term 'boy wonder' can be applied to any exceptionally talented young man or boy. ➤ See also *The* CAPED *Crusader*.

Bozzy   James Boswell (1740–95), Scottish lawyer, author, and biographer, best known for his celebrated biography *The Life of Samuel Johnson* (1791). Boswell records in his *Journal of a Tour to the Hebrides* (1785) an occasion when Johnson calls him this, adding 'He has a way of contracting the names of his friends'.

Brab   John Theodore Cuthbert Moore-Brabazon, 1st Baron Brabazon of Tara (1884–1964), British pioneer aviator and politician. He was the first British citizen to hold a pilot's licence (1910) and served as Minister of Transport and Minister of Aircraft in the coalition government during the Second World War. His long name was popularly shortened to *Brab*.

Brandy Nan   Anne (1665–1714), queen of England and Scotland (known as Great Britain from 1707) and Ireland 1702–14. She was known for her love of brandy. The position of Queen Anne's statue, erected in 1712 in front of St Paul's Cathedral, prompted the following rhyme: 'Brandy Nan, Brandy Nan, you're left in the lurch,/ Your face to the gin shop, your back to the church.' ➤ See also MRS *Bull*, MRS *Morley*.

The Bravest of the Brave Michel Ney (1768–1815), French marshal. He was one of Napoleon's leading generals, commanding the French cavalry at Waterloo (1815). Napoleon called him '*le brave des braves*', the *Bravest of the Brave*, after Ney commanded the rearguard of the French army during the retreat from Moscow in 1812. Displaying great personal courage, he was the last Frenchman to leave Russian soil. ➤ See also *Le* ROUGEAUD.

The Brazilian Bombshell Carmen Miranda (born Maria de Carmo Miranda da Cunha) (1909–55), Portuguese dancer and singer, who lived in Brazil from childhood. She starred in such Hollywood musicals as *Down Argentina Way* (1940) and *The Gang's All Here* (1943). She had a flamboyant style and wore exotic costumes which typically incorporated an elaborate hat or turban bedecked with tropical fruit and flowers.

Brenda Elizabeth II (b.1926), daughter of George VI, queen of the United Kingdom since 1952. *Brenda* is the nickname used in the satirical magazine *Private Eye*. ➤ See also LILIBET.

Brian Charles, Prince of Wales (b.1948). *Brian* is the nickname used in the satirical magazine *Private Eye*. ➤ See also ACTION *Man*.

The Bride of the Sea The city of Venice, emphasizing her traditional role as a sea power. The epithet the *Bride of the Sea* alludes to an 11th-century ceremony held on Ascension Day in Venice and known as the 'Marriage of the Adriatic'. During this ceremony, which symbolized the city's marriage to the sea, the doge dropped a ring into the Adriatic from his official barge. Venice is also known as the *Jewel of the Adriatic*. ➤ See also *The* SEA-BORN *City*.

The Bristol Boy Thomas Chatterton (1752–70), English poet. Born in Bristol, Chatterton is chiefly known for writing at the age of 15 poems professing to be the work of an imaginary 15th-century Bristol monk called Thomas Rowley. When these poems were first published in 1777, they deceived many prominent literary figures of the time. By this time, though, Chatterton was already dead; depressed by poverty and lack of literary recognition, he had committed suicide by taking arsenic aged 17. Chatterton was admired by the Romantic poets, Wordsworth referring to him as 'the marvellous boy,/The sleepless soul that perished in its pride' and Keats dedicating 'Endymion' (1818) to his memory.

The British Solomon James I (1566–1625), son of Mary, Queen of Scots, king of Scotland (as James VI) 1567–1625, and of England and Ireland 1603–25. James, a Scot, inherited the throne of England on the death of Elizabeth I. Although renowned as a scholar, James's reputation for Solomon-like wisdom seems to have been conferred either sycophantically or ironically. He was also sometimes known as the ENGLISH SOLOMON and the *Scotch Solomon*. ➤ See also *The* WISEST *Fool in Christendom*.

Broadway Joe Joe (Joseph William) Namath (b.1943), US American football player. He played for the New York Jets 1965–77, leading them to an upset victory over the Baltimore Colts in the 1969 Super Bowl. Namath's nickname *Broadway Joe* fitted his glamorous image as a metropolitan playboy.

The Brockton Blockbuster Rocky Marciano (born Rocco Francis Marchegiano) (1923–69), US boxer. In 1952 he became world heavyweight champion and successfully defended his title six times. After 49 professional fights as a heavyweight, he retired undefeated in 1956, the only heavyweight champion to do so. His nickname derives from his home town of Brockton, Massachusetts, and the ferocity of his punching.

The Bronx Bull Jake LaMotta (born Jacob LaMotta) (b.1921), US boxer. He was the first man to beat Sugar Ray Robinson (in 1943) and became world middleweight champion in 1949. In the ring he would charge with a low crouching stance, which, together with his birthplace of the Bronx, New York, accounted for his nickname. He was portrayed by Robert De Niro in the film *Raging Bull* (1980).

The Brown Bomber Joe Louis (born Joseph Louis Barrow) (1914–81), US boxer. Louis was heavyweight champion of the world for nearly 12 years (1937–49), defending his title 25 times during that period, a record for any weight. All but four of these victories were knockouts, evidence of the powerful punching which earned him his nickname the *Brown Bomber*. He retired undefeated in 1949 but subsequently returned to the ring and lost to Ezzard Charles and Rocky Marciano, only his second and third defeats in 71 professional bouts.

The Brown Eminence Martin Bormann (1900–c.1945), German Nazi politician, who succeeded Rudolf Hess as Party chancellor in 1941. Considered to be Hitler's closest collaborator, he disappeared at the end of the Second World War. He was sentenced to death *in absentia* at the Nuremberg trials in 1945. Long rumoured to have escaped to Argentina, his skeleton, exhumed in Berlin, was identified in 1973. Bormann was known as the *Brown Eminence* in a conscious echo of the GREY EMINENCE, as Cardinal Richelieu's influential private secretary was called. The sobriquet alludes to the Brownshirts, the Nazi storm troopers founded by Hitler in Munich in 1921, whose brown uniforms resembled those of Mussolini's Blackshirts.
➤ See also *The* GREY *Eminence, The* RED *Eminence*.

Brum The city of Birmingham, England. *Brum* is a shortened form of Brummagem, originally (in the mid-17th century) a dialect form of Birmingham. The term Brummagem came to be applied to the cheap plated goods and imitation jewellery once manufactured there and hence came to mean 'cheap, tatty, showy'. An inhabitant of Birmingham is known as a Brummie. ➤ See also *The* TOYSHOP *of Europe*.

Bubbles[1] William James (1881–1973), British Admiral of the Fleet. As a four-year-old boy, he modelled for a portrait by his grandfather John Everett Millais. The picture of a curly-headed boy blowing bubbles became widely known when it was used in an advertisement by Pears' soap. It was popularly known as 'Bubbles' and in later life the name was applied to William James himself.

Bubbles[2] Beverly Sills (born Belle Miriam Silverman) (b.1929), US operatic soprano, one of the leading bel canto stylists. At the age of three she made her first public performance on the radio under the name of *Bubbles*, a nickname she gained at birth from a large bubble of saliva in her mouth. She has been known by the name all her life. In 1955 she made her debut with the New York City Opera and in 1979 she retired to become its general director.

The Bubbly Jocks The Royal Scots Greys (2nd Dragoons), a regiment of the British army. The regiment used to be nicknamed the *Bubbly Jocks* (old Scottish slang for 'turkey cocks') because of the eagle on their regimental badge.

The Buckeye State The US state of Ohio. The state has an abundance of buckeye trees (*Aesculus glabra*), an American tree related to the horse chestnut, with showy red or white flowers. Its fruit is supposed to bear a resemblance to a deer's eye, hence the nickname *Buckeye State*. A Buckeye is a native of Ohio.

Buck House Buckingham Palace, the London residence of the British sovereign since 1837. Built in 1703 for the Duke of Buckingham, it was originally called Buckingham House. The affectionate and once fashionable nickname *Buck House* is recorded from the early 1920s. ➤ See also BECKINGHAM *Palace*.

Buddy Marlon Brando (1924–2004), US film and stage actor, a leading exponent of method acting. His early films included *A Streetcar Named Desire* (1951) and *On the Waterfront* (1954), for which he won an Academy Award. His later career included memorable roles in *The Godfather* (1972), *Last Tango in Paris* (1972), and *Apocalypse Now* (1979). *Buddy* was Brando's family nickname from childhood.

Buffalo Bill William Frederick Cody (1846–1917), US army scout and showman. He earned his nickname *Buffalo Bill* for killing 4 280 buffalo in eighteen months to supply meat to the Union Pacific Railroad labourers. It was apparently coined by the dime novelist Ned Buntline (1823–86). In 1883 Cody established his travelling Wild West Show, which toured the US and Europe.

Bugsy Siegel Benjamin Siegel (1906–47), US racketeer and gangland killer, often credited with founding the casino resort of Las Vegas in the Nevada Desert. His tendency to 'go bugs', that is, to fly into a violent rage, earned him the nickname *Bugsy* from his underworld acquaintances, though he would not tolerate its use in his presence.

Building Bess Elizabeth Talbot, Countess of Shrewsbury (1518–1608). ➤ See BESS *of Hardwick*.

The Bullfrog of the Pontine Marshes Benito Mussolini (1883–1945), Italian Fascist statesman, Prime Minister of Italy 1922–43. Known as *Il Duce* ('the leader'), he established a totalitarian dictatorship and allied Italy with Germany, entering the Second World War on Germany's side in 1940. During the war Winston Churchill's disparaging title for Mussolini was the *Bullfrog of the Pontine Marshes*. This refers to an area of reclaimed marshland in western Italy, on the Tyrrhenian coast south of Rome.

The Bullion State The US state of Missouri. *Old Bullion* was the nickname of Missouri senator Thomas Hart Benton (1782–1858) because he advocated using gold and silver in preference to paper currency. The nickname subsequently transferred to the state itself. ➤ See also *The* PUKE *State, The* SHOW *Me State*.

Bull Moose Theodore Roosevelt (1858–1919), US Republican statesman, 26th President of the US 1901–9. During the 1900 vice-presidential campaign, Roosevelt declared 'I am as strong as a bull moose'. It was a phrase he would continue to use, and he himself became known as *Bull Moose*. After serving two terms as president,

Roosevelt tried to make a comeback in 1912. Failing to win the Republican party's presidential nomination, he formed the Progressive Party to fight the election. This new party became popularly known as the Bull Moose Party. ➤ See also *The* ROUGH *Rider.*

Bumble David Lloyd (b.1947), English cricketer, who played for Lancashire and England in the 1970s. He is affectionately known as *Bumble* because of his cheerful garrulousness.

Butch Cassidy Robert Leroy Parker (1866–*c.*1909), US train robber and outlaw. His gang the Wild Bunch was responsible for numerous train and bank robberies and murders in the US. His nickname *Butch* stemmed from the fact that he had once worked as a butcher. ➤ See also *The* SUNDANCE *Kid.*

The Butcher Ulysses S(impson) Grant (1822–85), US general and 18th President of the US 1869–77. As Supreme Commander of the Unionist armies in the American Civil War, he defeated the Confederate army in 1865 with a policy of attrition. His readiness to accept heavy casualties to his command in order to secure a victory caused his own soldiers to label him the *Butcher* or *Butcher Grant.* He was troubled by this criticism for the rest of his life, once saying to an old friend: 'They call me a butcher. But do you know, I sometimes could hardly bring myself to give an order for battle. When I contemplated the death and misery that were sure to follow, I stood appalled.' The title was also attached to William Augustus, Duke of Cumberland (1721–65), English military commander and third son of George II, who suppressed the Jacobite clans in the aftermath of his victory at the Battle of Culloden (1746). ➤ See also *The* AMERICAN *Caesar, The* BLOODY *Butcher,* UNCONDITIONAL *Surrender.*

The Butcher of Baghdad Saddam Hussein (full name Saddam bin Hussein at-Takriti) (b.1937), President of Iraq 1979–2003. His Iraqi forces invaded and occupied Kuwait in August 1990, precipitating the Gulf War of 1991. Because of his harsh treatment of Kurdish rebels in Iraq (involving the use of chemical weapons against civilian populations) and the atrocities reported to have been committed by the army of occupation in Kuwait, Saddam was demonized as the *Butcher of Baghdad* in the western popular press. He was deposed as President following the Second Gulf War of 2003.

The Butcher of Broadway Alexander (Humphreys) Woollcott (1887–1943), US drama critic, noted for the savagery of some of his reviews. Dubbed the *Butcher of Broadway,* he was the inspiration for the character of the unwelcome house-guest Sheridan Whiteside in Moss Hart and George S. Kaufman's play *The Man Who Came to Dinner* (1939).

The Butcher of Lyons Klaus Barbie (1913–91), head of the Gestapo in Lyons between 1942 and 1944. He is held to have been responsible for the deaths of 4 000 people and the deportation of over 7 000 others. Barbie was extradited from Bolivia to France in 1983 and in 1987 was tried in Lyons for 'crimes against humanity'. He was sentenced to life imprisonment.

Cc

The Cabbage Garden   The state of Victoria, Australia. The Australian nickname the *Cabbage Garden* dates from the 1920s and probably alludes to its relatively small size or the crops grown there. It has also been suggested that there may be a reference to the mallee, a low-growing scrubby eucalyptus, that grows profusely in the state. A later variant of the nickname is the *Cabbage Patch*. ➤ See also *The* HANGING *State*.

Calamity Jane   Martha Jane Burke (born Martha Jane Canary) (*c.*1852–1903), US frontierswoman, noted for her skill at shooting and riding. She often dressed in men's clothes. She is said to have warned that 'calamity' would come to any man who had the temerity to court her. The name *Calamity Jane* has come to be applied to any female prophet of doom.

Caligula   Caligula (born Gaius Julius Caesar Germanicus) (AD 12–41), Roman emperor 37–41. He was brought up in a military camp, where he gained the nickname *Caligula* (meaning 'little boot') as an infant because of the miniature military boots he wore. Caligula's brief reign as an emperor, which began when he succeeded Tiberius and ended with his assassination, became notorious for its tyrannical excesses. He made his horse Incitatus a consul.

The Canaries   Norwich City football club. Soon after the club's founding in 1902, they acquired the nickname the *Canaries* from Norwich's trade in breeding and exporting pet birds. They duly named their ground The Nest and changed their strip to appropriately yellow shirts and green shorts.

Canmore   Malcolm III (*c.*1031–93), son of Duncan I, king of Scotland 1058–93. Malcolm came to the throne after killing Macbeth in battle in 1057. He was known to his contemporaries as *Ceann Mor* (or *Canmore*), Gaelic for 'Great Head', probably quite literally alluding to the size of the king's head.

Cannibal   Eddy Merckx (b.1945), Belgian racing cyclist. He won the Tour de France five times (1969–72 and 1974), also gaining five victories in the Tour of Italy between 1968 and 1974. His strength and endurance were such that he seemingly 'devoured' his opponents, earning him the nickname the *Cannibal*.

The Cannonball Kid   (Leonard) Roscoe Tanner (b.1951), US tennis player, winner of the Australian Open in 1977 and a Wimbledon finalist in 1979. Tanner was renowned for his powerful serve, earning himself the nickname the *Cannonball Kid*.

Capability Brown   Lancelot Brown (1716–83), English landscape gardener who evolved an English style of natural-looking landscape parks. Examples of his work can be found at Blenheim Palace in Oxfordshire, Chatsworth House in Derbyshire, and Kew Gardens. He earned his nickname *Capability Brown* from his habit of assuring his patrons that their estates had 'great capabilities'.

The Caped Crusader   Batman, a US comic-book superhero, a masked and costumed crime-fighter with a bat-like cape. He made his first appearance in a 1939 comic strip by Bob Kane and Bill Finger, and, with his young partner Robin, has subsequently appeared in comics, a TV series, and films. His real identity is Bruce Wayne, a millionaire socialite. ➤ See also *The* BOY *Wonder*.

Captain Bob   Robert Maxwell (1923–91), Czech-born publisher and media tycoon. ➤ See *The* BOUNCING *Czech*.

Captain Marvel   Bryan Robson (b.1957), English football player and manager. In 1981 the midfielder Robson was bought by Manchester United for £1.5 million, a record British fee at the time. He won 90 international caps, 65 as England captain. An inspirational captain of club and country, he was known as *Captain Marvel*, after the US comic-book superhero.

Caracalla   Aurelius Antoninus (born Septimus Bassanius; later called Marcus Aurelius Severus Antoninus Augustus) (188–217), Roman emperor 211–17. He became known as *Caracalla*, the name deriving from the long hooded Celtic cloak which he wore and made fashionable.

The Card   Denry Machin, the young social-climbing clerk in Arnold Bennett's novel *The Card* (1911), filmed in 1952 with Alec Guinness in the title role. This slang term for an odd or amusing person was first used in the early 19th century.

Cat   Philip Clive Roderick Tufnell (b.1966), English cricketer, a left-arm spin bowler for Middlesex and England. Tufnell was nicknamed *Cat* by his Middlesex teammates because of his predilection for taking naps during the day. The nickname dates from August 1988 when he neglected his duties as twelfth man by sleeping through the whole of the morning's session of play.

The Cat   Peter (Philip) Bonetti (b.1941), English footballer. Goalkeeper for Chelsea and England, Bonetti was popularly known as the *Cat* because of his shot-saving agility.

Cat's Eyes   John Cunningham (1917–2002), British fighter pilot in the Second World War. He became a group captain in 1944, making his name in night-time defence against German bombers. His ability to locate enemy planes in the dark was attributed to his consumption of carrots, earning him his wartime nickname *Cat's Eyes*, though Cunningham himself later put his success down to the top secret radar on his Mosquito aeroplane.

The Centennial State   The US state of Colorado. The state was admitted into the Union in 1876, a hundred years after the founding of the United States, hence its nickname the *Centennial State*.

The Chairboys   Wycombe Wanderers football club. Their nickname the *Chairboys* derives from High Wycombe's tradition of furniture-making. The club was formed by a group of young furniture trade workers in 1884.

The Chairman of the Board   Frank Sinatra (1915–98), US singer and film actor. This was how Sinatra was often referred to in the 1960s as the leader of the 'Rat Pack', a group of Las Vegas-based entertainers including Dean Martin, Sammy Davis Jr, Peter Lawford, and Joey Bishop. The title is supposed to have been coined by

William B. Williams, a New York disc jockey. It was partly a reference to his being the head of Reprise Records, a record label Sinatra founded in 1961. Other titles for Sinatra during this period were the GOV'NOR and the *Pope*. ➤ See also BONES, OL' *Blue Eyes*, *The* VOICE.

The Champion W. G. Grace (1848–1915), English cricketer and doctor. ➤ See *The* GRAND *Old Man*.

Chariots Martin Offiah (b.1966), British rugby league and rugby union player, noted for his speed as a winger. His nickname *Chariots Offiah* is a clever pun on the title of the 1981 film *Chariots of Fire*. The film was about the two British runners Eric Liddell and Harold Abrahams who won gold medals in the 1924 Olympics.

Charlie Hustle Pete Rose (Peter Edward Rose) (b.1941), US baseball player, mainly with the Cincinnati Reds and the Philadelphia Phillies. He played for 24 years in the major leagues (1963–86), playing in more games (3 562) and getting more hits (4 256) than any player in baseball history. His nickname *Charlie Hustle* derived from his habit of sprinting to first base even when he did not need to.

The Cheeky Chappie Max Miller (born Thomas Henry Sargent) (1895–1963), British music-hall comedian. Garishly dressed on stage in a multicoloured plus-four suit and white trilby, he was the master of the vulgar *double entendre*, justifying his billing as the *Cheeky Chappie*.

The Cheesemongers The First Life Guards, a regiment of the British army. The term derived in the late 18th century from the sneering remark that the regiment was composed 'not of gentlemen but of cheesemongers' (that is, the sons of merchants). In later years the insult was proudly embraced by the regiment, whose battle-cry at Waterloo was 'Come on the Cheeses!'

Cheggers Keith Chegwin (b.1957), British actor and TV presenter. He appeared in various children's TV programmes in the late 1970s, including a music show called *Cheggers plays Pop*.

Chemical Ali Ali Hassan al-Majid (b. 1938), Iraqi general. Al-majid earned his nickname *Chemical Ali* for ordering the use of chemical weapons on Kurds in northern Iraq in 1988. He is held responsible for the deaths of over 100 000 Kurds, including 5 000 who died in a single day when Iraqi forces used poison gas on the town of Halabja. ➤ See also COMICAL *Ali*.

The Cherry-breeches The 11th Hussars, a regiment of the British army. In 1840 the regiment adopted their distinctive crimson trousers, hence their nickname the *Cherry-breeches*. A variation was *Cherry-bums*, which was itself punningly modified to the more respectable CHERUBIMS. ➤ See also *The* CHERRY-PICKERS.

The Cherry-pickers The 11th Hussars, a regiment of the British army. The nickname the *Cherry-pickers* originated as a taunting reference to an incident in which a detachment was captured by the French whilst picking cherries in an orchard at San Martin de Trebejo, on 15 August 1811. The name stuck and became doubly appropriate in 1840 when the regiment adopted their distinctive crimson trousers. ➤ See also *The* CHERRY-BREECHES.

The Cherubims   The 11th Hussars, a regiment of the British army. ➤ See *The* CHERRY-BREECHES.

Cheryl   Diana, Princess of Wales (1961–97). *Cheryl* was the nickname used in the satirical magazine *Private Eye.* ➤ See also *The* PEOPLE'S *Princess, The* QUEEN *of Hearts.*

The Chesterbelloc   G(ilbert) K(eith) Chesterton (1874–1936), English essayist, novelist, and critic and (Joseph) Hilaire (Pierre René) Belloc (1870–1953), French-born British writer, historian, and poet. The *Chesterbelloc* was a composite nickname, coined by George Bernard Shaw, for the two writers who shared social and political beliefs and collaborated on a number of literary works. Their contributions to *The Speaker* took an anti-imperialist, pro-Boer stance on the Boer War question. They collaborated in works critical of modern industrial society and socialism, such as *The Servile State* (1912). In particular they were opposed to the socialism of Shaw and H. G. Wells. In 1908 Shaw published a lampoon imagining the two writers as forming a single creature, 'a very amusing pantomime elephant', that he called 'the Chesterbelloc'. They also jointly produced a number of humorous books illustrated by Chesterton and written by Belloc. Both were prominent Roman Catholics, Chesterton having converted in 1922.

Chiantishire   Tuscany, a region of west central Italy. Its popularity with English middle-class holiday-makers and holiday-home buyers has earned the region the nickname *Chiantishire*, Chianti being a dry red Italian wine produced in Tuscany. The term may have been coined by the writer and barrister John Mortimer (b.1923).

The Chief[1]   Eamon de Valera (1882–1975), American-born Irish statesman, Taoiseach (Prime Minister) 1937–48, 1951–54, and 1957–59 and President of the Republic of Ireland 1959–73. He was involved in the Easter Rising, the leader of Sinn Fein 1917–26 and the founder of the Fianna Fáil Party in 1926. As President of the Irish Free State from 1932, de Valera was largely responsible for the new constitution of 1937 which created the state of Eire. He was known in Ireland as the *Chief* and also as *Dev.* ➤ See also *The* LONG *Fellow.*

The Chief[2]   Herbert C(lark) Hoover (1874–1964), US Republican statesman, 31st President of the US 1929–33, whose administration was dominated by the Great Depression of the early 1930s. Earlier in his career he had organized food production and distribution in the US and Europe during and after the First World War. His success in this relief work earned him the title the *Chief.* He served as Secretary of Commerce under Presidents Harding and Coolidge (1921–28).

Chilly   Chris(topher Middleton) Old (b.1948), English cricketer. A seam bowler for Yorkshire and England, he was known as *Chilly* on the cricket field, paraphrasing his name C. Old (i.e. *Cold*).

Chinese Gordon   Charles George Gordon (1833–85), British general and colonial adminstrator. He first won fame by commanding the Chinese army that crushed the Taiping Rebellion (1863–64), earning him the name *Chinese Gordon*. He was governor of the Sudan (1877–80), returning in 1884 to fight Mahdist forces led by Muhammad Ahmad, the Mahdi. Gordon was trapped at Khartoum and killed before a relief expedition could reach him. He is often referred to as *Gordon of Khartoum.*

The Chingford Strangler Norman (Beresford) Tebbit (b.1931), British Conservative politician, formerly MP for Chingford, Essex, and chairman of the Conservative
Party 1985–87. Known in the press as either the *Chingford Strangler* or the *Chingford
Skinhead*, Tebbit had a reputation for being abrasive and combative in political
debate.

The Chinook State The US state of Washington. The Chinook are an American
Indian people originally inhabiting the region around the mouth of the Columbia
River. The river flows through Washington state. ➤ See also *The* EVERGREEN *State*.

The Choirboy Walter (Robert John) Swinburn (b.1961), British jockey. He won his
first Derby in 1981, winning the race again in 1986 and 1995. In all he rode eight
Classic winners. Swinburn was called the *Choirboy* on account of his cherubic
appearance.

Chopper Ron Harris (b.1944), English footballer who played for Chelsea in the
1960s and 1970s. Like Norman 'BITES YER LEGS' Hunter, Ron '*Chopper*' Harris, one
of the acknowledged 'hard men' of football in his day, was known for his lunging
tackles which would 'chop down' players from the opposing team.

Chu Leon Berry (1910–41), US jazz saxophonist. He earned the nickname *Chu* in 1930
when Berry's goatee beard caused fellow musician Billy Stewart to remark that he
looked oriental, resembling the character Chu Chin Chow from the musical of that
title based on the Ali Baba story.

La Cicciolina Ilona Staller (b.1955), Hungarian-born Italian porn actress, elected to
the Italian parliament in 1987. Her adopted name *La Cicciolina* means 'the little
fleshy one'.

The Cincinnatus of the West George Washington (1732–99), US soldier and
statesman, 1st president of the US 1789–97. Having served two terms, Washington
declined a third term and retired to his Virginia estate at Mount Vernon. However,
in 1798 he was summoned from retirement for a few weeks to take command of the
American forces with the prospect of a war with France. This episode prompted
Byron, in his 'Ode to Napoleon Bonaparte' (1814), to dub Washington the
Cincinnatus of the West, after Lucius Quintus Cincinnatus, a legendary Roman hero
of the 5th century BC. According to tradition, Cincinnatus was twice called from the
plough to assume the dictatorship of Rome. ➤ See also *The* AMERICAN *Fabius*, *The*
FATHER *of his Country*.

The Cinderella Man James Joseph Braddock (1906–74), US boxer, world heavyweight champion 1935–37. In the early 1930s Braddock's boxing career had taken
such a downturn that he was surviving on public welfare. Then in 1935 he made the
most of his opportunity to contest the world heavyweight title by, as a 15-1 outsider,
unexpectedly defeating the champion Max Baer. This rags-to-riches story caused
Braddock to be dubbed the *Cinderella Man*.

The Citizen King Louis Philippe (1773–1850), king of France 1830–48. His father,
Philippe d'Orléans (1747–93), who had initially supported the French Revolution
against his cousin Louis XVI, had taken the name Égalité, and Louis Philippe had
fought with the revolutionary army before going into exile abroad in 1793. He
returned to France after the restoration of the Bourbons, becoming the focus for

liberal discontent, and after the overthrow of Charles X in 1830 he was proclaimed king of France. Thomas Carlyle in *The French Revolution* (1837) refers to him as 'young Égalité'.

The City College   Newgate Prison, a former London prison from the 13th century. Newgate, notorious in the 18th century for its unsanitary conditions, was finally demolished in 1902. The prison was ironically nicknamed the *City College* because of its location in the City of London and its likely provision of a criminal education.

The City of Bon-accord   The city of Aberdeen, Scotland. Its nickname the *City of Bon-accord* derives from *bon-accord*, which in Scottish usage (from French) means 'good will, fellowship'. ➤ See also *The* GRANITE *City*.

The City of Brotherly Love   The city of Philadelphia, Pennsylvania. It was the site in 1776 of the signing of the Declaration of Independence and in 1787 of the adoption of the Constitution of the United States. The city's name means 'brotherly love', and the *City of Brotherly Love* is an informal name for Philadelphia. ➤ See also *The* QUAKER *City, The* REBEL *Capital*.

The City of Dreaming Spires   The city of Oxford, England. The romantic nickname the *City of Dreaming Spires* is taken from the poem 'Thyrsis' (1866) by Matthew Arnold: 'And that sweet City with her dreaming Spires'. The phrase calls to mind the various steeples, towers, and domes of the Oxford skyline.

The City of Firsts   The US city of Kokomo, Indiana. Among the innovations the city proudly claims are the first mechanical corn-picker, the first push-button car radio, the first commercially built car and the first canned tomato juice.

The City of Lilies   The city of Florence, Italy. Lilies form part of the coat-of-arms of Florence, hence its nickname the *City of Lilies*.

The City of Magnificent Distances   The US city of Washington DC. The nickname the *City of Magnificent Distances* was coined in 1816 by the Portuguese Minister to the United States, José Correa da Serra. Washington is noted for its wide avenues, many parks, and impressive vistas.

The City of Masts   The city of London, England. In London's days as a major port, it was known as the *City of Masts*. ➤ See also *The* BIG *Smoke, The Great Wen*.

The City of Saints   The city of Montreal, Canada, in the French Catholic province of Quebec. It is known as the *City of Saints* because many of its streets are named after saints. The epithet has also been applied to Salt Lake City, Utah, because it is the world headquarters of the Church of Latter-Day Saints. ➤ See also *The* LAND *of the Saints,* MORMON *City*.

The City of the Seven Hills   The city of Rome, Italy. Its nickname the *City of the Seven Hills* (*Urbs Septacollis*) alludes to the seven hills on which the ancient city of Rome was built. These were called Aventine, Caelian, Capitoline, Esquilane, Quirinal, Viminal, and Palatine. ➤ See also *The* ETERNAL *City*.

The City of the Tribes   The town of Galway, Republic of Ireland. Its nickname the *City of the Tribes* alludes to the *tribes of Galway*, a term used for the fourteen Irish families or 'tribes' whose ancestors settled there in the 13th century.

The City of the Violated Treaty   The town of Limerick, Republic of Ireland. The nickname refers to the Treaty of Limerick, signed by Jacobite and Williamite forces in Ireland in 1691, but repeatedly dishonoured during the reigns of William III and Queen Anne.

The City of the Violet Crown   The city of Athens, Greece. The *City of the Violet Crown* (or the VIOLET-CROWNED CITY) translates an epithet used by the Greek poet Pindar and the dramatist Aristophanes, perhaps referring to the beautiful purple colour sometimes to be seen on the mountains round the city. The epithet also alludes to Ion, the legendary king of Athens. *Ion* is Greek for 'violet'.

Clockwork Ocwirk   Ernst Ocwirk (b.1926), Austrian footballer. A creative midfield player, Ocwirk played for FK Austria and the Italian club Sampdoria. He first played for Austria in 1947 and went on to win 62 caps. After his impressive performance at Wembley when Austria drew 2–2 against England in 1951, the British press dubbed him *Clockwork Ocwirk*.

The Clones Cyclone   Barry McGuigan (b.1961), Northern Irish boxer, WBA featherweight champion 1985–86. He was brought up in Clones, County Monaghan, on the border between the Republic of Ireland and Northern Ireland.

The Clothes Horse   Joan Crawford (born Lucille Le Sueur) (1908–77), US film actress, for over forty years one of Hollywood's leading film stars. A dancer in her early films, she went on to star in films such as *Rain* (1932), *The Women* (1939), and *Mildred Pierce* (1945), for which she won an Academy Award. She came to be associated with sultry roles in psychological melodramas. Crawford was dubbed the *Clothes Horse* because of her lavish wardrobe, even during the Depression.

The Clown Prince of Basketball   Meadowlark Lemon (born Meadow George Lemon) (b.1933), US basketball player. In 1954 Lemon joined the Harlem Globetrotters, a professional basketball team who tour the world giving exhibition matches combining ball skills with comedy routines. He became the most well-known member of the team and was dubbed the *Clown Prince of Basketball*.

The Coathanger   Sydney Harbour Bridge. Australians dubbed the single-span arch bridge (opened in 1932) the *Coat Hanger* because of its distinctive shape. Its main arch is 503m (1 652 ft) long.

The Cobblers   Northampton Town football club. They are known as the *Cobblers* on account of the town's once-dominant shoe- and boot-making industry.

The Cockade State   The US state of Maryland. A cockade is a rosette or knot of ribbons worn in a hat as a badge of office or as part of a livery. During the American War of Independence, cockades were worn by soldiers of the Old Line. ➤ See also *The* FREE *State, The* OLD *Line State, The* QUEEN *State.*

The Cock of the North   George, 5th Duke of Gordon (1770–1836), who formed the regiment later known as the Gordon Highlanders in 1795. His nickname the *Cock of the North* was originally applied to his ancestor Alexander, 2nd Duke of Gordon (*c.*1678–1728), whose son Lord Huntly was dubbed *Cockalorum*. A Jacobite song of *c.*1715 contains the lines: 'Hey for Sandy Don!/Hey for Cockalorum!/Hey for Bobbing John,/And his Highland quorum!'

The Cockpit of Europe Belgium, a part of Europe on which European conflicts have frequently been fought. Battles fought on Belgian soil have included Ramilles (1706), Waterloo (1815), Mons and Ypres in the First World War, and the German invasion of 1940. The term *cockpit*, historically an enclosure used for holding cockfights, can be applied to any arena of conflict. With reference to war in Europe, the idea is first recorded in the writings of the Anglo-Welsh man of letters James Howell (*c.*1594–1666): 'The Netherlands have been for many years, as one may say, the very cockpit of Christendom' (*Instructions for Foreign Travel*, 1642).

Cock Robin Robert Walpole (1676–1745), British Whig statesman, First Lord of the Treasury and Chancellor of the Exchequer 1715–17 and 1721–42. He is generally regarded as the first British Prime Minister. His nickname *Cock Robin* is a familiar name for a male robin, especially in nursery rhymes.

Coeur de Lion Richard I (1157–99), son of Henry II, king of England 1189–99. He spent all but six months of his reign absent from his kingdom. On succeeding to the throne, he left to lead the Third Crusade. His military prowess made him a medieval legend and accounts for his nickname *Coeur de Lion*, literally meaning 'heart of a lion'. According to one story associated with him, he was supposed to have once torn the heart out of a lion and eaten it.

The Colossus of Independence John Adams (1735–1826), US Federalist statesman, 2nd President of the US 1797–1801. As a member of the Continental Congress he argued eloquently for the Declaration of Independence (1776), which he helped to draft. In recognition of these achievements, Adams was given the nickname the *Colossus of Independence* by Thomas Jefferson. A 'colossus' is a person or thing of enormous size, importance, or ability. The word in this sense is recorded from the early 17th century, and derives from the Colossus of Rhodes, the huge bronze statue of the sun god Helios (built *c.*292–280 BC) that was one of the Seven Wonders of the World. ➤ See also OLD *Sink or Swim*.

The Comeback Kid Bill (William Jefferson) Clinton (b.1946), US Democratic statesman, 42nd President of the US 1993–2001. The nickname the *Comeback Kid* was first used by Clinton himself, then the Governor of Arkansas, following the Democratic primary in New Hampshire in 1992. His campaign had been derailed by charges of womanizing and draft-dodging, and he came a poor second to another candidate Paul Tsongas. Since 1952 every US president had won his party's New Hampshire primary so this defeat appeared to cast serious doubt on Clinton's presidential ambitions. The phrase, encapsulating Clinton's determination to recover from this apparent setback, was actually coined by his campaign strategist Paul Begala. Clinton went on to win the Democratic presidential nomination and was elected president in November 1992. The nickname proved appropriate during Clinton's presidency, as he sought to bounce back from further reverses, in particular allegations of financial impropriety during his period in office in Arkansas, sex scandals, and ultimately impeachment proceedings. ➤ See also SLICK *Willy*.

Comical Ali Ali Mohammed Saeed al-Sahaf (b. 1940), Iraqi minister of information during the Second Gulf War of 2003. He was dubbed *Comical Ali* (a nickname consciously modelled on *Chemical Ali*) when his defiantly optimistic denials of US and British military advances made him a cult figure in the Western media. Al-Sahaf refused to admit that US troops were in Baghdad even when the rumbling of tanks and the sound of gunfire could be heard just half a mile away. ➤ See also CHEMICAL *Ali*.

The Confessor Edward the Confessor (*c*.1003–66), son of Ethelred the Unready, king of England 1042–66. He gained a reputation for piety during his lifetime, devoting himself to religion and to the rebuilding of Westminster Abbey, where he is buried. Edward introduced to England the custom of touching people suffering from the skin disease scrofula, known as 'the King's Evil' and popularly supposed to be curable by the royal touch. He was canonized in 1161, a century after his death.

Conky Arthur Wellesley, 1st Duke of Wellington (1769–1852), British soldier and Tory statesman, Prime Minister 1828–30 and 1834. ➤ See OLD *Conky*.

The Conqueror William I (*c*.1027–87), reigned 1066–87, the first Norman king of England. As Duke of Normandy he invaded England in 1066, defeated Harold II at the Battle of Hastings, and was crowned king. The conquest of England led to the introduction of Norman institutions and customs, especially feudalism. Though known by contemporary writers as *William the* BASTARD because of his parentage, he became generally known as *William the Conqueror*. ➤ See also *The* BASTARD.

The Constitution State The US state of Connecticut. The Fundamental Orders drawn up in Hartford in 1639 are believed to be the first formal constitution written on American soil. The draft US constitution was partly based on this and was itself ratified in Connecticut in 1788. Connecticut's official nickname is accordingly the *Constitution State*. ➤ See also *The* NUTMEG *State*.

Copper Nose Oliver Cromwell (1599–1658), English general and statesman, Lord Protector of the Commonwealth 1653–58. Contemporary descriptions mention Cromwell's large red nose and ruddy complexion. A 1648 pamphlet speaks of 'the glow-worm glistening in his beak'. He accordingly acquired the nicknames *Copper Nose* and RUBY NOSE. ➤ See also *The* ALMIGHTY *Nose*, CRUM-HELL, IRONSIDES, KING *Oliver*, OLD *Noll*.

The Cornhusker State The US state of Nebraska, known as the *Cornhusker State*. The term Cornhusker, originally applied to the University of Nebraska's athletics and football teams, is used for any native or resident of Nebraska.

The Corn Law Rhymer Ebenezer Elliott (1781–1849), English poet born in Rotherham, Yorkshire. He was largely self-educated and worked as a master-founder in Sheffield. A former Chartist, he bitterly attacked the Corn Laws in his *Corn-Law Rhymes* (1831), which describe the miseries of rural poverty. The Corn Laws regulated the import and export of grain, but had the unintended effect of forcing up bread prices and were finally repealed in 1846.

The Corsican Ogre Napoleon I (known as Napoleon; full name Napoleon Bonaparte) (1769–1821), emperor of France 1804–14 and 1815. Napoleon was born in Ajaccio, Corsica and referred to affectionately by the French as the *Corsican*. His enemies called him the *Corsican Ogre* or the *Corsican Upstart*. ➤ See also BONEY, *The* LITTLE *Corporal*, *The* MAN *of Destiny*, *The* VIOLET *Corporal*.

The Cottagers Fulham football club. Fulham have played at Craven Cottage since 1896, hence their nickname the *Cottagers*.

Cottonopolis The city of Manchester, in NW England. The 19th-century nickname *Cottonopolis* (based on the word *metropolis*) confers a certain grandeur on the city that was then the centre of the Lancashire cotton manufacturing industry, which provided Britain's chief export. ➤ See also MADCHESTER.

The Cotton State The US state of Alabama. Cotton growing was at one time a dominant part of the state's economy, hence its nickname the *Cotton State*. ➤ See also The HEART *of Dixie*, The YELLOWHAMMER *State*.

Count William James Basie (1904–84), US jazz pianist, bandleader, and composer. The big band he formed in 1935, the Count Basie Orchestra, was an influential band of the swing era, noted for its strong rhythm section. It is generally supposed that Bill Basie was given the nickname *Count* by a Kansas City radio announcer in the 1930s, intentionally elevating him to the same ranks of jazz nobility as the well-established bandleader Duke Ellington. There is some evidence, though, that Basie had given himself the title earlier, even having business cards printed with the words 'Beware the Count is Here'.

The Cowboy Philosopher Will Rogers (born William Penn Adair) (1879–1935), US actor and humorist. Rogers began his career as a rodeo cowboy and rope-twirler in vaudeville shows such as the Ziegfeld Follies. He also appeared in films. He later became a perceptive political commentator, known for his aphorisms and home-spun wisdom. His popular newspaper articles and columns were eventually syndicated, reaching an estimated audience of 40 million readers. He was widely known as the *Cowboy Philosopher*.

The Coyote State The US state of South Dakota. Its official nickname the *Coyote State* comes from the name of the wolf-like wild dog (*Canis latrans*), native to western North America and also known as the prairie wolf. The term Coyote is also used to denote an inhabitant of South Dakota.

The Crab Ray(mond Colin) Wilkins (b.1956), English footballer. He played for a number of clubs including Chelsea, Manchester United, and Milan, and won 84 England caps. Complaining that the player was over-cautious, manager Ron Atkinson nicknamed him the *Crab* for continually passing the ball sideways: 'the only time he goes forward is to toss the coin'.

The Cracker State The US state of Georgia. There are various explanations offered for the origin of the state's nickname the *Cracker State*, dating from the late 19th century. It may allude to early settlers cracking their whips over their mules. It may derive from the practice of cracking corn to make cornmeal. It may even refer to the harsh Georgian dialect, sometimes thought to resemble a cracking sound. ➤ See also The GOOBER *State*, The PEACH *State*.

The Cradle of Liberty The US city of Boston, Massachusetts. Boston was the centre of opposition to the British before and during the War of American Independence, hence its nickname the *Cradle of Liberty*. ➤ See also The ATHENS *of America*.

The Crafty Cockney Eric (John) Bristow (b.1957), English darts player, the leading player of the early 1980s. He won the world championship in 1980, going on to win a further four world titles (1981, 1984, 1985, 1986). According to the London-born

Bristow, he took his nickname from a shirt given to him by the owner of the *Crafty Cockney* bar in Beverley Hills.

Crawfie Marion Crawford (1909–88), British governess to the Princesses Elizabeth and Margaret in the 1930s, known in the press as *Crawfie*. The unauthorized publication of her reminiscences in 'The Little Princesses', an article that appeared in *Women's Own* magazine, caused her to fall out of royal favour.

Crazy Horse Emlyn (Walter) Hughes (1947–2004), English footballer. Hughes played for Liverpool and England, winning 62 international caps (23 as captain). Noted for his whole-hearted enthusiasm and stamina, he was dubbed *Crazy Horse* by his Liverpool teammates. The historical Crazy Horse was a Sioux chief Ta-Sunko-Witko (*c.*1849–77), leader of the Indian force that defeated General Custer at Little Bighorn in 1876.

Crescent City The US city of New Orleans, Louisiana. The nickname *Crescent City* refers to the city's location on the east bank of a bend in the Mississippi River. ➤ See also *The* BIG *Easy.*

The Crocodile Ernest Rutherford (1871–1937), New Zealand physicist, regarded as the founder of nuclear physics. Working with him at the Cavendish laboratories in Cambridge, the Russian physicist Peter Kapitza (1894–1984) used to call Rutherford the *Crocodile*. Kapitza's explanation was that the sobriquet was often given to great men in Russian folklore. The real reason was probably more mischievous: just as the crocodile in *Peter Pan* could be heard approaching by the ticking of Captain Hook's watch that it had swallowed, so Rutherford's arrival was usually preceded by the sound of his booming voice. In Rutherford's honour, Kapitza commissioned the sculptor Eric Gill to carve a crocodile on the outer wall of one of the Cavendish laboratories.

Crookback Richard III (1452–85), brother of Edward IV, king of England 1483–85. Many modern historians have argued that the traditional image of Richard as a physically deformed hunchback has little basis in fact but derives from Tudor propaganda. Shakespeare's depiction of Richard cemented this image: 'And where's that valiant crook-back prodigy,/Dicky your boy' (3 *Henry VI* (1592)). According to Robert Fabyan's *Chronicle* (1494), the nickname *Crookback* was earlier applied to Edmund of Lancaster (1245–96), who is also known as CROUCHBACK. ➤ See also *The* BOAR.

Crouchback Edmund of Lancaster (1245–96), second son of Henry III. He had a hunchback, hence his nickname. Like Richard III, he is also sometimes called *Crookback.* ➤ See also CROOKBACK.

Crum-Hell Oliver Cromwell (1599–1658), English general and statesman, Lord Protector of the Commonwealth 1653–58. His name was pronounced 'Crumwell' in his lifetime, hence the Royalist toast 'God send this *crumb well* down!' and the condemnatory nickname *Crum-Hell*. ➤ See also *The* ALMIGHTY *Nose*, COPPER *Nose*, IRONSIDES, KING *Oliver*, OLD *Noll.*

Cuddly Ken Kenny Everett (born Maurice Cole) (1944–95), British disc jockey and comedian. He made his name as an anarchic DJ, initially on pirate radio, before transferring his zany brand of humour to television in the late 70s and early 80s. Everett used to refer to himself as *Cuddly Ken.*

Cunctator Quintus Fabius (full name Quintus Fabius Maximus Verrucosus) (d.203 BC), Roman general and statesman. After Hannibal's defeat of the Roman army at Cannae in 216 BC, Fabius successfully pursued a strategy of caution and delay in order to wear down the Carthaginian invaders with guerrilla tactics of raids and ambushes in the hills without risking a pitched battle on the plains. This earned him his nickname *Cunctator,* which means 'delayer'. ➤ See also *The* AMERICAN *Fabius.*

The Curate of Meudon François Rabelais (*c.*1494–1553), French satirist, best known for the allegories *Pantagruel* (*c.*1532) and *Gargantua* (1534), characterized by bawdy humour and an exuberant use of language. Rabelais spent a period in his early life as a Franciscan monk, although his works were later denounced by the Church. He spent the last years of his life as a non-resident curate at Meudon near Paris.

The Currant Bun *The Sun* newspaper. *Currant bun* is Cockney rhyming slang for 'sun'.

Curthose Robert II, Duke of Normandy (1054?–1134), eldest son of William the Conqueror. On the death of William Rufus, the throne should have passed, by right, to him but while Robert was away on a crusade his younger brother Henry opportunistically seized the throne. The name *Curthose* means 'short boot' or 'short legging': Robert was short and stocky-legged.

Curtmantle Henry II (1133–89), son of Matilda, king of England 1154–89. He was the first Plantagenet king. The nickname means 'Short Mantle'. Henry introduced to English society the Anjou mantle, a knee-length garment which was particularly suitable for riding and hunting. His predecessors wore ankle-length robes.

Dd

Dame Harold   Harold Evans (b.1928), British newspaper editor. He edited the *Sunday Times* (1967–81) and the *Times* (1981–82), and later went on to run the Random House publishing group in the US. While editor of the *Sunday Times*, he was dubbed *Dame Harold Evans* by Lord Arran because of his supposed resemblance to the great theatrical Dame, Edith Evans. The nickname was gleefully taken up by the satirical magazine *Private Eye*.

The Dancing Chancellor   Christopher Hatton (1540–91), Lord Chancellor 1587–91. He is said to have first attracted the attention of Queen Elizabeth by his graceful dancing at a court masque, especially in a dance called the galliard. Sheridan alludes to this in *The Critic* (1779): 'You'll know Sir Christopher, by his turning out of his toes—famous you know for his dancing.'

The Dancing Destroyer   Herbie Hide (b.1971), Nigerian-born British boxer, WBO heavyweight champion 1994–95. Noted for his fast hands and nimble footwork, he was billed as the *Dancing Destroyer*.

The Dapper Don   John Gotti (1940–2002), US Mafia boss, head of the Gambino crime family. He was known by the New York tabloids as the *Dapper Don* because of his expensively tailored Italian suits. Another nickname was the Teflon Don because none of the charges brought against him in three criminal trials could be made to 'stick' and he was acquitted on each occasion. In 1992 he was finally convicted of murder, racketeering, and conspiracy and died in prison of throat cancer having served ten years of a life sentence.

The Dark and Bloody Ground   The US state of Kentucky. This name for Kentucky was popularized by the US poet Theodore O'Hara (1820–67): 'Sons of the dark and bloody ground' ('The Bivouac of the Dead', 1847). The phrase is said to derive from a warning given by a Cherokee chief in the late 18th century, that the land was already 'a bloody ground' because of fierce battles fought between American Indian tribes and that it would be dark for prospective settlers. ➤ See also *The* Bluegrass *State*.

The Dark Continent   Africa. The *Dark Continent* was a 19th-century epithet given to Africa at a time when it was little known to Europeans, suggesting both that the continent was relatively unexplored and mysterious and that its inhabitants were dark-skinned. The term is first recorded in H. M. Stanley's *Through the Dark Continent* (1878).

The Dark Horse President   James A(bram) Garfield (1831–81), US Republican statesman, 20th President of the US March–September 1881. He was assassinated within months of taking office. A 'dark horse' is a person about whom little is known. In US politics the term describes a candidate who is unexpectedly elected or appointed, and has been applied to several presidential candidates, but to Garfield in particular. In 1880 he emerged as the compromise Republican candidate for the presidential nomination. Rutherford B. Hayes (1822–93) was another *Dark Horse President*. ➤ See also *The* FIRST *Dark Horse*.

The Darling of the Halls   George Robey (born George Edward Wade) (1869–1954), British comedian and actor who performed in music-halls from the 1890s. In response to Mr Justice Darling's courtroom enquiry 'And who is George Robey?', the lawyer (later statesman) F. E. Smith (1872–1930) replied: 'Mr George Robey is the Darling of the music halls, m'lud.' The comedian subsequently became known as the *Darling of the Halls*. ➤ See also *The* PRIME *Minister of Mirth*.

Daubaway Weirdsley   Aubrey (Vincent) Beardsley (1872–98), English artist and illustrator. ➤ See AWFULLY *Weirdly*.

Dazzler   Darren Gough (b.1970), English cricketer for Yorkshire and England. His nickname *Dazzler* suits his ebullient personality, his lively fast bowling, and his cavalier batting. He had earlier been known as *Guzzler* because of his large appetite.

Deadly[1]   Doug Ellis (Herbert Douglas Ellis) (b.1924), British football club chairman. Ellis became chairman of Aston Villa in December 1968. During his long tenure in that post he has acquired a not altogether justified reputation for sacking a succession of managers, hence his nickname *Deadly*. The name is thought to have been coined by the former player Jimmy Greaves.

Deadly[2]   Derek Leslie Underwood (b.1945), English cricketer, a left-arm spin bowler for Kent and England. The attritional consistency and accuracy of Underwood's bowling earned him the nickname *Deadly*.

The Death-or-Glory Boys   The 17th Lancers (later the 17th/21st Lancers), a regiment of the British army. The regimental badge depicts a death's head with the motto 'or glory'. The badge commemorates the death of General Wolfe at Quebec in 1759, the year the regiment was formed. ➤ See also *The* HORSE *Marines*, WOLFE'S *Own*.

The Delhi Spearmen   The 9th (Queen's) Royal Lancers, a regiment of the British army. The nickname the *Delhi Spearmen* commemorates an incident at the siege of Delhi in 1857, during the Indian Mutiny. The regiment fought off a force of mutineers who are said to have shouted '*Delhi Bhala Wallah!*' ('Delhi Spearman!') as they fled.

The Demon Barber of Fleet Street   Sweeney Todd, the legendary barber who murdered his customers, the central character of a play by George Dibdin Pitt (1799–1855) and of later plays and musicals. He was said to cut his victims' throats while they sat waiting to be shaved. The bodies were then disposed of through a trapdoor and made into pies or sausages.

The Demon Bowler   Frederick Robert Spofforth (1853–1926), Australian cricketer. The greatest bowler of his time, he was often thought to be 'unplayable'. In 1881 he clean-bowled all 20 wickets in a match in Australia. The following year at the Oval he claimed 14 wickets for 90 runs, in Australia's first victory over England on English soil. Gaunt-faced with a large nose, Spofforth was known as the *Demon Bowler*, or simply as the *Demon*.

Der Alte Konrad Adenauer (1876–1967), German statesman, first Chancellor of the Federal Republic of Germany 1949–63, who presided over the political and economic reconstruction of his country after the Second World War. Taking office at the age of 73, Adenauer was known in Germany as *Der Alte* or 'the Old Man'. He finally resigned as Chancellor at the age of 87.

Der Bingle Bing Crosby (1904–77), US singer and film actor, as he was known by German soldiers in the Second World War. ➤ See also *The* OLD *Groaner*.

The Desert Fox Erwin Rommel (1891–1944), German field marshal, acclaimed for his brilliant generalship in North Africa in the Second World War. As commander of the Afrika Korps he became known as the *Desert Fox* for outwitting Allied forces with a series of surprise manoeuvres. He succeeded in capturing Tobruk (1942), but was defeated by Montgomery at El Alamein later that year. Rommel was forced to commit suicide after being implicated in the officers' plot against Hitler in 1944.

The Desert Rats The 7th British armoured division, a unit of the 8th army in the North African desert campaign of 1941–42. It called itself the *Desert Rats* after the jerboa (also known as a desert rat) depicted on the divisional badge.

The Devil's Own The 88th Foot, a regiment of the British army. The nickname the *Devil's Own* was bestowed on the 88th Foot by General Picton (1758–1815) in recognition of their bravery during the Peninsular War. The nickname is also associated with the Inns of Court Rifle Corps of Volunteers, who were so-named by George III when he learned that the regiment was composed mainly of lawyers.

Diamond City The city of Amsterdam, the Netherlands. It is a major centre of the diamond-cutting industry. ➤ See also *The* VENICE *of the North*.

Diamond Jim James Buchanan Brady (1856–1917), US millionaire. A former bellboy in a New York hotel, Brady rose from a job as a railway worker to amass a fortune selling railway equipment. He was known as *Diamond Jim* because of his extravagant tastes and fondness for wearing diamond jewellery, for example shirt-studs, tie-pins, and cuff-links.

Diamond Pitt Thomas Pitt (1653–1726), East India merchant and governor of Madras, known as *Diamond Pitt* because of the famous Pitt Diamond he owned. In 1702 he bought a 137-carat diamond, found in the Parteal mines in India, from a merchant. He later sold it to the Duke of Orleans for over six times the amount he had paid for it. At one time the Pitt Diamond was set in the hilt of Napoleon's sword.

The Diamond State The US state of Delaware. Though small in size (only Rhode Island is smaller), Delaware has great historical importance: it was the first of the thirteen founding states of the Union. From this derives its nickname the *Diamond state*. ➤ See also *The* BLUE *Hen State*, *The* FIRST *State*, NEW *Sweden*.

Dictionary Johnson Samuel Johnson (1709–84), English lexicographer, writer, critic, and conversationalist. Johnson was widely known by this sobriquet after the publication of his *Dictionary of the English Language* (1755), a landmark in lexicography which established his literary reputation. ➤ See also *The* GREAT *Cham of Literature*, URSA *Major*.

The Diehards The 57th Foot (later the Duke of Cambridge's Own Middlesex Regiment), a regiment of the British army. They won their nickname the *Diehards* at the Battle of Albuera (May 1811) in the Peninsular Wars, when the regiment was defending an important position against the French. The commanding officer Colonel Inglis was badly wounded but refused to be moved to the rear. Lying where he had fallen, he urged his men to 'Die hard, 57th, die hard!' Heavily outnumbered, 80% of the regiment were killed or wounded.

Dippermouth Louis Armstrong (1900–71), US jazz musician. Before he became known as *Satchelmouth* (or SATCHMO or *Satch*), Armstrong enjoyed the nickname *Dippermouth*, similarly denoting a person with a large mouth. In this case, Armstrong's mouth was being compared to a dipper, that is a ladle or long-handled pan. In 1923 King Oliver's band (with whom Armstrong then played) recorded 'Dippermouth Blues', which may have been named after him. ➤ See also POPS, SATCHMO.

Dirty Den Dennis Watts, the landlord of the *Queen Vic* pub in the BBC soap opera *EastEnders*, set in the East End of London and first broadcast in 1985. Played by Leslie Grantham, he was dubbed *Dirty Den* by the British tabloids, because of the character's womanizing and the early storyline in which he seduced the schoolgirl Michelle Fowler.

Dirty Dick Nathaniel Bentley (1735?–1809), English hardware shop-owner. He had been a well-known London dandy (the *Beau of Leadenhall Street*, as he was called) but, when his fiancée died on the eve of their wedding, he deteriorated into slovenliness, becoming known as *Dirty Dick*. He hardly ever washed, saying 'If I wash my hands today, they will be dirty again tomorrow', and his premises on Leadenhall Street became famous for their dirt and squalor.

The Dirty Digger (Keith) Rupert Murdoch (b.1931), Australian-born newspaper and media tycoon. His international media empire comprises newspapers in Australia, Britain, and the US, together with film and television companies. Murdoch took out US citizenship in 1985. In Australia and New Zealand, *digger* is an informal term for a man, especially a private soldier. The term derived (in the early 20th century) from digger 'miner', reinforced by association with the digging of trenches on the battlefields.

The Dirty Half-hundred The 50th Foot (later the 1st Battalion Royal West Kent), a regiment of the British army. Their nickname the *Dirty Half-hundred* stems from an incident at the Battle of Vimiero in 1808, during the Peninsular War. As the men wiped their sweating brows with their black coat cuffs, the dye left black marks on their faces. *Half-hundred* refers to the regimental number. ➤ See also *The* BLIND *Half-hundred*.

The Dirty Shirts The 101st Foot (later the 1st Battalion Munster Fusiliers), a regiment of the British army. The regimental nickname the *Dirty Shirts* dates from the siege of Delhi in 1857, during the Indian Mutiny. Discarding their coats, they fought in their shirtsleeves.

The Divine Callas Maria Callas (born Maria Cecilia Anna Kalageropoulos) (1923–77), operatic soprano, born in New York of Greek parents. Callas, generally acknowledged as the greatest singing actress of the 20th century, is celebrated for the intensity of her acting and the power and range of her voice. Her bel canto style of singing especially suited her to early Italian opera and she excelled in such roles as Bellini's Norma, Cherubini's Medea, and Puccini's Tosca.

The Divine Miss M Bette Midler (b.1945), US singer, comedienne, and actress. The *Divine Miss M* was the persona Midler created for her outrageous stage act, developed early on in her career when she performed at gay venues in New York City: a brassy and bawdy cabaret star modelled on the likes of Mae West and Sophie Tucker. Midler's first album was entitled *The Divine Miss M* (1972). She also liked to refer to herself as the *Last of the Tacky Ladies*.

The Divine One Sarah Lois Vaughan (1924–90), US jazz singer and pianist, noted for her vocal range and improvisational skills. She began by performing with bebop bands in the early 1940s, later becoming an international star recording both jazz numbers and romantic ballads. Sometimes described as jazz's diva, Vaughan was called *Sassy* by those who knew her and the *Divine One* by her many admirers.

The Divine Pagan Hypatia (*c*.370–415), Greek philosopher, astronomer, and mathematician. The head of the Neoplatonist school at Alexandria, she wrote several learned treatises as well as devising inventions such as an astrolabe. Hypatia was murdered by a Christian mob opposed to her Neoplatonist philosophy.

The Divine Ponytail Roberto Baggio (b.1967), Italian footballer. Considered one of the best centre forwards of the 1990s, he was named both World and European Player of the Year in 1993. He played for Italy in three World Cup tournaments. The clubs he has played for include Fiorentina, Juventus, AC Milan, Bologna, and Inter Milan. His nickname the *Divine Ponytail* refers to the hairstyle he wore for much of his career.

The Divine Sarah Sarah Bernhardt (born Henriette Rosine Bernard) (1844–1923), French actress. Internationally acclaimed as the greatest tragic actress of her day, she is probably best known for her portrayal of Marguerite in *La Dame aux camélias* by Alexandre Dumas *fils*. Bernhardt was noted for her great beauty, the clarity of her speaking voice, and her charismatic personality. In 1915 she had one of her legs amputated, but she continued to act until her death. It was Oscar Wilde who first called her the *Divine Sarah*. ➤ See also SARAH *Heartburn*.

Dixie William Ralph Dean (1907–80), British footballer. He made his debut for Everton in 1925 and is remembered for scoring 60 league goals for the club in the 1927–28 season, a tally for a season that has never been beaten. His famous nickname *Dixie Dean* is said to have derived from his swarthy complexion, supposedly reminiscent of that of inhabitants of the southern USA, known as Dixieland. Dean hated his nickname but it has subsequently been applied to many other men sharing his surname.

Dizzy Benjamin Disraeli, 1st Earl of Beaconsfield (1804–81), British Tory statesman, of Italian-Jewish descent. He was Prime Minister 1868 and 1874–80. *Dizzy* was a contemporary nickname, its informality reflecting his popularity in the country. It is recorded that when after a successful vote in the House of Commons, Disraeli refused a supper party at the Carlton to go home, his wife told people proudly, 'Dizzy came home to *me*.'

The Doc Tommy Docherty (b.1928), Scottish football player and manager. After a successful career as a player, he went on to manage a succession of clubs, including Chelsea, Queen's Park Rangers, Aston Villa, and Manchester United, once joking that he had 'had more clubs than Jack Nicklaus'. Known for his forthright views on the game, Docherty's managerial career was often marked by controversy. His nickname the *Doc* is an abbreviation of his surname.

The Dockers' KC Ernest Bevin (1881–1951), British Labour statesman and trade unionist. As secretary of the dock workers' union, Bevin successfully argued the dockers' case for higher wages and better conditions before the Commission of Inquiry of 1920. This advocacy won him the nickname the *Dockers' KC* (that is, King's Counsel). He was one of the founders of the Transport and General Workers' Union, serving as its first General Secretary (1921–40), and was a leading organizer of the General Strike (1926). He was later to serve as Foreign Secretary (1945–51).

Doctor Mirabilis Roger Bacon. ➤ See *The* ADMIRABLE *Doctor*.

Doctor Subtilis John Duns Scotus (*c*.1265–1308), Scottish theologian and scholar. ➤ See *The* SUBTLE *Doctor*.

Doctor Universalis St Albertus Magnus (*c*.1200–80), German Dominican theologian, philosopher, and scientist who was a pioneer in uniting Aristotelianism and Christian theology. Among his pupils was the young Thomas Aquinas. His wide learning and the breadth of his knowledge earned him the nickname *Doctor Universalis*.

The Dog Diogenes (*c*.400–*c*.325 BC), Greek philosopher, the most famous of the Cynics. He lived in Athens in extreme poverty and asceticism, hence his nickname *Kuōn* ('the Dog'), from which the Cynics were then said to have derived their name. According to legend he lived in a barrel, to demonstrate his belief that the virtuous life is the simple life.

Dolly Basil Lewis d'Oliveira (b.1931), South African-born cricketer who played for England in 44 Test matches. At the start of the 1968 MCC tour of South Africa, d'Oliveira was the central figure in an international incident when the player was refused entry to the country because he was a 'Cape Coloured'. As a result the tour was cancelled. His nickname *Dolly* is a shortening of his surname.

The Don Donald George Bradman (1908–2001), Australian cricketer. An outstanding batsman who dominated the sport in his day, he began his career in 1927 with New South Wales and played for his country from 1928 until his retirement in 1948. He captained Australia from 1936 to 1948. A prolific run-maker, Bradman scored 117 first-class centuries, 29 of them in Test matches. His Test match batting average of 99.94 is well above that of any other cricketer of any era. Although generally known as the *Don* (from his first name), he was also nicknamed the LITTLE MASTER because of his relatively diminutive stature.

The Doog Derek Dougan (b.1938), Northern Irish footballer. During the 1960s and 1970s he made 244 league appearances for Wolverhampton Wanderers, scoring 95 goals. The centre forward, who won 43 caps for Northern Ireland, was popularly known by the Wolverhampton fans as the *Doog*.

Doomsday Sedgwick William Sedgwick (1610?–69?), English puritan and mystic. In 1646, following the prophecy of a woman in the neighbourhood of Swaffham Prior, Cambridge, he announced that doomsday, or the day of judgement, was at hand. Although nothing happened on the appointed day, during the following night there was a considerable storm.

Doris Karloff Ann (Noreen) Widdecombe (b.1947), British Conservative politician. In the 1990s, as a Home Office minister with responsibility for prisons, she acquired a reputation for uncompromising toughness and combativeness. Her tabloid nickname *Doris Karloff* was based on the name of Boris Karloff (1887–1969), a British-born US actor, noted for his roles in horror films.

Le Douanier Henri (Julien) Rousseau (1844–1910), French painter. Before taking up painting full time at the age of 41, Rousseau had served in the army and then worked for the Paris customs service as a toll-collector, hence his nickname *Le Douanier*, 'The Customs Officer'. A self-taught artist, he is known for his bold, colourful paintings of exotic jungle landscapes and haunting dream-like scenes painted in a naive style.

Doubting Thomas St Thomas, one of the twelve apostles, also called Didymus ('the twin'). He said that he would not believe that Christ had risen again until he had seen and touched his wounds (John 20:24–9). His nickname *Doubting Thomas* has come to be applied to any person who is sceptical and refuses to believe something without proof.

Dracula Ray(mond) Reardon (b.1932), Welsh snooker player who won the world championship in 1970, 1973–76, and 1978. He was known as *Dracula* because of his facial resemblance to movie incarnations of Bram Stoker's fictional vampire and his prominent eye-teeth.

Dr Brighton Brighton, resort town on the south coast of England. In the late 18th and 19th centuries Brighton was a fashionable health resort, for some years patronized by the Prince Regent (later George IV). The nickname *Dr Brighton* first gained currency towards the end of the Regency period (c.1820).

Dr Death[1] David (Anthony Llewellyn) Owen (b.1938), British politician. Owen served as Foreign Secretary 1977–79 in the Labour government. Growing increasingly dissatisfied with the Labour Party's policies, in 1981 he broke away to become a founding member of the Social Democratic Party (SDP). He led the SDP from 1983 to 1987, resigning to form a breakaway SDP when the main party decided to merge with the Liberals. He owed his nickname *Dr Death* to his earlier career as a neurologist, to his saturnine looks, and to his alleged political ruthlessness.

Dr Death[2] Harold Frederick Shipman (1946–2004), British serial killer. A general practitioner from Hyde in Greater Manchester, Shipman was sentenced to life imprisonment in 2000 for the murders of 15 patients, mainly elderly women, by lethal injections of the drug diamorphine. A subsequent inquiry concluded that he had been responsible for the deaths of at least 215 patients over a 23-year period. During Shipman's trial the British tabloids dubbed him *Dr Death*.

Dr Presto Jonathan Swift (known as Dean Swift) (1667–1745), Irish satirist, poet, and Anglican cleric, best known for his satire *Gulliver's Travels* (1726). This punning nickname was, according to Swift's *Journal to Stella*, given to him by the Italian-born Duchess of Shrewsbury: 'The secretary and I have been walking three or four hours to-day. The duchess of Shrewsbury asked him, was not that Dr. Dr. and she could not say my name in English, but said Dr. Presto, which is Italian for Swift. Whimsical enough, as Billy Swift says' (2 August 1711). It appealed to Swift and he subsequently used the name to refer to himself, both in the journal and elsewhere.

Dr Slop John Stoddart (1773–1856), British journalist. As an opinionated contributor to *The Times* (1812–16) and editor of 'The New Times' (*c.*1817–28), he was the subject of several satires, such as 'A Slap at Slop' (1820). The nickname *Dr Slop* had earlier been applied to the antiquary and physician John Burton (1710–71), who was satirized as Dr Slop in Sterne's *Tristram Shandy* (1759–67).

Dr Squintum George Whitefield (1714–70), English evangelist, one of the founders of Methodism. *Dr Squintum* was the nickname under which he was ridiculed by Samuel Foote in his comedy *The Minor* (1760), a satire on Methodists.

Dubya George W(alker) Bush (b.1946), US Republican statesman, 43rd President of the US. Before entering politics, he worked first in the oil business and later as managing partner of the Texas Rangers baseball franchise. Elected Governor of Texas in 1994, he became president in 2001. To distinguish him from his father, the former president George Bush, the son is widely known as George W. Bush, or simple as George W. The nickname *Dubya* represents the Texan pronunciation of the letter W. Another way to differentiate between the two presidents has been to refer to one as '41' (i.e. the 41st president) and the other as '43'.

The Dude President Chester Alan Arthur (1830–86), US Republican statesman, 21st President of the US 1881–85. He was appointed Garfield's vice-president in 1881 and became president after Garfield's assassination. The dapper Arthur, the *Dude President*, was noted for his polished manners and stylish clothes. In the late 19th century a 'dude' was a fop or a dandy.

Dugout Doug Douglas MacArthur (1880–1964), US general. He commanded the US defence of the Philippines against the Japanese 1941–42. The front line troops under heavy bombardment on the Bataan peninsula felt that MacArthur, conducting operations from his underground shelter on Corregidor Island, had abandoned them. Their scathing name for him, *Dugout Doug*, pursued him for the rest of the war. ➤ See also *The* AMERICAN *Caesar*.

Duke[1] Edward Kennedy Ellington (1899–1974), US jazz composer, pianist, and bandleader, one of the leading figures in the history of jazz. He wrote over 900, often complex, compositions, including 'Mood Indigo' and 'Satin Doll'. Ellington, whose father was a butler at the White House, acquired his nickname long before he started playing jazz. As a teenager his school friends used to call him *Duke*, apparently because he was always so elegantly dressed and had a somewhat aristocratic bearing.

Duke[2] John Wayne (1907–79), US film actor, chiefly associated with roles in such westerns as *Stagecoach* (1939), *Red River* (1948), and *True Grit* (1969). He acquired the nickname *Duke* in childhood, when he was still known by his real name of Marion Morrison. Duke was the name of the family's pet dog, an Airedale terrier. When as a boy he walked the dog around the neighbourhood, people referred to the dog and his master as Little Duke and Big Duke respectively. The childhood name stuck and he began his film career in 1927 under the name Duke Morrison. Although he soon changed this to John Wayne, he continued to be known as 'the Duke', a nickname that well suited the tough plain-speaking persona adopted in his film roles.

The Dumb Ox St Thomas Aquinas (1225–74), Italian philosopher, theologian, and Dominican friar. He was nicknamed the *Dumb Ox* by his schoolfellows because they thought his habitual silence indicated stupidity. Albertus Magnus (*c.*1200–80) is said to have commented, 'We call him the dumb ox, but he will give such a bellow of learning as will be heard all over the world.' ➤ See also *The* ANGELIC *Doctor*.

Dutch[1] Marlene Dietrich (born Maria Magdelene von Losch) (1901–92), German-born US film actress and singer. She won international fame in the 1930 German film *Der Blaue Engel* (*The Blue Angel*). Her Hollywood films include *Morocco* (1930), *Shanghai Express* (1932), and *Destry Rides Again* (1939). From the 1950s she was an internationally successful cabaret star, noted for her husky, sultry singing voice. Among her circle of friends in Hollywood, she was affectionally known as *Dutch*, a humorous corruption of *Deutsche* 'German'.

Dutch[2] Ronald (Wilson) Reagan (1911–2004), US Republican statesman, 40th President of the US 1981–89. According to Reagan's own account, his family nickname *Dutch* came from his father's remark after his birth: 'For such a little bit of a fat Dutchman, he makes a hell of a lot of noise.' ➤ See also *The* GIPPER, *The* GREAT *Communicator*, OLD *Hopalong*, *The* TEFLON *President*.

Dutch Billy William III, also known as William of Orange (1650–1702), grandson of Charles I, king of Great Britain and Ireland 1689–1702. William was *stadtholder* (chief magistrate) of the Netherlands from 1672. In 1688 he landed in England with a Dutch fleet at the invitation of parliamentary opponents to James II and, having accepted the Declaration of Rights, was crowned as joint sovereign with his wife Mary II (daughter of James II) the following year. ➤ See also *The* GREAT *Deliverer*, KING *Billy*.

Ee

Eddie the Eagle Eddie Edwards (b.1963), British ski-jumper. Edwards shot to fame at the 1988 Winter Olympics in Calgary when his hopeless performance representing Britain made him a folk-hero. He came 56th in a field of 57 competitors, the 57th having been disqualified. At the closing ceremony, the IOC president Juan Antonio Samaranch singled out the ski-jumper's heroic failure for special mention: 'At this Olympic Games some competitors have won gold, some have broken records, and one has even flown like an eagle.'

Edward the Caresser Edward VII (1841–1910), king of Great Britain and Ireland 1901–10. Punning on the name of Edward the Confessor, this nickname alludes to his notorious womanizing. ➤ See also BERTIE, EDWARD *the Peacemaker*, TUM-TUM, *The* UNCLE *of Europe*.

Edward the Peacemaker Edward VII (1841–1910), king of Great Britain and Ireland 1901–10. He was nicknamed *Edward the Peacemaker* in recognition of his efforts in diplomacy. Related to many of the crowned heads of Europe, Edward used his visits abroad to help prevent the outbreak of a European war. The *Entente Cordiale* between Britain and France was established in his reign. His affair with Lillie Langtry earned him the punning alternative nickname *Edward the Piecemaker*. ➤ See also BERTIE, EDWARD *the Caresser*, TUM-TUM, *The* UNCLE *of Europe*.

Eisenhower Platz Grosvenor Square, London. During the Second World War, this square in the West End of London, where the US embassy is situated, was informally known as *Eisenhower Platz*. Many of the buildings in the square were occupied by the headquarters of the US military forces in Europe, under the command of General Dwight D. Eisenhower. ➤ See also LITTLE *America*.

El Beatle George Best (b.1946), Northern Irish footballer, an exceptionally skilful striker and winger. In 1963 he made his debut for Manchester United at the age of 17 and made 349 league appearances for them over the next ten years. With his good looks, charisma, and high-living lifestyle, Best was the first British football superstar, a sporting equivalent of the Beatles rock group. In 1966 the British press dubbed him *El Beatle* when he was photographed wearing an enormous sombrero on the team's triumphant return from Portugal having beaten the Lisbon club Benfica 5–1.

El Cid Rodrigo Díaz de Vivar (c.1043–99), Count of Bivar, Spanish soldier and national hero. A champion of Christianity against the Moors, in 1094 he captured Valencia, which he went on to rule. He was nicknamed *El Cid*, from the Arabic *sayyid* meaning 'lord', by the Moors. He is immortalized in the Spanish *Poema del Cid* (12th century) and in Corneille's play *Le Cid* (1637).

The Elephant Man Joseph Carey Merrick (1862–90), known as the *Elephant Man*. Merrick was born with severe facial deformities caused by a rare disease, now thought to be Proteus syndrome. As an adult he was exhibited as a fairground freak, 'The Elephant Man, Half-a-Man and Half-an-Elephant'. He was finally rescued by the surgeon Sir Frederick Treves and given sanctuary in the London Hospital, where he spent the few remaining years of his life.

El Gran Capitán Gonzalo Fernández de Córdoba (1453–1515), Spanish military leader, famous for his military exploits in support of the king of Naples against the French. He was known as *El Gran Capitan* ('the Great Captain').

El Greco Domenikos Theotokopoulos (1541–1614), Cretan-born Spanish painter, generally known as *El Greco*, 'The Greek'. He was born in Crete of Greek descent and, after studying in Italy, possibly as a pupil of Titian, moved to Spain in 1570. His portraits and religious works are characterized by elongated and distorted figures and vibrant use of colour. His works include the altarpiece *The Assumption of the Virgin* (1577–79) and the painting *The Burial of Count Orgaz* (1586).

El Tel Terry Venables (b.1943), football player and manager. Although Venables is by no means the only British football manager to have worked in Spain, his affectionate and tabloid-friendly nickname is a reference to his time as coach of Barcelona FC (1984–87), during which period the club won the Spanish league title. When he later returned to English football to manage Tottenham Hotspur and subsequently to coach the England national side (1994–96), he continued to be popularly known as *El Tel*.

Elvis the Pelvis Elvis (Aaron) Presley (1935–77), US pop and rock-and-roll singer, one of the biggest stars of the 20th century. He shot to fame in 1956 with such records as 'Heartbreak Hotel', 'Blue Suede Shoes', and 'Hound Dog'. His performances on stage were noted for their vigorous sexuality, particularly as manifested in the suggestive hip gyrations from which he gained his nickname. When he first appeared on national television he was shown only from the waist up. ➤ See also *The* KING[2].

The Emerald Isle Ireland. The epithet the *Emerald Isle* refers to the prevailing lush green of its countryside. The name is first recorded in the nationalist poem *Erin* by William Drennan (1754–1820): 'Nor one feeling of vengeance presume to defile/The cause, or the men, of the Emerald Isle' (1795). ➤ See also *The* LAND *of Saints and Scholars*.

Éminence Grise François Leclerc du Tremblay (1577–1638), also known as Père Joseph, French cleric and private secretary of Cardinal Richelieu. Richelieu was known as the RED CARDINAL or as *L'Éminence Rouge*. Du Tremblay, who wore a grey habit, became known as the GREY CARDINAL or as *L'Éminence Grise*. Although he was not a cardinal, he exercised the power of one behind the scenes. The term 'éminence grise' has come to be applied to anyone who exercises influence without holding an official position.

Éminence Rouge Armand Jean du Plessis, duc de Richelieu (1585–1642), French cardinal and statesman. As chief minister of Louis XIII 1624–42 he dominated French government. He destroyed the power base of the Huguenots in the late 1620s and supported Gustavus Adolphus in the Thirty Years War from 1635. In 1635 he established the Académie française. Richelieu was known as the *Red Cardinal* or as *L'Éminence Rouge*, because he wore a red habit, which was unusual for the time.

The Emperor of Pugilism John Jackson (1769–1845), English boxer. This was a nickname bestowed on him by Lord Byron, who was one of his pupils at the boxing school Jackson opened on his retirement. ➤ See also GENTLEMAN *Jackson.*

The Emperor's Chambermaids The 14th King's Hussars, a regiment of the British army. After the Battle of Vittoria in June 1813, they captured the coach of Joseph Bonaparte, brother of Napoleon. Among the contents they seized as trophies was an ornate silver chamber pot, hence the nickname the regiment acquired, the *Emperor's Chambermaids.*

Empire City New York City. It takes its nickname *Empire City* from that of New York State, the EMPIRE STATE. ➤ See also *The* BIG *Apple,* GOTHAM.

The Empire State The US state of New York. In 1784 George Washington referred to New York as 'the seat of Empire', the origin of its nickname (dating from *c.*1820) the *Empire State.* ➤ See also *The* EMPIRE *City.*

The Empress Maud Matilda (1102–67), English princess and claimant to the English throne, daughter of Henry I. Her marriage to the Holy Roman Emperor Henry V caused her to be known as *Empress Matilda* or more commonly *Empress Maud.* After her husband's death she married Geoffrey Plantagenet, count of Anjou. She had been nominated by her father Henry I as his heir but when the king died in 1135, her cousin Stephen seized the throne and Matilda was forced to flee. She waged an unsuccessful civil war with Stephen for the English throne, her supporters crowning her queen in 1141 and declaring her *Lady of the English* (or *Lady of England*). Her son became Henry II, the first in a long line of Plantagenet monarchs.

The Empress of Emotion Elissa Landi (Elizabeth Kuhnelt) (1904–48), Austrian-Italian film actress who made films in several countries before becoming a Holly-wood leading lady in the 1930s, starring in such films as *The Sign of the Cross* (1932) and *The Count of Monte Cristo* (1934).

The Empress of the Blues Bessie Smith (1894–1937), US blues singer. A hugely influential singer and unchallenged recipient of the title *Empress of the Blues,* Bessie Smith established herself as the pre-eminent female singer of the blues in the 1920s and made over 150 recordings. She is remembered for the strength and intensity of her voice and the vitality of her performances.

The English Alexander Henry V (1387–1422), son of Henry IV, king of England 1413–22. Soon after coming to the throne, he invaded France, thus renewing the Hundred Years War. He defeated the French at Agincourt in 1415 and conquered Normandy in 1419. His military genius and early death (from dysentery) made the *English Alexander* an appropriate nickname for him. In Shakespeare's *Henry V,* the Welsh soldier Fluellen compares the king to Alexander the Great: 'If you mark Alexander's life well, Harry of Monmouth's life is come after it indifferent well'.

The English Palladio Inigo Jones (1573–1652), English architect and stage designer. ➤ See *The* ENGLISH *Vitruvius.*

The English Roscius David Garrick (1717–79), English actor, manager, and dramatist. He was regarded as the foremost Shakespearean actor of 18th-century England and was manager of Drury Lane Theatre for nearly 30 years (1747–76).

Quintus Roscius Gallus (d.62 BC) was the most celebrated of Roman comic actors, after whom many great actors were nicknamed. ➤ See also *The* YOUNG *Roscius*.

The English Solomon James I (1566–1625), son of Mary, Queen of Scots, king of Scotland (as James VI) 1567–1625, and of England and Ireland 1603–25. ➤ See *The* BRITISH *Solomon*.

The English Vitruvius Inigo Jones (1573–1652), English architect and stage designer, best known as the architect of the Queen's House at Greenwich (1616) and the Banqueting Hall at Whitehall (1619). Having studied architecture in Italy, Jones introduced the Palladian style to England, earning the titles the *English Vitruvius* and the *English Palladio*. Vitruvius (Marcus Vitruvius Pollio, *fl.* 1st century BC) was a Roman architect and military engineer, whose comprehensive ten-volume treatise on architecture influenced the Italian Renaissance architect, Andrea Palladio (1508–80). Palladio's theoretical works and neoclassical style in turn inspired the English Palladian movement.

The Equality State The US state of Wyoming. In 1869 Wyoming became the first state in the US to grant votes to women, hence its nickname the *Equality State*. An earlier variation was the *Suffrage State*.

Eric the Eel Eric Moussambani (b.1980), Equatorial Guinean swimmer. At the 2000 Sydney Olympic Games, he swam a heat of the 100m freestyle in a time of 1 minute 52.72 seconds, one of the slowest times in Olympic history. He became an overnight celebrity, his nickname deliberately modelled on that of EDDIE THE EAGLE.

Est-il Possible Prince George of Denmark (1653–1708), consort of Queen Anne. On hearing a piece of news, especially bad news, he would invariably remark 'Est-il possible?' (French, literally 'Is it possible?'). This became his nickname, probably coined by his father-in-law James II. It was said that when in 1688, the prince was one of those to desert James for William of Orange, the king commented, 'So Est-il possible is gone too.'

The Eternal City The city of Rome, Italy. It has been known as the *Eternal City* since classical times, the epithet being a translation of Latin *urbs aeterna*, occurring in Ovid and Tibullus, and frequently found in the official documents of the Empire. ➤ See also *The* CITY *of the Seven Hills*.

The Ettrick Shepherd James Hogg (1770–1835), Scottish poet who worked as a shepherd in the Ettrick Forest. His poetic talent was discovered by Walter Scott and he soon acquired the nickname the *Ettrick Shepherd*. The name was perpetuated by *Noctes Ambrosianae*, a regular and popular editorial feature in *Blackwood's Magazine* (on which Hogg worked as a member of its editorial staff). This took the form of a series of imaginary conversations between 'Christopher North' (the pseudonym of John Wilson, who wrote most of the conversations), the 'Ettrick Shepherd' (Hogg), and others. The dialogues were lively, witty, and convivial and covered a wide range of topics. Wilson's impersonation of the Ettrick Shepherd was particularly entertaining.

Evans of the Broke Edward Ratcliffe Garth Russell Evans, 1st Baron Mountevans (1881–1957), British admiral and explorer. He was known as *Evans of the Broke* from an incident in the First World War when, as commander of HMS *Broke* (pronounced 'brook'), he sank six German destroyers.

The Evergreen State   The US state of Washington. Its mountains are covered by forests of spruce and Douglas fir, reflected not only in the state's nickname but also in its green flag. The *Evergreen State* was adopted as Washington's official nickname in 1893. ➤ See also *The* CHINOOK *State*.

Evita   María Eva Duarte de Perón (1919–52), Argentinian politician. She married Juan Perón in 1945, becoming de facto Minister of Health and of Labour after he became president. In this capacity she organized female workers, secured the vote for women, and earmarked substantial government funds for social welfare. Idolized by the Argentine public for her charitable work, she was popularly known as *Evita*. She died of cancer at the age of 33. The stage musical *Evita*, based on her life, is by Andrew Lloyd Webber and Tim Rice.

The Factory King   Richard Oastler (1789–1861), English reformer. He earned the sobriquet the *Factory King* because of his campaigning to improve conditions in Yorkshire factories. In particular he helped to introduce the ten-hour day and to improve the lot of child labour.

The Fair Maid of Kent   Joan (1328–85), daughter of Edmund Earl of Kent, and wife of her cousin Edward, the Black Prince. She was the mother of Richard II. Although the sobriquet the *Fair Maid of Kent* is not found in contemporary sources, she is called '*cette jeune damoiselle de Kent*' in Jean Froissart's *Chronicle* (1325–1400).

The Fair Maid of Norway   Margaret of Norway (1283–90). ➤ See *The* MAID *of Norway.*

Fair Perdita   Mary Robinson, actress and mistress of George, Prince of Wales. ➤ See PERDITA.

Fair Rosamond   Rosamond de Clifford (d.1176?), mistress of Henry II, known as *Fair Rosamond*. According to legend, the king concealed her in a maze at Woodstock to protect her from the jealousy of his queen, Eleanor of Aquitaine. In an elaboration of the legend, Eleanor finds her rival by following a silken thread through the maze, and then offers Rosamond the choice of a dagger or a bowl of poison. Whether this story is true or not, Rosamond was buried in the choir of Godstow Abbey near Oxford, though her remains were removed to the Chapter House there around 1191.

The Famine Queen   Victoria (1819–1901), queen of Great Britain and Ireland 1837–1901 and empress of India 1876–1901. This was a derogatory nickname for Queen Victoria, coined by Maud Gonne (1867–1953) in reference to the Irish Potato Famine of 1846–47. ➤ See also *The* GRANDMOTHER *of Europe*, MRS *Brown*, *The* WIDOW *at Windsor.*

Famous Seamus   Seamus (Justin) Heaney (b.1939), Irish poet, born in Northern Ireland and an Irish citizen since 1972. His early poetry, such as *Death of a Naturalist* (1966), reflects the rural life of his youth, while later work deals with wider social and cultural themes, including the conflict in Northern Ireland. Among his collections are *North* (1975), *The Haw Lantern* (1987), *Spirit Level* (1996), and *Electric Light* (2001). Heaney was awarded the Nobel Prize for Literature 1995. His subsequent celebrity has won him the rhyming nickname *Famous Seamus* in literary circles.

Farmer George   George III (1738–1820), grandson of George II, king of Great Britain and Ireland 1760–1820, Elector of Hanover 1760–1815 and king of Hanover 1815–20. During his reign he was known as *Farmer George* because of his keen interest in agricultural schemes and model farms. Under the pseudonym Ralph Robinson he contributed to the periodical *Annals of Agriculture*, edited by the writer and agricultural theorist Arthur Young. He was lampooned in satires and caricatures for earning a profit from his farm near Windsor.

The Fat Adonis George, Prince of Wales, later George IV (1762–1830). ➤ See *The* ADONIS *of Fifty*.

Fatha Earl Kenneth Hines (1905–83), US jazz pianist, conductor, and songwriter. He formed his own band in 1929, later playing with Louis Armstrong's All Stars (1948–51). While such members of the jazz nobility as Duke Ellington, Count Basie, and King Oliver owe their titles to nicknames, Earl Hines was born with that name. His own nickname of *Fatha* was originally given him by the radio announcer/ engineer Ted Pearson.

The Father of Chemistry Robert Boyle (1627–91), Irish-born scientist, often acknowledged as the *Father of Chemistry*. His precise definitions of chemical elements and chemical reactions helped to separate the discipline from alchemy. A founder member of the Royal Society, Boyle is best known for his experiments with the air pump, which led to the law named after him. ➤ See also *The* FATHER *of Modern Chemistry*.

The Father of Comedy Aristophanes (*c*.450–*c*.385 BC), Greek comic dramatist. His eleven surviving comedies caricature contemporary politicians and intellectuals (such as Socrates in *The Clouds*), parody living poets such as Aeschylus and Euripides, and comment on current affairs. These plays are notable for the exuberance of their language and fantasy-like inventiveness of their settings. The actor and dramatist Samuel Foote (1720–77) was known to his contemporaries as the *English Aristophanes*, on account of the satirical portraits of living people that most of his plays contain. Likewise, Molière (1622–73) was known as the *French Aristophanes*.

The Father of English History St Bede (*c*.673–735), English monk, theologian, and historian, known as the VENERABLE BEDE. His *Ecclesiastical History of the English People* (completed in 731) is a primary source for early English history. It has vivid descriptions of life in the 7th century and is based on careful research, separating fact from hearsay and tradition wherever possible. ➤ See also *The* VENERABLE *Bede*.

The Father of English Music Thomas Tallis (*c*.1505–85), English composer, known chiefly for his choral church music, such as the forty-part motet *Spem in Alium*. As organist of the Chapel Royal jointly with William Byrd, he served under Henry VIII, Edward VI, Mary, and Elizabeth I.

The Father of English Poetry Geoffrey Chaucer (*c*.1342–1400), English poet. His most famous work the *Canterbury Tales* (*c*.1387–1400) is a cycle of linked tales told by a group of pilgrims journeying from London to Canterbury. His other works include the long narrative poem *Troilus and Criseyde* (1385). Chaucer's skills of vivid characterization, humour, and stylistic versatility established him as the first great English poet; according to John Dryden, he was the *Father of English Poetry*.

The Father of English Prose Roger Ascham (*c*.1515–68), English humanist scholar and writer. He was tutor to the future Elizabeth I and Latin secretary to Queen Mary and later to Elizabeth. His works include *Toxophilus* (1545), his treatise on archery, and *The Scholemaster* (1570), a practical and influential treatise on education.

Ascham, writing in English at a time when scholarly works were usually written in Latin, did much to help the development of a simple, clear English prose style.

The Father of Greek Drama Thespis (6th century BC), Greek dramatic poet. He is credited by Aristotle with originating the role of the actor in addition to the traditional chorus, thus allowing spoken dialogue to develop. The word *thespian* comes from his name. ➤ See also *The* FATHER *of Tragedy.*

The Father of His Country The title the *Father of His Country* has been bestowed on a number of historical figures, most notably Cicero and George Washington. Marcus Tullius Cicero (106–43 BC), Roman statesman, orator, and writer, was given the title by the Roman senate. George Washington (1732–99), US general and statesman, 1st President of the US 1789–97, earned the title during his lifetime. It was first used, in the form of the German *Das Landes Vater,* on a calendar published in Pennsylvania in 1778. ➤ See also *The* AMERICAN *Fabius, The* CINCINNATUS *of the West.*

The Father of History Herodotus (5th century BC), Greek historian. His *History,* generally regarded as the first major work of narrative history, is an account of the Persian Wars of the early 5th century BC. It also deals with the earlier history of the Persian empire and its relations with the Greeks to explain the origins of the conflict. Herodotus is commonly known as the *Father of History* because he was the first historian to collect his materials systematically, critically evaluate their accuracy to a degree, and arrange them in a well-constructed and vivid narrative. However, his use at times of dubious anecdotes has also caused him to be called the FATHER OF LIES.

The Father of Lies Herodotus (5th century BC), Greek historian. ➤ See *The* FATHER *of History.*

The Father of Medicine Hippocrates (*c.*460–377 BC), Greek physician, traditionally regarded as the *Father of Medicine.* His name was attached to a body of ancient Greek medical writings which contained diverse opinions on the nature of illness and treatment. The Hippocratic oath, named after him, is an oath stating the duties and proper conduct of doctors, formerly taken by those beginning medical practice.

The Father of Modern Chemistry Antoine Laurent Lavoisier (1743–94), French chemist, acclaimed as the *Father of Modern Chemistry.* He developed a new rational system for naming chemical substances. Lavoisier identified and named oxygen and described its role in combustion and respiration. He was guillotined in the French Revolution because of his involvement in the collection of indirect taxes. ➤ See also *The* FATHER *of Chemistry.*

The Father of Reform John Cartwright (1740–1824), English radical politician. Cartwright was a political reformer, who advocated annual parliaments and universal suffrage, and founded the Society for Constitutional Information.

The Father of the Atomic Bomb Julius Robert Oppenheimer (1904–67), US physicist. As director of the laboratory at Los Alamos, New Mexico, during the Second World War, he supervised the development and construction of the first atomic bomb, known as the Manhattan Project. He later opposed the development of the hydrogen bomb.

The Father of the Blues W(illiam) C(hristopher) Handy (1873–1958), US blues musician, composer, and bandleader. Although by no means the first musician to play the blues, he was one of the first to write this music down in such compositions as 'Memphis Blues' (1912), one of the first blues ever published, and 'St Louis Blues' (1914). Many of these compositions were inspired by the rural blues songs Handy had heard and were not therefore entirely original, a fact he readily acknowledged. Nevertheless he earned the title the *Father of the Blues*, which was also to be the title of his 1941 autobiography. Handy's reputation as the originator of the blues (and indeed jazz) has been scornfully disputed by many, notably Jelly Roll Morton.

The Father of the Constitution James Madison (1751–1836), US Democratic Republican statesman, 4th President of the US 1809–17. Throughout the 1780s Madison was a key figure in national constitutional reform. He played a leading part in calling the Federal Constitutional Convention at Philadelphia in 1787, and in drawing up the US Constitution and the Bill of Rights.

The Father of the Hole Henry (Spencer) Moore (1898–1986), English sculptor and draughtsman. His massive semi-abstract sculptures, typically of reclining forms and family groups, characteristically have holes or hollows within them. These empty spaces in his work have led Moore to be dubbed the *Father of the Hole*.

The Father of the Skyscraper The title *Father of the Skyscraper* is shared by two US architects, William Le Baron Jenney (1832–1907) and Cass Gilbert (1859–1934). Jenney designed the first steel-frame building, the 10-storey Home Insurance Building in Chicago (1883), usually regarded as the first skyscraper. Gilbert was a major figure in the development of the skyscraper, designing many tall buildings. His 60-storey Woolworth Building in New York City (1913) was the tallest building in the US at the time.

The Father of Tragedy Aeschylus (*c.*525–*c.*456 BC), Greek dramatist, the earliest writer of Greek tragic drama whose works survive. He is best known for his trilogy the *Oresteia* (458 BC), consisting of the tragedies *Agamemnon*, *Choephoroe*, and *Eumenides*. These tell the story of Agamemnon's murder at the hands of his wife Clytemnestra and the vengeance of their son Orestes. Aeschylus was the first dramatist to introduce a second actor to what had previously been a dialogue between a single actor and the chorus. The title is also sometimes accorded to the Greek dramatic poet Thespis. ➤ See also *The* FATHER *of Greek Drama*.

The Father of Waters The river Mississippi in North America, which rises in Minnesota near the Canadian border and flows south to a delta on the Gulf of Mexico. The Mississippi is known informally as the *Father of Waters*, with its chief tributary, the Missouri, regarded as its offspring. During the American Civil War, the Union forces under General Grant regained control of the Mississippi by besieging the town of Vicksburg and eventually capturing it on 4 July 1863. Abraham Lincoln was moved to comment, 'the Father of Waters again goes unvexed to the sea.' ➤ See also OL' *Man River*.

The Fat Owl of the Remove Billy Bunter, a schoolboy character in stories about Greyfriars school by Frank Richards (pseudonym of Charles Hamilton 1876–1961). These stories first appeared in the *Magnet* comic in 1908. Bunter is greedy,

overweight, and wears large, round spectacles, hence the nickname his fellow
pupils give him, the *Fat Owl of the Remove*. A 'remove' is a class or form.

The Faugh-a-Balaghs The Royal Irish Fusiliers/87th Foot, a regiment of the
British army. The regimental war-cry, used at the Battle of Barossa in 1811, was the
Irish *fág an bealach* 'clear the way', hence their nickname the *Faugh-a-Balaghs*.
The variant *Old Fogs* is a corruption of the Irish phrase.

FDR Franklin Delano Roosevelt (1882–1945), US Democratic statesman, 32nd
President of the US 1933–45. His New Deal of 1933 helped to lift the US out of the
Great Depression, and he played an important part in Allied policy during the
Second World War. He was the only US President to be elected three times, and
subsequently secured a fourth term in office. His initials were used as a nickname,
as with several other presidents. ➤ See also *The* SPHINX.

The Female Howard Elizabeth Fry (born Elizabeth Gurney) (1780–1845), English
Quaker prison reformer, a leading figure in the early 19th-century campaign for
penal reform. She campaigned in particular to improve the conditions of women in
Newgate and other prisons and those of convicts transported to Australia. Fry was
called the *Female Howard* after her famous predecessor John Howard (1726–90), the
English philanthropist and prison reformer. Howard travelled widely in Britain
inspecting prison conditions and wrote *The State of Prisons in England and Wales*
(1777). His work is continued by the Howard League for Penal Reform (founded
1844), named after him.

Fiery Face James II (1430–60), king of Scotland 1437–60. James had a large red
birth-mark covering one side of his face, earning him the nickname *Fiery Face*.

Fiery Fred Frederick Sewards Trueman (b.1931), English cricketer. A fast bowler for
Yorkshire and England, he was the first bowler to take 300 test wickets (1964), ending
his test career with 307 wickets altogether. Trueman was known as *Fiery Fred* because
of his aggressive fast bowling and his truculent manner.

The Fifth Beatle This sobriquet has been applied to both George Martin and Brian
Epstein, in each case suggesting that their contribution to the Beatles' success was
substantial enough for them to be considered effectively an additional member of
the band. George Martin (b.1926) was a producer for the EMI Parlophone record
label who worked with Lennon and McCartney on the arrangements of many of
their songs and brought innovative four-track studio techniques to the recording of
such albums as *Revolver* (1966) and *Sgt Pepper's Lonely Hearts Club Band* (1967).
Brian Epstein (1934–67) first heard the Beatles play at the Cavern Club in Liverpool
in 1961 and became their manager. He is credited with conceiving the band's image
in its early years. Following Epstein's death by suicide in 1967, John Lennon said that
they would not have made it without him. Yet another candidate for the title is
Stuart Sutcliffe, the band's original bass guitarist, who left the Beatles in 1961 and
died the following year.

The Fighting Bishop Henry Despencer (also known as Henry Spenser) (d.1406),
English bishop of Norwich. He put down insurrection in Norfolk during the
Peasants' Revolt of 1381, and later fought in Flanders and France on behalf of Pope

Urban VI against the supporters of the antipope. His sobriquets include the *Fighting Bishop*, the *Fighting Prelate*, and the WARLIKE BISHOP.

The Fighting Boilermaker James J. Jeffries (1875–1953), US boxer. When he started boxing professionally Jim Jeffries was known as the *Fighting Boilermaker* because he had earlier worked at the Lacey Manufacturing Company, a boiler-making factory near Los Angeles. He became world heavyweight champion in 1899, holding the title until his retirement in 1905. He was talked into making an ill-advised comeback six years later in an attempt to reclaim the title from the first black champion Jack Johnson. ➤ See also *The* GREAT *White Hope*.

The Fighting Fifth The 5th Foot (Royal Northumberland Fusiliers), a regiment of the British army. Their nickname comes from a remark made by the Duke of Wellington during the Peninsular War, when he referred to 'the ever fighting, often tried, but never failing Fifth'. They are also known as the *Old Bold Fifth*.

The Fighting Marine Gene Tunney (James Joseph Tunney) (1897–1978), US boxer. Not long after turning professional, Tunney was drafted into the US Marine Corps. While stationed in France in 1919 he won the US Expeditionary Force's light-heavyweight championship. When he resumed his professional career he was therefore known as the *Fighting Marine*. Tunney beat Jack Dempsey in 1926 to become world heavyweight champion. He defended the title the following year against Dempsey in a famous fight that has become known as the 'Battle of the Long Count'. He retired undefeated in 1928, and subsequently became a successful businessman.

Finality Jack Lord John Russell (1792–1878), British Whig statesman, Prime Minister 1846–52 and 1865–66. As a member of Lord Grey's government (1830–34), he was responsible for introducing the Reform Bill of 1832 into Parliament. He subsequently characterized it as 'a finality', indicating that he was not prepared to pursue further measures of electoral reform.

The First Dark Horse James K(nox) Polk (1795–1849), US Democratic statesman, 11th President of the US 1845–49. Polk became known as the *First Dark Horse* when, at the 1844 Democratic convention, he unexpectedly won the presidential nomination instead of better known candidates including Martin van Buren. He narrowly defeated Henry Clay in the presidential election. ➤ See also *The* DARK *Horse President*, YOUNG *Hickory*.

The First Gentleman in Europe George, Prince of Wales, later George IV (1762–1830), reigned 1820–30. George enjoyed a reputation as a man of style and good manners, a leader of fashion, and a patron of the arts. All this earned him his admiring nickname. It was however applied satirically by Cruikshank in a caricature (1820) which showed the 'First Gentleman in Europe' recovering from a debauch. The name *First Gentleman of Europe* had in the 17th century been applied by the political economist William Petty to the Catholic and Royalist Irish peer the Duke of Ormonde (1610–88). ➤ See also *The* ADONIS *of Fifty*, FLORIZEL, FUM *the Fourth*, *The* PRINCE *of Whales*, PRINNY.

The First Gentleman of the Screen George Arliss (George Augustus Andrews) (1868–1946), English actor. He had a distinguished career as a stage actor, becoming a film star only in middle age. Suave and elegant on screen, he usually played monarchs, statesmen, millionaires, and the like, hence his nickname. He won an Oscar for *Disraeli* (1929), having previously played the part on stage in 1911 and in a silent film version in 1921.

The First Lady of Hollywood (Edith) Norma Shearer (1900–83), Canadian film actress. She was a major star of the 1920s and 30s, her films including *The Divorcee* (1930), for which she won an Academy Award, and *Marie Antoinette* (1938). Shearer was dubbed both the *First Lady of Hollywood* and the *First Lady of the Screen*.

The First Lady of the Screen Norma Shearer, Canadian film actress. ➤ See *The* FIRST *Lady of Hollywood*.

The First State The US state of Delaware. It is known as the *First State* because in 1787 Delaware became the first state to ratify the new Constitution of the Union. ➤ See also *The* BLUE *Hen State*, *The* DIAMOND *State*, NEW *Sweden*.

The Flanders Mare Anne of Cleves (1515–57), fourth wife of Henry VIII, whom the king divorced. A flattering portrait of her painted by Holbein had deceived Henry into agreeing to a marriage advised by his minister Thomas Cromwell. According to Smollett's *A Complete History of England* (3rd ed., 1759), 'The King found her so different from her picture...that...he swore they had brought him a Flanders mare.'

Flash Harry (Harold) Malcolm (Watts) Sargent (1895–1967), English conductor. He was the conductor of the BBC Symphony Orchestra (1950–57) and chief conductor of the annual Promenade Concerts at London's Royal Albert Hall (1957–67). His nickname derives from his dapper appearance and urbane charm. The term can be generally applied to any extrovert and loudly-dressed show-off or to someone with the air of a 'spiv'.

The Flickertail State The US state of North Dakota. A flickertail is a popular name for Richardson's ground squirrel, a burrowing rodent found in North Dakota. The state is accordingly known as the *Flickertail State*. ➤ See also *The* PEACE *Garden State*, *The* SIOUX *State*.

Flo-Jo Florence Griffith-Joyner (born Delorez Florence Griffith) (1959–98), US track athlete. She won three gold medals at the 1988 Seoul Olympics (the 100m and 200m and the sprint relay). A glamorous figure in the world of athletics, she wore garishly coloured one-piece bodysuits and painted her six-inch fingernails in rainbow colours or in the Stars and Stripes. She was widely known as *Flo-Jo*, an abbreviation of her name. Her lucrative sponsorship deals also earned her the nickname *Cash Flo*.

Florizel George, Prince of Wales, later George IV (1762–1830), reigned 1820–30. As a young man he saw a performance at Drury Lane of Shakespeare's *The Winter's Tale* and was captivated by the actress Mary Robinson who was playing the part of Perdita. He began an affair with the actress, signing his letters to her 'Florizel', the name of Perdita's lover in the play. The nickname *Florizel* stuck for a time. ➤ See also *The* ADONIS *of Fifty*, *The* FIRST *Gentleman in Europe*, FUM *the Fourth*, PERDITA, *The* PRINCE *of Whales*, PRINNY.

Fluff Alan Freeman (b.1927), Australian disc jockey. Beginning his career on British radio in the early 1960s, he has mainly worked for the BBC and Capital Radio. His catchphrases include 'Greetings, pop pickers!' and 'Not 'arf!' Freeman's long-time nickname *Fluff* apparently relates to an old fluffy jumper that he once wore.

The Flying Dutchman Honus Wagner (John Peter Wagner) (1874–1955), US baseball player, mostly with the Pittsburgh Pirates. He was an exceptional right-handed hitter and is widely recognized as the greatest shortstop in baseball history. He was dubbed the *Flying Dutchman*, after the legendary ghost ship of that name, because of his Dutch ancestry and his exceptional speed as a base runner. He stole over 20 bases every year from 1898 to 1915.

The Flying Dutchwoman Fanny Blankers-Koen (1918–2004), Dutch athlete. At the 1948 Olympics held in London, Blankers-Koen, a 30-year-old mother of two, was the oldest female competitor taking part in the Games. She caused a sensation by winning four gold medals in the 100m, the 200m, the 80m hurdles, and the sprint relay. She was inevitably dubbed the *Flying Dutchwoman*, after the legendary ghost ship *The Flying Dutchman*.

The Flying Finn Paavo (Johannes) Nurmi (1897–1973), Finnish athlete who dominated middle- and long-distance running in the 1920s. Known for revolutionizing training methods, he won a total of nine Olympic gold medals, five of them at the 1924 Paris Olympics in the 1500m, 3000m steeplechase, 5000m, and the cross-country team and individual events. Nurmi's statue stands outside the Olympic stadium in Helsinki. He was alliteratively nicknamed the *Flying Finn*. The title has been subsequently applied to the Finnish Formula One motor-racing driver Mika Hakkinen (b.1968), world champion in 1998 and 1999.

The Flying Peacemaker Henry (Alfred) Kissinger (b.1923), German-born US statesman and diplomat, Secretary of State 1973–77. In an era of shuttle diplomacy, Kissinger helped negotiate the withdrawal of US troops from South Vietnam, for which he shared the Nobel Peace Prize. He subsequently mediated between Israel and Syria in the wake of the Yom Kippur War.

Foggy Bottom The US State Department in Washington DC. It is often referred to as *Foggy Bottom*, from the traditional name of the swampy piece of land on which the office buildings were built. The term was first used in connection with the State Department by James Reston in the *New York Times* in 1947.

Fonthill Beckford William Beckford (1759–1844), English writer, author of the fantastic oriental romance *Vathek* (1786). He inherited a large fortune from his father and spent it lavishly. Beckford's nickname derives from his building of an immense Gothic folly, Fonthill Abbey in Wiltshire, south England, where he lived in seclusion 1796–1822. Shortly after he sold the building, its 260-foot bell tower collapsed.

The Fonz Arthur Fonzarelli, a character played by Henry Winkler in the 1950s-set US comedy series *Happy Days* (1976–85). Known as the *Fonz*, he wore a black leather jacket, rode a motorcycle, and was the epitome of teenage 'cool'.

The Forbidden City Two cities are known as the *Forbidden City*, Lhasa and Beijing. Lhasa, the capital of Tibet and the spiritual centre of Tibetan Buddhism, gained the epithet because of its remoteness and the fact that it was closed to foreign visitors until the 20th century. The name is also applied to a walled section of Beijing, the capital of China, containing the former imperial palaces, temples, and other buildings of the former Chinese Empire. Entry was forbidden to all except the members of the imperial family and their servants.

The Forces' Sweetheart   Vera Lynn (born Vera Margaret Lewis) (b.1917), English singer. During World War II she sang to British servicemen, becoming known as the *Forces' Sweetheart*. She is mainly remembered for such songs as 'We'll Meet Again' and 'White Cliffs of Dover'. Her radio series *Sincerely Yours* was aimed at the troops serving overseas. She had a number of postwar successes, including 'Auf Wiederseh'n, Sweetheart' (1952). In 1975 she was made a Dame.

The Fordham Flash   Frankie Frisch (full name Frank Francis Frisch) (1898–1973), US baseball player. During his career (1919–37), he played with the New York Giants and St Louis Cardinals. An outstanding fielder, his nickname the *Fordham Flash* derived from his time as an undergraduate at Fordham University, where he was an all-round sportsman.

The Foreigner State   The US state of New Jersey. Its nickname the *Foreigner State* alludes to Joseph Bonaparte (1768–1844), king of Spain, who lived in New Jersey for a time, having fled there in about 1812. ➤ See also *The* GARDEN *State, The* MOSQUITO *State*.

The Fortunate Islands   The Canary Islands. In Greek legend the *Fortunate Islands* (*Fortunatae Insulae*) were fabulous islands in the Western Ocean (i.e. the Atlantic Ocean), supposedly beyond the Pillars of Hercules. They were believed to be the abode of the blessed dead, where the souls of the virtuous were placed after death. The name was later applied to the Canary Islands.

Foul-Weather Jack   John Byron (1723–86), British naval officer. He commanded the frigate *Dolphin* in a voyage round the world 1764–66. His nickname *Foul-Weather Jack* alluded to his reputation for encountering bad weather on every voyage. In 1768 he published an account of his shipwreck on the coast of Chile in 1741, which was later used by his grandson Lord Byron in his poem *Don Juan*.

The Fowler   Henry I (*c*.876–936), king of Germany 919–36 and duke of Saxony from 912. He became known as the *Fowler* because he was said to have been fowling (hunting wildfowl) with a hawk on his wrist when informed of his election to the throne on the death of Conrad I.

The Foxes   Leicester City football club. The club was originally known as Leicester Fosse because its founders' inaugural meeting in 1884 was held at a house on the Fosse Way, an old Roman road. For some years they were nicknamed the *Fossils*, but in 1919 the club was renamed Leicester City and a new nickname was adopted, the *Foxes*.

Fra Diavolo   Michele Pezza (1771–1806), Italian brigand who led a revolt against the French occupation of Naples between 1799 and 1806. He was known as *Fra Diavolo*, 'Brother Devil'. In folk legends he appears as a popular guerrilla leader and is the subject of the opera by Auber which bears his name (1831).

Fraud   Rutherford B(irchard) Hayes (1822–93), US Republican statesman, 19th President of the US 1877–81. In the 1876 presidential election, Hayes ran against the Democrat Samuel J. Tilden. Tilden won the popular vote and led the electoral college 184–166, with the allocation of a further 19 votes (the returns of Louisiana, Florida, and South Carolina) in dispute. A special electoral commission was appointed by Congress to decide the result. The commission, voting 8–7 along party lines, awarded all 19 disputed votes to Hayes, giving him the presidency by a majority of one in the electoral college. His administration was inevitably undermined by his controversial victory and by the scornful nicknames the president's opponents bestowed on him, including *Fraud*, the *Fraud President*, *His Fraudulency*, and *Rutherfraud B. Hayes*. ➤ See also *The* DARK *Horse President*.

Fred's   Fortnum & Mason, London department store, an upmarket purveyor of provisions. Its nickname *Fred's*, dating from around 1945, was intended to form a pair with ROD's, that other upmarket London store Harrods. ➤ See also ROD's.

Free-O   Fremantle, the principal port of Western Australia, near the city of Perth. A refreshing sea breeze that blows into Fremantle and Perth on warm evenings is known locally as the *Fremantle Doctor*.

The Free State   The US state of Maryland. In 1923 Hamilton Owens, the editor of the *Baltimore Evening Sun*, invented the name *Maryland Free State* to promote the state's claim to be a sanctuary from the oppressive legislation suffered by the rest of the country. The name caught on within Maryland and was later shortened to the *Free State*. ➤ See also *The* COCKADE *State*, *The* OLD *Line State*, *The* QUEEN *State*.

Frisco   The US city of San Francisco, California. The abbreviation *Frisco* is sometimes used by non-residents and is disliked by San Franciscans themselves. ➤ See also *The* GOLDEN *Gate City*.

Fritz   Walter (Frederick) Mondale (b.1928), US Democratic politician, Vice President under Jimmy Carter 1977–81. Mondale was known as *Fritz*, from his middle name Frederick. Fritz is the traditional short form of the German name Friedrich.

Fum the Fourth   George IV (1762–1830), son of George III, reigned 1820–30. Byron refers to the king as *Fum the Fourth* in his poem *Don Juan* (1819–24): '. . . Where's George the Third?/Where is his will? (That's not so soon unriddled.)/And where is "Fum" the Fourth, our "royal bird"?/Gone down, it seems, to Scotland to be fiddled/Unto by Sawney's violin, we have heard.' In Chinese legend, the Fum was a fabulous bird believed to symbolize royal dignity. ➤ See also *The* ADONIS *of Fifty*, *The* FIRST *Gentleman in Europe*, FLORIZEL, *The* PRINCE *of Whales*, PRINNY.

Gg

The Gabba The Queensland Cricket Association's ground at Woollongabba, a suburb of Brisbane, Australia. A venue for Test matches, its informal name the *Gabba* is a shortening of Woollongabba.

The Galloping Gourmet Graham Kerr (b.1934), British television cook of the late 1960s and early 1970s. He was promoted as the *Galloping Gourmet* because of his frenetic style, dashing around the kitchen set as he prepared each dish.

The Galloping Major Ferenc Puskás (b.1927), Hungarian footballer. He was a prominent member of the great Hungarian national team of the early 1950s, playing in the stunning 6–3 victory over England at Wembley in 1952. In all Puskás played for Hungary 84 times, scoring 83 goals. In 1956 he left Hungary to play for Real Madrid, scoring four goals in their 1960 European Cup Final victory and a hat trick in the corresponding 1962 final, in which Real Madrid lost. Puskás was known as the *Galloping Major* because of his rank when he played for the Hungarian army club Honved.

The Gamecock State The US state of South Carolina. A *gamecock* is a cock bred and trained for cockfighting. South Carolina's nickname the *Gamecock State* refers to the supposed belligerence of its inhabitants and in particular to its determined opposition to the abolition of slavery. It was the first state to secede from the Union in 1860. ➤ See also *The* PALMETTO *State, The* SANDLAPPER *State*.

The Gang of Four In China, the *Gang of Four* was a group of four associates involved in implementing many of Mao Zedong's policies during the Cultural Revolution. The four members were Wang Hongwen, Zhang Chunjao, Yao Wenyuan, and Mao's wife Jiang Qing. They attempted to take power on Mao's death in 1976, but were arrested and imprisoned. In the UK, the name was applied to a group of four Labour MPs (Shirley Williams, Roy Jenkins, David Owen, and William Rodgers) who broke away from the Labour Party in 1981 to form the Social Democratic Party.

The Garden of England The English county of Kent and, formerly, Worcestershire. Both counties are noted for their fertility and fruit production.

The Garden State The US state of New Jersey. As a producer of vegetables, fruit, and dairy products, it is known as the *Garden State*, though its economy is actually dominated by chemicals and pharmaceuticals manufacturing. ➤ See also *The* FOREIGNER *State, The* MOSQUITO *State*.

Gaseous Cassius Muhammad Ali (b.1942), US boxer. ➤ See *The* LOUISVILLE *Lip*.

Gazza Paul (John) Gascoigne (b.1967), English footballer. An exceptionally gifted midfielder, he has played for England and for clubs including Newcastle United,

Tottenham Hotspur, and the Italian club Lazio. During England's World Cup semi-final with West Germany in 1990, Gascoigne received a second yellow card which would have ruled him out of the final, had England beaten West Germany. His tearful reaction endeared him to the British public and he became a hugely popular national figure overnight. His nickname *Gazza*, which he had acquired at the age of 12, caught on to such an extent that it was registered as a trademark by Gascoigne's agent and it inspired a succession of similar '-zza' coinages. After Gascoigne signed for Lazio the Italian fans continued to call him *Gazza* ('magpie' in Italian), coincidentally appropriate for a player who had previously played for Newcastle United (nicknamed the MAGPIES). ➤ See also HEZZA, PREZZA.

The Gem State   The US state of Idaho. The name Idaho is popularly though erroneously supposed to come from an Indian word meaning 'mountain gem', hence the state's nickname the *Gem State*.

The Geneva Bull   Stephen Marshall (1594?–1655), English presbyterian divine. A follower and exponent of John Calvin, the French Protestant leader who was based in Geneva, Marshall was noted for the bellowing delivery of his Calvinist sermons, hence his nickname the *Geneva Bull*.

Gentleman Jackson   John Jackson (1769–1845), English boxer. Jackson defeated Daniel Mendoza in 1795 to become champion of England, a title he held until 1803. One of the most celebrated figures of his day, he gained his nickname *Gentleman Jackson* (or *Gentleman Jack*) because of his dandyish dress, refined speech, and good manners. ➤ See also *The* EMPEROR *of Pugilism.*

Gentleman Jim   James J(ohn) Corbett (1866–1933), US boxer. He defeated John L. Sullivan in 1892 to become the first world heavyweight champion of the gloved era, a title he held until 1897. Well-mannered outside the ring, he introduced a style of boxing that relied on speed and technical skill rather than brute strength.

The Gentle Shepherd   George Grenville (1712–70), British Whig statesman, Prime Minister 1763–65. The nickname the *Gentle Shepherd* stuck to Grenville following an exchange with the elder Pitt in the House of Commons. During a debate on the imposition of a cider tax, in March 1763, Grenville reminded the house that the recent war had made the imposition of new taxes a necessity, and he 'wished gentlemen would show him *where* to lay them.' Pitt, mimicking his languid mode of speech, responded by quoting the refrain of an old song, 'Gentle shepherd, tell me where!'

George Cross Island   The island of Malta. An important British naval base in the Mediterranean in the Second World War, Malta sustained heavy Italian and German air attacks between 1940 and 1942, throughout which the people of the island put up steadfast resistance. In April 1942 George VI awarded the island the George Cross, a British medal given to civilians for courage in circumstances of extreme danger, in recognition of the bravery and endurance of its inhabitants. Malta duly became known as *George Cross Island* and a representation of the medal appears on the Maltese flag.

The Georgia Peach   Ty(rus Raymond) Cobb (1886–1961), US baseball player with the Detroit Tigers and Philadelphia Athletes (1905–28). One of the greatest players in the history of the game, the Georgia-born Cobb became the first player elected to baseball's Hall of Fame in 1936. He holds the record for runs scored (2 254) and lifetime batting average (0.367). His career total of 4 191 hits was a major league record for almost 60 years. ➤ See also *The* PEACH *State*.

The Gipper Ronald (Wilson) Reagan (1911–2004), US Republican statesman, 40th President of the US 1981–89. A former film actor, Reagan appeared in the 1940 film *Knute Rockne—All American* in the role of the real-life American footballer George Gipp (1895–1920). Nicknamed the *Gipper*, Gipp died young from pneumonia. On his deathbed he said to Knute Rockne, his team's coach, 'Someday, when things look real tough for Notre Dame, ask the boys to go out there and win one for the Gipper.' As president, Ronald Reagan frequently exhorted his supporters to 'win one for the Gipper' and the nickname became associated with him too. ➤ See also DUTCH², *The* GREAT *Communicator*, OLD *Hopalong*, *The* TEFLON *President*.

The Girl with the Million Dollar Legs Betty Grable (born Ruth Elizabeth Grable) (1916–73), US film actress, singer, and dancer who appeared in comedies and musicals such as *Million Dollar Legs* (1939) and *Pin Up Girl* (1944). Her shapely legs were reportedly insured for a million dollars (in fact $250 000) with Lloyds of London. Grable herself said: 'There are two reasons why I'm in show business, and I'm standing on both of them'. A picture of her wearing a white bathing suit made her the most popular pin-up of the Second World War.

Give 'Em Hell Harry Harry S. Truman (1884–1972), US Democratic statesman, 33rd President of the US 1945–53. As Vice-president to Franklin Roosevelt, Truman assumed the presidency on the death of Roosevelt in 1945. He subsequently fought and won the election of 1948. During the presidential campaign he told his running mate Alben W. Barkley, 'I'm going to fight hard. I'm going to give 'em hell.' Suiting his combative personality, *Give 'Em Hell Harry* became his nickname, though he later said in an interview, 'I never give them hell. I just tell the truth. And they think it is hell.' ➤ See also *The* MAN *from Missouri*.

The Glaziers Crystal Palace football club. The club was named after the Crystal Palace, originally built in 1851 to house the Great Exhibition in Hyde Park and moved to Sydenham Hill in South London soon afterwards. Their nickname the *Glaziers* alluded to this enormous glass-and-iron structure. In the 1970s the club dropped their old nickname in favour of the *Eagles*.

The Gloomy Dean William Ralph Inge, (1860–1954), English theologian and dean of St Paul's Cathedral 1911–34. He wrote a column for the London *Evening Standard* in the 1930s. His pessimistic outlook on numerous political and social matters won him the sobriquet the *Gloomy Dean*.

Gloriana Elizabeth I (1533–1603), daughter of Henry VIII, queen of England and Ireland 1558–1603. Spenser uses the name *Gloriana* for the character representing the queen in his *Faerie Queene* (1590, 1596). Benjamin Britten's opera composed for the coronation of Elizabeth II (1952), was entitled *Gloriana*. ➤ See also GOOD *Queen Bess*, ORIANA, *The* VIRGIN *Queen*.

Glorious John John Dryden (1631–1700), English poet, dramatist, and critic. He is known especially for his satires written in heroic couplets, such as *Absalom and*

Achitophel (1681), and for such plays as *Marriage à la mode* (1673) and *All for Love* (1678). Dryden was appointed poet laureate in 1668, though he lost the post in 1688. He was nicknamed *Glorious John* by Walter Scott in *The Pirate* (1821): ' "You forget glorious John," said Mordaunt. "Ay, glorious you may well call him." ' ➤ See also *The* POET *Squab*.

The Gnome   Keith William Robert Fletcher (b.1944), English cricketer, who played for Essex and England. He was nicknamed the *Gnome*, partly from his slight appearance and partly from his somewhat hunched, introspective style of batting.

The Goat   David Lloyd George (1863–1945), British Liberal statesman, Prime Minister 1916–22. His lecherous reputation and extra-marital affairs, the subject of much gossip, earned him the sobriquet the *Goat*. It was coined by Robert Chalmers, a senior civil servant, when Lloyd George was Chancellor of the Exchequer. ➤ See also *The* WELSH *Wizard*[1].

Godlike Daniel   Daniel Webster (1782–1852), US lawyer and politician, secretary of state 1841–43 and 1850–52. His efforts as a senator to secure a compromise on the slavery issue in order to preserve the Union angered abolitionists. Regarded as the greatest American orator of the 19th century, he was *Godlike Daniel* to his admirers.

The Gold Coast   An affluent residential area along Lake Shore Drive in Chicago, bordering Lake Michigan. It comprises luxurious hotels, private mansions, and high-rise apartment houses. The *Gold Coast* was the former name (until 1957) for Ghana in West Africa, so called because it was an important source of gold.

Goldenballs   David Beckham (b.1975), English footballer. In September 2001 his wife Victoria revealed on the *Parkinson* television chat show that her own nickname for him was *Goldenballs*. This was enthusiastically taken up by the press. ➤ See also BECKS.

The Golden Bear   Jack (William) Nicklaus (b.1940), US golfer, often regarded as the greatest player ever. He won 18 professional major championships, including six wins in the Masters, five in the PGA, four in the US Open, and three in the British Open. His nickname the *Golden Bear* alluded to his sturdy build and blond hair.

The Golden Boy   Two pop singers were dubbed the *Golden Boy*, Frankie Avalon and Paul Anka. Frankie Avalon (Francis Thomas Avalone) (b.1939) was a US teen idol of the 1950s, successful both as a pop singer and a film actor, especially in a series of beach movies. His hits included 'Venus' (1959) and 'Why' (1959). Paul Albert Anka (b.1941) was a Canadian pop singer, known for such songs as 'Diana' and for writing the English lyrics of the French singer-songwriter Claude François's song 'My Way'. A cinema short about Anka, released in 1962, had the title *Golden Boy*. The term was originally the title of a play by Clifford Odets (1937), subsequently filmed. It can be applied to any popular, talented, or successful young man.

The Golden Foghorn   Ethel Merman (born Ethel Agnes Zimmerman) (1909–84), US musical comedy star with a dynamic personality and an ear-splitting voice, hence her nickname. She starred in such Broadway shows as *Annie Get Your Gun* (1946), *Call Me Madam* (1950), and *Gypsy* (1958). The first of these contained one of the songs with which she is most associated, 'There's No Business Like Show Business'.

The Golden Gate City The US city of San Francisco, California. The Golden Gate is the mile-wide strait connecting San Francisco Bay with the Pacific Ocean. It is spanned by the Golden Gate single-span suspension bridge (completed 1937). ➤ See also FRISCO.

The Golden State The US state of Calfornia. The nickname originally referred to the discovery of gold in the Sierra Nevada in 1848, which led to the gold rush of 1849–56. Later the name was taken to be a reference to California's sunshine. California's state flower is the Golden Poppy.

Goldy Oliver Goldsmith (1728–74), Irish novelist, poet, essayist, and dramatist. He is best known for his novel *The Vicar of Wakefield* (1766), the pastoral poem *The Deserted Village* (1770), and the comic plays *She Stoops to Conquer* (1773) and *The Good-Natur'd Man* (1768). According to James Boswell in his *Journal of a Tour to the Hebrides* (1785), Samuel Johnson had a habit of contracting the names of his friends: 'Goldsmith feels himself so important now, as to be displeased with it. I remember one day, when Tom Davies was telling that Dr. Johnson said, "We are all in labour for a name to Goldy's play," Goldsmith cried, "I have often desired him not to call me Goldy."'

GOM William Ewart Gladstone (1809–98), British Liberal statesman, Prime Minister 1868–74, 1880–85, 1886, and 1892–94. In his later years Gladstone was known as the *Grand Old Man*, or simply as *GOM*. The abbreviation was first used by Lord Rosebery in 1882. The initials were interpreted by Gladstone's opponents as 'God's Only Mistake'. GOM was subsequently transposed into MOG, standing for 'Murderer of Gordon', referring to the death of Gordon of Khartoum. ➤ See also *The* GRAND *Old Man*[1], *The* GREAT *Commoner*.

The Goober State The US state of Georgia. Famous for its peanut farming, Georgia is known as the *Goober State*. *Goober* is a 19th-century Southern US word for a peanut, ultimately of Bantu origin. ➤ See also *The* CRACKER *State*, *The* PEACH *State*.

Good Duke Humphrey Humphrey, Duke of Gloucester (1391–1447), youngest son of Henry IV. Although devout, he is thought to have earned the epithet 'Good' as a patron of learning who encouraged such men of letters as the poet John Lydgate and the historian John Capgrave. A great book-collector, he donated the books which now form the oldest part of Oxford's Bodleian Library. He is referred to as *Good Duke Humphrey* in Shakespeare's 2 *Henry VI*.

Good Queen Bess Elizabeth I (1533–1603), daughter of Henry VIII, queen of England and Ireland 1558–1603. This contemporary nickname demonstrates the affection her subjects felt for her. ➤ See also GLORIANA, ORIANA, *The* VIRGIN *Queen*.

The Good Regent James Stewart, Earl of Moray (d.1570), illegitimate elder brother of Mary Queen of Scots, and Regent of Scotland from 1567 after Mary's flight to England until his murder in 1570.

Goodtime George George Melly (b.1926), English jazz singer, writer, and bon viveur. His nickname *Goodtime George* comes from John Chiltern's song of that title, which Melly regularly performs.

GOP The US Republican Party. ➤ See *The* GRAND *Old Party*.

The Gopher State   The US state of Minnesota. A Gopher is an informal term for a native or inhabitant of Minnesota, with reference to the burrowing rodent of the same name. The nickname the *Gopher State* dates back to the late part of the 19th century. ➤ See also *The* NORTH *Star State*.

Gorby   Mikhail (Sergeevich) Gorbachev (b.1931), Soviet statesman, General Secretary of the Communist Party of the USSR 1985–91 and President 1988–91. His foreign policy brought about an end to the Cold War, while within the USSR he introduced major reforms known as *glasnost* and *perestroika*. He enjoyed immense popularity in the West in the late 1980s, his trips outside the Soviet Union meeting with an enthusiastic public response. Gorbachev was affectionately nicknamed *Gorby* in the press and the term Gorbymania was used to describe the public reaction to his visits abroad.

Gorgeous George   George Raymond Wagner (1915–63), US professional wrestler. A master of self-promotion, he had long curly hair dyed platinum blond and wore elaborate robes to enter the ring. The name *Gorgeous George* was supposedly first shouted at him by female spectators. ➤ See also *The* GREATEST.

Gorgeous Gussie   Gertrude Moran (b.1923), US tennis player. Gussie Moran caused a sensation at Wimbledon in 1949 by wearing frilly lace panties under her tennis dress, designed by the ex-player and fashion designer Teddy Tinling (1910–90). Although hugely popular with the public, she was accused by the Wimbledon authorities of 'bringing vulgarity and sin into tennis'.

Gotham   New York City. The nickname *Gotham* was coined by Washington Irving in *Salmagundi* (1807). It alludes to a village in Nottinghamshire associated with the English folk tale 'The Wise Men of Gotham', in which the inhabitants of the village demonstrated cunning by feigning stupidity. The fictional Gotham City, based on New York, is the setting of the Batman stories. ➤ See also *The* BIG *Apple*, *The* EMPIRE *City*.

The Gov'nor   Frank Sinatra (1915–98), US singer and film actor. ➤ See *The* CHAIRMAN *of the Board*.

The Grand Canyon State   The US state of Arizona. The Grand Canyon is a deep gorge in Arizona, formed by the Colorado River, which is about 440km (277 miles) long, 8–24km (5 to 15 miles) wide, and, in places, 1 800m (6 000ft) deep. The *Grand Canyon State* is the official state nickname and appears on licence plates. ➤ See also *The* APACHE *State*, *The* AZTEC *State*, *The* VALENTINE *State*.

La Grande Mademoiselle   Anne de Montpensier (1627–93), cousin of Louis XIV. The tall and wealthy French princess was called *La Grande Mademoiselle*. Her formal title was 'Mademoiselle' as her father, brother of Louis XIII, had the designation 'Monsieur'.

Grandma Moses   Anna Mary Robertson Moses (1860–1961), US primitive painter, generally known as *Grandma Moses*. Self-taught, she did not begin to paint until she was nearly 70, going on to produce more than a thousand paintings in naive style, mostly of rural life in New England. She was still painting at the age of 100.

Le Grand Monarque   Louis XIV (1638–1715), son of Louis XIII, king of France 1643–1715. This sobriquet literally means 'the Great Monarch'. ➤ See also *The* sun *King.*

The Grandmother of Europe   Victoria (1819–1901), queen of Great Britain and Ireland 1837–1901 and empress of India 1876–1901. Victoria had nine children and by the time of her death her descendents occupied most of the thrones of Europe and Russia, a consequence of a succession of diplomatic marriages. Victoria thus became known as the *Grandmother of Europe*. ➤ See also *The* famine *Queen,* mrs *Brown, The* widow *at Windsor.*

The Grand Old Man[1]   William Ewart Gladstone (1809–98), British Liberal statesman, Prime Minister 1868–74, 1880–85, 1886, and 1892–94. He achieved a series of social and political reforms, including the introduction of elementary education, voting by secret ballot, and the passing of the Irish Land Act and the third Reform Act. The widely used sobriquet the *Grand Old Man*, often abbreviated to GOM, was coined by the MP Henry Labouchère in April 1881. The term soon caught on and, as Roy Jenkins notes in his biography of Gladstone, 'there was a touch of mockery as well as affection about its use'. In 1882 the Earl of Iddesleigh remarked in a speech, 'Argue as you please, you are nowhere; that grand old man, the Prime Minister, insists on the other thing.' ➤ See also gom, *The* great *Commoner.*

The Grand Old Man[2]   W(illiam) G(ilbert) Grace (1848–1915), English cricketer and doctor. He began playing first-class cricket for Gloucestershire in 1864 and played in his last Test match at the age of 50. In a first-class career that lasted nearly 45 years, he made 126 centuries, scored 54 896 runs, and took 2 864 wickets. Grace twice captained England in Test matches against Australia (1880 and 1882). Enormously influential in popularizing cricket and establishing it as the English national game, this huge, bearded figure was acclaimed as the *Grand Old Man*. He was also known as w.g., the champion and, as a qualified surgeon, the *Doctor.*

The Grand Old Party   The Republican Party, a US political party formed in 1854. The term *Grand Old Party* is recorded from the late 19th century. It is sometimes abbreviated to gop.

Grandpa England   George V (1865–1936), son of Edward VII, king of Great Britain and Northern Ireland 1910–36. This is supposedly how the king was known to his young granddaughters, the Princesses Elizabeth and Margaret. ➤ See also *The* sailor *King.*

Grandpa's Grandson   Benjamin Harrison (1833–1901), US Republican statesman, 23rd President of the US 1889–93. He was the grandson of William Henry Harrison, the 9th President. An 1888 Republican campaign song had the title 'Grandfather's Hat Fits Ben!'

The Granite City   The city of Aberdeen, Scotland. Its nickname is the *Granite City* because of the local granite used in many of its public buildings. ➤ See also *The* city *of Bon-accord.*

The Granite State   The US state of New Hampshire. Its nickname is the *Granite State* because New Hampshire's mountain region is composed mainly of granite, the quarrying of which was once a major industry.

The Grauniad   *The Guardian* newspaper. The paper is affectionately known as the *Grauniad* (an anagram of its name) because of its reputation for misprints. The nickname was coined in the 1970s by the satirical magazine *Private Eye*.

The Great   This honorific has been applied to numerous rulers, most notably: (i) Alexander (356–323 BC), son of Philip II, king of Macedon 336–323. (ii) Alfred (849–99), king of Wessex 871–99. (iii) Peter I (1672–1725), tsar of Russia 1682–1725. (iv) Frederick II (1712–86), king of Prussia 1740–86. (v) Catherine II (1729–96), empress of Russia, reigned 1762–96.

The Great Cham of Literature   Samuel Johnson (1709–84), English lexicographer, writer, critic, and conversationalist. This famous nickname was coined by the writer Tobias Smollett (1721–71) in a letter to John Wilkes: 'I am again your petitioner, in behalf of that great Cham of literature, Samuel Johnson' (16 March 1759, quoted in Boswell's *Life of Johnson*). *Cham* (pronounced 'kam') is an obsolete form of the word *Khan*, formerly applied to the rulers of the Tartars and the Mongols, and to the emperor of China. As such the word fitted Johnson's magisterial position as the dominant literary authority of his time. In the first edition of Boswell's *Life of Johnson*, the word was mistakenly printed as 'Chum', which seems much less appropriate. ➤ See also DICTIONARY *Johnson*, URSA *Major*.

The Great Commoner   William Pitt (1708–78), 1st Earl of Chatham, known as Pitt the Elder, British Whig statesman. As Secretary of State (effectively Prime Minister), he headed coalition governments 1756–61 and 1766–68. He brought the Seven Years War to an end in 1763 and also masterminded the conquest of French possessions overseas, particularly in Canada and India. He became known as the *Great Commoner* for his oratory in the House of Commons and his defence of constitutional rights. The term was also applied to William Ewart Gladstone. Another masterly parliamentary orator and debater, Gladstone partly earned the title in recognition of his refusal of a peerage. ➤ See also *The* GRAND *Old Man*¹.

The Great Communicator   Ronald (Wilson) Reagan (1911–2004), US Republican statesman, 40th President of the US 1981–89. Reagan was immensely popular with the American public. His background as a film actor was evident in the folksy, conversational delivery of his speeches and in his skilful use of television and radio. He became known as the *Great Communicator*. ➤ See also DUTCH, *The* GIPPER, OLD *Hopalong*, *The* TEFLON *President*.

The Great Compromiser   Henry Clay (1777–1852), US statesman and orator. He was called the *Great Compromiser* and the GREAT PACIFICATOR because of his efforts to resolve sectional conflict between North and South over the issue of slavery and so avoid civil war. Clay was a key figure behind the Missouri Compromise (1820–21) and also sponsored the Compromise of 1850. ➤ See also *The* MILL *Boy of the Slashes*.

The Great Deliverer   William III (1650–1702), king of Great Britain and Ireland 1689–1702. Following the Glorious Revolution of 1688–89, William became known as the *Great Deliverer* since he (jointly with his wife Mary II) had preserved the Protestant succession from the son of the Catholic James II. ➤ See also DUTCH *Billy*, KING *Billy*.

The Great Elector Frederick William (1620–88), Elector of Brandenburg 1640–88. An Elector was a German prince entitled to take part in the election of the Holy Roman Emperor. Frederick William earned the title the *Great Elector* for rehabilitating his state following the Thirty Years War and, through military success against Sweden and Poland, laying the basis for the expansion of Prussian power in the 18th century.

The Great Emancipator Abraham Lincoln (1809–65), US Republican statesman, 16th President of the US 1861–65. Lincoln succeeded in uniting the Union side behind the anti-slavery cause and the emancipation of slaves was formally proclaimed on New Year's Day, 1863. The abolition of slavery was made part of the Constitution in 1864. ➤ See also HONEST *Abe*, OLD *Abe*, *The* RAIL *Splitter*.

The Greatest Muhammad Ali (formerly Cassius Clay) (b.1942), US boxer. Even before he won the gold medal in the 1960 Olympic Games, he was bragging 'I'll be the greatest of all time.' After he defeated Sonny Liston in 1964 to become world champion, he shouted to the press: 'I told you, I told you, I AM the Greatest!' He later revealed that he acquired his catchphrase from a wrestler called GORGEOUS GEORGE (born George Raymond Wagner), who had a similarly bombastic style of self-promotion. ➤ See also *The* LOUISVILLE *Lip*.

Great Head Malcolm III (*c*.1031–93), king of Scotland 1058–93. ➤ See CANMORE.

The Great Lake State The US state of Michigan. The Great Lakes, a group of five connected freshwater lakes along the US–Canada border, are made up of Lakes Superior, Michigan, Huron, Erie, and Ontario. Michigan state is comprised of two peninsulas in the midst of the Great Lakes and divided by Lake Michigan, hence its nickname the *Great Lake State*. ➤ See also *The* AUTO *State*, *The* WOLVERINE *State*.

The Great Lover Two screen actors have attracted the promotional title the *Great Lover*, Rudolph Valentino and Charles Boyer. Rudolph Valentino (born Rodolfo Guglielmi di Valentina d'Antonguolla) (1895–1926). The Italian-born US actor became a leading star of silent films in the 1920s, playing the archetypal romantic lover in films such as *The Sheikh* (1921) and *Blood and Sand* (1922). Valentino was one of the screen's first sex symbols. After his sudden death from peritonitis his funeral resulted in scenes of mass hysteria. Charles Boyer (1897–1977), French-born US actor, was noted for playing romantic leading roles in films such as *Mayerling* (1936).

The Great Magician Walter Scott (1771–1832), Scottish novelist and poet. According to Lockhart's *Life of Scott*, this name was first coined in 'a set of beautiful stanzas, inscribed to Scott by Mr Wilson [that is, the poet and critic John Wilson] under the title of "The Magic Mirror"'; the name afterwards became 'one of his standing titles'. Scott was also known as the MAGICIAN OF THE NORTH and the WIZARD OF THE NORTH. ➤ See also *The* ARIOSTO *of the North*, *The* GREAT *Unknown*.

The Great One Wayne Gretzky (b.1961), Canadian ice-hockey player, often considered the best player in the history of the sport. He played with the Edmonton Oilers 1979–88 and with the Los Angeles Kings from 1988. He holds the records for the most goals scored in a season (92, in 1981–82) and the most career points. Gretzky is universally acknowledged the *Great One*.

The Great Pacificator Henry Clay (1777–1852), US statesman and orator. ➤ See *The* GREAT *Compromiser.*

The Great Profile John Barrymore (1882–1942), US actor. Barrymore was both a distinguished stage actor, celebrated for his Hamlet (1922), and a flamboyant matinee idol, starring in such films as *Don Juan* (1926), *Grand Hotel* (1932), *Dinner at Eight* (1933), and *Twentieth Century* (1934). His handsome looks and aquiline nose earned him the nickname the *Great Profile* or simply the *Profile.*

The Great Unknown Walter Scott (1771–1832), Scottish novelist and poet. Well known as a poet, Scott published his first novel *Waverley* anonymously in 1814; subsequent novels were 'by the author of Waverley'. The author of these highly popular historical novels was commonly referred to as the *Great Unknown,* a sobriquet coined by Scott's publisher James Ballantyne. Scott only acknowledged authorship of them in 1827, though it was by then widely known. ➤ See also *The* ARIOSTO *of the North, The* GREAT *Magician.*

The Great Wen The city of London. This archaic and derogatory nickname was originally coined by the radical writer William Cobbett: 'But what is to be the fate of the great wen of all? The monster, called "the metropolis of the empire"?' (*Rural Rides,* 1821). A *wen* is a wart or tumour, and Cobbett was applying the word to the abnormal and unsightly growth of a congested and sprawling city into the surrounding countryside. ➤ See also *The* BIG *Smoke, The* CITY *of Masts.*

The Great White Hope This informal title was applied to a succession of white challengers to the first black heavyweight champion Jack Johnson (1878–1946). After Johnson knocked out Tommy Burns to win the heavyweight title in 1908, many white American fans looked for a *Great White Hope* to win it back. Stanley Ketchel was Johnson's first challenger in 1909. James J. Jeffries, who had retired in 1905, was talked into making a comeback six years later to take on the champion Johnson in Reno, Nevada. Billed as the 'Battle of the Century' and taking place in front of a racially hostile crowd, the contest was a one-sided affair won by the champion. Johnson had three further successful defences. Finally in 1915 Jess Willard (1883–1968), from Pottawatomie County, Kansas, challenged Johnson in Havana, Cuba. Also known as *Cowboy Jess* and the *Pottawatomie Giant* (he was over 6½ ft tall), Willard won by a knockout in the 26th round. Many have suspected that the fight was fixed. Nearly 70 years later the designation was revived for Gerry Cooney (Gerald Arthur Cooney) (b.1956) when he unsuccessfully challenged Larry Holmes in a highly publicized fight for the WBC heavyweight title in 1982. ➤ See also *The* FIGHTING *Boilermaker.*

The Great White Shark Greg (Gregory John) Norman (b.1955), Australian golfer, one of the world's leading players in the 1980s and 1990s. He won the world matchplay championship three times (1980, 1983, 1986) and the British Open twice (1986, 1993). The blond-haired Norman became known as the *Great White Shark* or the WHITE SHARK because he used to fish for shark off the Brisbane coast. The name was apparently coined in 1981 by a newspaper in Augusta, Georgia, following an interview Norman gave during the US Masters. Norman now presides over a multinational business, involved in such activities as golf course design and property development, called Great White Shark Enterprises.

The Great White Way Broadway, in New York City, especially the part that runs between 41st and 53rd Streets. The nickname the *Great White Way* refers to the brilliant illumination used for theatres, cinemas, clubs, and advertising signs. It is the title of a novel written by Albert Bigelow Paine in 1901.

The Great Whore Anne Boleyn (1507–36), second wife of Henry VIII and mother of Elizabeth I. This was how Henry and his court referred to her once she had fallen from favour having failed to produce a male heir. She was alleged by them to have had many lovers and to have committed incest with her brother. She was executed in 1536. ➤ See also ANNE *of the Thousand Days*.

The Green Goddess Diana Moran (b.1940), keep-fit demonstrator on BBC breakfast television from 1983. She was billed as the *Green Goddess* because of the green catsuit she wore. The original Green Goddess was a green-painted military fire engine first used during the Second World War.

The Green Howards The 19th Foot, a regiment of the British army. They were known as the *Green Howards* on account of the green facings on their uniform and the name of their colonel from 1738 to 1748, Sir Charles Howard. The nickname distinguished the 19th Foot from the 3rd Buffs, also commanded by a Colonel Howard, and accordingly known as *Howard's Buffs*. It was adopted as part of the regiment's official name in 1920, when they were renamed the Green Howards (Alexandra, Princess of Wales's Own Yorkshire Regiment).

The Green Linnets The 39th Foot (later the Dorsetshire Regiment), a regiment of the British army. The nickname the *Green Linnets* dates from the mid-18th century and refers to the green facings on their uniform.

The Green Mountain State The US state of Vermont. The name Vermont comes from the French *vert mont*, 'green mountain'. The state takes both its name and its nickname the *Green Mountain State* from the Green Mountains, a range in the northern Appalachians covered with evergreen forests.

The Grey Cardinal François Leclerc du Tremblay (1577–1638), also known as Père Joseph, French cleric and private secretary of Cardinal Richelieu. ➤ See ÉMINENCE *Grise*.

The Grey Eminence François Leclerc du Tremblay (1577–1638), also known as Père Joseph, French cleric and private secretary of Cardinal Richelieu. ➤ See ÉMINENCE *Grise*.

Grim Grom Andrei (Andreevich) Gromyko (1909–89), Soviet statesman, Foreign Minister of the USSR 1957–85 and President of the USSR 1985–88. The humourless, severe demeanour with which he conducted diplomatic negotiations during his 28 years as foreign minister earned him the sobriquet *Grim Grom*.

The Grinder Cliff Thorburn (b.1948), Canadian snooker player who won the World Professional championship in 1980. He was known by his fellow-players as the *Grinder* because of his attritional, tenacious style of play and stubborn refusal to consider himself beaten.

The Grocer Edward (Richard George) Heath (1916–2005), British Conservative statesman, Prime Minister 1970–74. The satirical magazine *Private Eye* called Heath the *Grocer*, a reference to his role as chief negotiator for British entry into the Common Market in 1961–62, when much of his time was spent haggling over the price of hundreds of foodstuffs. During Heath's premiership, the magazine featured a cartoon strip called 'Grocer Heath and His Pals'.

The Grocer's Daughter   Margaret (Hilda) Thatcher (b.1925), British Conservative stateswoman, Prime Minister 1979–90. While Thatcher was indeed the daughter of a Grantham grocer, her nickname the *Grocer's Daughter* was apt for another reason. Her predecessor as leader of the Conservative Party was Edward Heath, known as the GROCER. ➤ See also ATTILA *the Hen*, *The* BLESSED *Margaret*, *The* IRON *Lady*, *The* LEADERENE, MAGGIE, *The* MILK *Snatcher*, TINA.

The Guinea Pig State   The US state of Arkansas. It earned its nickname the *Guinea Pig State* in the 1930s when its farmers volunteered to take part in the agricultural experiments suggested by the federal government. ➤ See also *The* TOOTHPICK *State*.

The Gunners   Arsenal football club. The club was formed by workers at the Royal Arsenal Armaments Factory in Woolwich in 1886, hence their nickname the *Gunners*.

Guy the Gorilla   Ian (Terence) Botham (b.1955), English cricketer. His nickname *Guy the Gorilla*, referring to his powerful build, derives from the name of an actual gorilla that used to be a popular exhibit at London Zoo. ➤ See also BEEFY.

Hh

The Hammer David Blackstock McNee (b.1925), Commissioner of the Metropolitan Police (1977–82). He had earlier gained both a reputation for toughness and his nickname the *Hammer* from his robust approach to law and order while serving as Chief Constable of Glasgow (1971–75).

The Hammer and Scourge of England William Wallace (*c.*1270–1305), Scottish national hero. He was a leader of Scottish resistance to Edward I, defeating the English army at Stirling in 1297 and mounting campaigns against the north of England. After Edward's second invasion of Scotland in 1298 he was defeated and subsequently executed. While Edward was himself known as the HAMMER OF THE SCOTS, Wallace was given the matching nickname the *Hammer and Scourge of England*. The sobriquet *Braveheart* has also become associated with Wallace since the 1995 film of that title. ➤ See also *The* HAMMER *of the Scots*.

Hammerin' Hank Hank (Henry Louis) Aaron (b.1934), US baseball player. He played for the Milwaukee (later Atlanta) Braves and Milwaukee Brewers (1954–76). His batting prowess earned him the nickname *Hammerin' Hank*. In 1973 he overtook Babe Ruth's record of 714 career home runs, ending his career with a total of 755. When he broke Ruth's legendary record (which had stood since 1935), he was the object of racist abuse from many resentful baseball fans.

The Hammer of the Monks Thomas Cromwell (*c.*1485–1540), English statesman, chief minister to Henry VIII 1531–40. He presided over the king's divorce from Catherine of Aragon (1533) and his break with the Roman Catholic Church. Appointed Vicar-General in 1535, Cromwell supervised the dissolution of the monasteries from 1536 to 1539, for which task he was rewarded with some of their confiscated lands. His suppression of the monasteries won him the sobriquet *Malleus Monachorum*, the *Hammer of the Monks* or the *Maul of the Monks*.

The Hammer of the Scots Edward I (1239–1307), son of Henry III, king of England 1272–1307. Inscribed on his tomb in Westminster Abbey are the words *Edwardus Primus Malleus Scotorum hic est* ('Here lies Edward I Hammer of the Scots'). Edward fought a persistent campaign against Scotland, though his efforts to conquer the country failed. He had a successful first campaign there in 1296, deposing the Scottish king, John de Baliol (*c.*1250–1313), who had made an alliance with the French against him. Later he defeated a Scottish revolt under William Wallace (himself known as the HAMMER AND SCOURGE OF ENGLAND) at Falkirk in 1298. ➤ See also LONGSHANKS, MARTEL.

The Hammers West Ham United football club. The club was formed in 1895 as the company team of the Thames Ironworks, hence their nickname the *Hammers*, or, formerly, the *Irons*.

The Handcuff King   Harry Houdini (born Erik Weisz) (1874–1926),
Hungarian-born US magician and escape artist. In the early 1900s he became famous
for his ability to escape from handcuffs and chains, from straitjackets, from locked
containers, and from prison cells. He was billed as the *Handcuff King*.

Hands of Stone   Roberto Duran (b.1951), Panamanian boxer. Born in Guarare,
Panama, Duran was a ferocious puncher known as *Manos de Piedra* or *Hands of
Stone*. In the 1970s and 80s he was world champion at lightweight, welterweight,
super-welterweight, and middleweight.

The Hanging Judge   George Jeffreys, 1st Baron Jeffreys of Wem (*c*.1645–89), Welsh
judge. He took part in the Popish Plot prosecutions and from 1683 was Chief Justice
of the King's Bench. Judge Jeffreys became popularly known as the *Hanging Judge*
because of his brutal sentencing at the Bloody Assizes of 1685, when he condemned
to the gallows 300 or so supporters of the Duke of Monmouth's rebellion. The
nickname is also associated with John Toler, 1st Earl of Norbury (1745–1831), Chief
Justice of the Common Pleas in Ireland in the early 1800s.

The Hanging State   The state of Victoria, Australia. It became the last Australian
state to abolish capital punishment in 1975. ➤ See also *The* CABBAGE *Garden*.

The Hangman of Europe   Reinhard (Tristan Eugen) Heydrich (1904–42), German
Nazi leader. As second-in-command of the Gestapo and head of the security service,
Heydrich was responsible for ordering numerous mass executions in the occupied
countries, hence his nickname the *Hangman of Europe*. He was assassinated by Czech
patriots, reprisals for which included the execution of 1300 civilian inhabitants of
the village of Lidice.

Hannibal the Cannibal   Hannibal Lecter, the psychopathic serial-killer anti-hero of
The Silence of the Lambs (1988, film 1991) and other books by Thomas Harris
(b.1940). Dr Lecter, who eats his victims after killing them, is otherwise known as
Hannibal the Cannibal.

Hanoi Jane   Jane Fonda (b.1937), US film actress. Her films include *Klute* (1971), for
which she won an Oscar, and *The China Syndrome* (1979). Active in left-wing
politics, she campaigned against American involvement in the Vietnam War, and in
1972 made a trip to Hanoi to denounce the US bombing campaigns against North
Vietnam. During this visit she volunteered to make a number of propaganda
broadcasts over Radio Hanoi intended to demoralize US servicemen. This made her
unpopular with many Americans at the time: the disapproving nickname was
consciously modelled on that of TOKYO ROSE, notorious for broadcasting
propaganda to GIs from Japan during the Second World War.

Harefoot   Harold I (d.1040), king of England 1035–40. Harold was an illegitimate
son of Canute and first came to the throne when his half-brother Hardecanute
(Canute's legitimate heir) was king of Denmark and thus absent at the time of his
father's death. The epithet *Harefoot* derives from an Old Norse word *harfotr*, a
nickname for a swift runner.

The Hatters   Luton Town football club. Their nickname is the *Hatters* from the
town's once-thriving millinery industry, especially the manufacture of straw hats.

The Havercake Lads The 33rd Foot (Duke of Wellington's Regiment), a regiment of the British army. The regimental recruiting sergeants during the Napoleonic Wars are said to have attracted potential recruits with oatcakes (known as havers) skewered to the end of their swords. As a result the regiment became known as the *Havercake Lads*.

Hawk Coleman Randolph Hawkins (1904–69), US jazz saxophonist. ➤ See BEAN.

Hawkeye Natty Bumppo, the tracker in James Fenimore Cooper's five *Leatherstocking* novels of American frontier life (1823–41). Bumppo is given various names throughout the novels, including *Leatherstocking*, *Deerslayer*, and *Pathfinder*. In *The Last of the Mohicans* (1826) he is known as *Hawkeye*, because of his keen-sightedness. The character Hawkeye Pierce in the book and US television series *MASH* is said to have been named after him. ➤ See also *The* LAST *of the Mohicans*, LEATHERSTOCKING.

The Hawkeye State The US state of Iowa. The nickname the *Hawkeye State* is first recorded around 1859. The informal term Hawkeye for a native of Iowa may have originated with the newspaper editor J. G. Edwards who was the editor of the Burlington *Patriot* and himself nicknamed *Old Hawkeye*. The newsaper was later retitled the *Hawkeye and Patriot*.

The Head Waiter Harry Wragg (1902–85), British jockey. He won the Derby in 1928, 1930, and 1942, and rode another ten classic winners. Wragg was champion jockey in 1941. Tactically astute, he would wait until the very end of a race before taking the front and crossing the line first, hence his nickname the *Head Waiter*.

The Heart of Dixie The US state of Alabama. Dixie is an informal name for the Southern states of the US. The origin of the term is uncertain, although it has been suggested that the name comes from French *dix* 'ten' on ten-dollar notes printed before the Civil War by the Citizens Bank of Louisiana, and circulating in the Southern States. ➤ See also *The* COTTON *State, The* YELLOWHAMMER *State*.

The Heart of Midlothian The old Edinburgh Tolbooth, or prison, which once stood on a site near St Giles' Cathedral and was demolished in 1817. Its nickname the *Heart of Midlothian* was taken by Walter Scott as the title of a novel (1818), set in 18th-century Edinburgh and opening with the Porteous riot of 1736. Midlothian is a former county of central Scotland, in which Edinburgh was situated. It became a part of Lothian region in 1975. Heart of Midlothian (more commonly known as Hearts) is the name of one of Edinburgh's football teams.

Heff Hugh (Marston) Hefner (b.1926), US publisher and entrepreneur. In 1953 he founded *Playboy*, an erotic magazine for men, and later set up the Playboy chain of nightclubs, whose 'Bunny girl' hostesses wore skimpy costumes with ears and a tail suggestive of a rabbit.

Hell Bruegel Pieter Bruegel the Younger (1564–1638), Flemish artist, the son of the more famous Pieter Bruegel the Elder, whose work he often copied. He is also noted for his paintings of devils and the infernal regions, hence his nickname *Hell Bruegel*. ➤ See also PEASANT *Bruegel*, VELVET *Bruegel*.

Hell's Kitchen   A district on the West Side of New York City once regarded as the haunt of criminals. The term can be applied to any area or place regarded as very disreputable or unpleasant.

The Herring Pond   The North Atlantic Ocean. First recorded in the late 17th century, the *Herring Pond* (or the *Pond*) is a humorous nickname for the North Atlantic.

Hezza   Michael (Ray Dibdin) Heseltine (b.1933), English Conservative politician. *Hezza* is one of a number of nicknames that consciously echo that of the footballer Paul Gascoigne, known as GAZZA. Heseltine mentions in his autobiography that it is said to have been invented by Alastair Campbell when he was a journalist, before Campbell became Tony Blair's press secretary. ➤ See also TARZAN.

The Highland Laddie   Charles Edward Stuart (1720–88), also known as BONNIE PRINCE CHARLIE and the YOUNG PRETENDER.

The Hill   Capitol Hill, a small hill in Washington DC. Informally known as the *Hill*, Capitol Hill is where the Congress buildings and Supreme Court stand. By extension, the term can be used to refer to Congress itself.

His Accidency   ➤ See *The* ACCIDENTAL *President*.

His Royal Badness   Prince (born Prince Rogers Nelson) (b.1958), US rock singer, musician, and songwriter. His albums include *1999* (1982), *Purple Rain* (1984), and *Sign O'The Times* (1987). In 1993 Prince announced that he had changed his name to an unpronounceable symbol and should thereafter be referred to as 'the Artist formerly known as Prince'. Another nickname is the *Purple Pixie*, from his early preference for dressing in purple and his diminutive stature.

Hitch   Alfred (Joseph) Hitchcock (1899–1980), English film director. Working in Hollywood, he became best known for such thrillers as *Strangers on a Train* (1951), *North by Northwest* (1959), *Psycho* (1960), and *The Birds* (1963). These films are notable for their ability to generate suspense and for their technical ingenuity. He was known informally as *Hitch* and on film posters as the MASTER OF SUSPENSE.

Hit 'em Where They Ain't   Willie (William Henry) Keeler (1872–1923), US baseball player. He mostly played with the Baltimore Orioles and New York Yankees (1892–1910). His nickname comes from his own summary of his batting style: 'Keep your eye on the ball and hit 'em where they ain't'. Only 5ft 4in (1.64m), he was also known as WEE WILLIE.

The Hit Man   Thomas Hearns (b.1958), US boxer, the first to win championships at five different weights: welterweight, light-middleweight, middleweight, light-heavyweight, and super-middleweight. Hearns was an explosive puncher, hence his nickname.

The Hog and Hominy State   The US state of Tennessee. Its nickname the *Hog and Hominy State* refers to the traditional local diet of fatback pork and cornmeal. ➤ See also *The* MONKEY *State*, *The* VOLUNTEER *State*.

Hollywood   Shane Keith Warne (b.1969), Australian cricketer. A prodigious spinner of the ball, he made his Test debut in 1992. His nickname *Hollywood* was coined by the Australian Rules footballer Trevor Barker in Warne's early days playing that sport. It fits well with the cricketer's superstar image and the amount of press attention he attracts. Teammates also call him *Truman*, after the film *The Truman Show*, starring Jim Carrey, in which a man's life is filmed 24 hours a day for a television show. Another of his nicknames is the SULTAN OF SPIN.

Hollywood's Mermaid   Esther Jane Williams (b.1923), US swimming champion and film actress. She made her film debut in 1942 and subsequently appeared in a series of MGM musicals whose spectacular aquatic sequences made full use of her superb swimming ability, among them *Bathing Beauty* (1944), *Neptune's Daughter* (1949), *Million Dollar Mermaid* (1952), and *Dangerous When Wet* (1953). In the memorable words of producer Joe Pasternak, 'Wet she was a star'.

The Holy Boys   The 9th Foot (East Norfolk) Regiment, a regiment of the British army. Their nickname the *Holy Boys* is thought to come from the regimental badge, which depicts Britannia. During the Peninsular War, she was often mistaken by the Spanish for the Virgin Mary. An alternative explanation points to the soldiers' practice of selling off their issue bibles.

Homicide Hank   Henry Armstrong (born Henry Jackson) (1912–88), US boxer. Armstrong is the only boxer to have held three world titles simultaneously, namely featherweight, lightweight, and welterweight. He was also known as HURRICANE HANK and the *Human Buzzsaw*, because of the speed and ferocity with which he assaulted his opponents.

Honest Abe   Abraham Lincoln (1809–65), US Republican statesman, 16th President of the US 1861–65. His election as president on an anti-slavery platform helped precipitate the American Civil War. He was assassinated by John Wilkes Booth shortly after the war ended. Before entering politics, Lincoln worked as a lawyer where he acquired a reputation for scrupulous integrity and his nickname *Honest Abe*. ➤ See also *The* GREAT *Emancipator*, OLD *Abe*, *The* RAIL *Splitter*.

Honkers   Hong Kong. The informal name *Honkers* was used from the 1920s by British expatriates living and working in Hong Kong, when it was a British Crown Colony.

The Hoosier State   The US state of Indiana. A Hoosier is a native or inhabitant of Indiana. The term, dating from around 1826, is of unknown origin. Around the same time Indiana began to be referred to as the *Hoosier State*.

The Horse Marines   The 17th Lancers (later the 17th/21st Lancers), a regiment of the British army. In 1795 a detachment of the regiment served aboard the frigate HMS *Hermione* in the West Indies. The 17th Lancers accordingly became known as the *Horse Marines*. The expression *tell that to the horse marines* is used to express scornful disbelief, the horse marines being taken as an imaginary corps of mounted marine soldiers. The phrase is more commonly found in the form *tell that to the marines*. ➤ See also *The* DEATH-OR-GLORY *Boys*.

Hotspur   Henry Percy (1364–1403), English soldier, son of the 1st Earl of Northumberland. He was killed in battle at Shrewsbury during a rebellion against Henry IV. He was commonly known as *Hotspur* or *Harry Hotspur* because of his fiery temper and impetuous nature. 'Hotspur' was an archaic term for a rash or reckless person.

The Hotspur of Debate   Edward Stanley, later 14th Earl of Derby (1799–1869).
➤ See *The* RUPERT *of Debate*.

Hudibras Butler   Samuel Butler (1612–80), English poet, writer of the verse satire *Hudibras* (1663–78), a mock-heroic romance parodying the Puritan sects and the Civil War, which enjoyed an enormous popularity in England at the time. Its chief character is Hudibras (a name taken from Spenser's *Faerie Queene* (1590; 1596)), a fat and pedantic Presbyterian. The poet's subsequent designation as *Hudibras Butler* is partly to distinguish him from the other literary Samuel Butler (1835–1902), the author of the satirical romance *Erewhon* (1872) and the semi-autobiographical novel *The Way of All Flesh* (1903). The later writer is sometimes known as *Erewhon Butler*.

Hunt the Shunt   James (Simon Wallis) Hunt (1947–93), British motor-racing driver. He won the World Motor-racing Championship in 1976 by one point. In his early years of racing Minis and in Formula Three, he became disparagingly known as *Hunt the Shunt* because of the number of crashes he was involved in.

Hurricane   Alex(ander) Higgins (b.1949), Northern Irish snooker player. Known for his volatile and controversial personality, Higgins won the World Professional championship in 1972 and 1982. His first manager John McLaughlin gave him his nickname *Hurricane Higgins*, which well suited his quick-fire style of play.

Hurricane Hank   Henry Armstrong, US boxer. ➤ See HOMICIDE *Hank*.

I i

Iceberg[1] Grace (Patricia) Kelly (1928–82), US film actress of the 1950s, later Princess Grace of Monaco. She starred in such films as *High Noon* (1952), *Rear Window* (1954), *Dial M for Murder* (1954), and *High Society* (1955). A cool blonde beauty, she projected an aloof presence on screen and, according to some of her co-stars, on set too. She accordingly attracted nicknames such as *Iceberg*, the *Ice Princess*, and *Fair Miss Frigidaire*, this last coined by Frank Sinatra. Kelly retired from her film career in 1956 to marry Prince Rainier III of Monaco. She died in 1982 in a road accident.

The Iceberg[2] Björn (Rune) Borg (b.1956), Swedish tennis player. He won five consecutive men's singles titles at Wimbledon (1976–80) and six French Open singles titles (1974–75 and 1978–81). Borg's cool, undemonstrative demeanour on court led the press to call him the *Iceberg*, or, echoing his surname, the *Iceborg*.

IDS Iain Duncan Smith (b.1954), British Conservative politician, leader of the Conservative Party 2001–03. Since the leadership campaign of 2001, when he first became widely known to the British public, Duncan Smith has been known as *IDS*, coined by his supporters on the model of the US presidents FDR, JFK, and LBJ.

Ike Dwight D(avid) Eisenhower (1890–1969), US general and Republican statesman, 34th President of the US 1953–61. Eisenhower was the Allied Commander in Europe during the Second World War. *Ike* was a childhood nickname, derived from his surname, which he carried into adult life. It gained wide currency with the slogan 'I Like Ike', used in Eisenhower's presidential campaigns of 1952 and 1956, though the phrase was used as early as 1947 when he was first being courted as a presidential candidate.

The Immortal Dreamer John Bunyan (1628–88), English writer and preacher, the author of *The Pilgrim's Progress* (1678–84), an allegory recounting the spiritual journey of its hero Christian. The nickname is a reference to the fact that the book takes the form of a dream by the author. ➤ See also *The* IMMORTAL *Tinker*.

The Immortals The 76th Foot (later the Duke of Wellington's Regiment (West Riding)), a regiment of the British army. The nickname the *Immortals* (or the OLD IMMORTALS) dates from the Mahratta War (1803–5) in India, when most of the men in the regiment were wounded, though few of them were killed.

The Immortal Tinker John Bunyan (1628–88), English writer and preacher. Bunyan was born at Elstow, near Bedford, the son of a tinker. He worked with his father until he was conscripted into the Parliamentary army in 1644. He later became a Nonconformist lay preacher, spending several years in prison for unlicensed preaching. ➤ See also *The* IMMORTAL *Dreamer*.

The In and Out The Naval and Military Club, in Piccadilly, London, founded in 1862. Its nickname the *In and Out* refers to the words 'In' and 'Out' painted on the pillars flanking the approach to the courtyard, and is thought to have originated with London cabbies. The club moved to new premises in St James's Square in 1998.

The Invincible Doctor William of Occam (or Ockham) (1285–1349), English philosopher and Franciscan friar. He is best known for the maxim called 'Occam's razor', according to which no more assumptions should be made in explaining a thing than are necessary. His sobriquet the *Invincible Doctor* is a translation of the Latin phrase *Doctor Invincibilis*.

The Iron Scunthorpe United football club. Its nickname the *Iron* stems from the town's steel mills.

The Iron Butterfly Jeanette (Anna) Macdonald (1901–65), US singer and film star. In the 1930s she appeared with Nelson Eddy (1901–67) in an immensely popular series of film operettas, such as *Naughty Marietta* (1935) and *Rose Marie* (1936). Probably the most successful singing duo in the history of cinema, the pair were unkindly dubbed the *Iron Butterfly* and the SINGING CAPON.

The Iron Chancellor[1] Otto (Eduard Leopold) von Bismarck (1815–98), German statesman, Chancellor of the German Empire 1871–90. As Minister-President and Foreign Minister of Prussia under Wilhelm I from 1862, Bismarck was the driving force behind the unification of Germany. He was nicknamed the *Iron Chancellor* after he used the phrase 'blood and iron' in a speech to the Prussian parliament in 1862, referring to military force as an instrument of foreign policy.

The Iron Chancellor[2] Gordon Brown (b.1951), British Labour politician, Chancellor of the Exchequer from 1997. In May 1995, while still in Opposition, Brown undertook to be an 'iron chancellor' if Labour were elected: 'Nobody should doubt my iron commitment to macroeconomic stability and financial prudence.' The use of the title *Iron Chancellor* was a deliberate echo of the phrase associated with Bismarck.

Iron City The US city of Pittsburgh, Pennsylvania. Following the discovery of iron deposits and rich coalfields, Pittsburgh, with its large steel mills, was for a century (until the 1980s) a centre of iron and steel production in the US.

The Iron Duke Arthur Wellesley, 1st Duke of Wellington (1769–1852), British soldier and Tory statesman, Prime Minister 1828–30 and 1834. He served as Commander of the British forces in the Peninsular War (1808–14), receiving a dukedom in 1814. In 1815 Wellington defeated Napoleon at the Battle of Waterloo, so ending the Napoleonic Wars. His famous nickname does not, however, derive from his military achievements. During his first tenure as Prime Minister, he suffered a period of unpopularity and was forced to put up iron shutters outside his London home Apsley House after angry crowds had stoned the windows. Together with his reputation for iron determination, this prompted the press to dub him the *Iron Duke*. He was also referred to as the *Great Duke*. ➤ See also *The* ACHILLES *of England,* OLD *Conky.*

Iron-hand Götz von Berlichingen (1480–1562), German knight. His artificial iron hand replaced one that had been shot away at the siege of Landshut (1505), and his life exploits in battle against various feudal rulers were the subject of a play by Goethe.

The Iron Horse Lou Gehrig (Henry Louis Gehrig) (1903–41), US baseball player. In his 17-year career, he played 2 130 consecutive major-league games for the New York Yankees (1925–39), a record games-played streak that was finally surpassed in 1995 by Carl Ripken. Gehrig's great stamina earned him his nickname the *Iron Horse*. To his teammates he was known as BISCUIT PANTS, because of his heavy build. He died aged 38 from a form of motor neuron disease now often called Lou Gehrig's disease.

The Iron Lady Margaret (Hilda) Thatcher (b.1925), British Conservative states-woman, Prime Minister 1979–90. In January 1976, before she became prime minister, she was dubbed the *Iron Lady* by the Soviet defence ministry newspaper *Red Star*, which accused her of trying to revive the Cold War. She immediately responded to the name: 'I stand before you tonight in my red chiffon evening gown, my face softly made up, my fair gently waved … the Iron Lady of the Western World! Me? A cold war warrior? Well, yes—if that is how they wish to interpret my defence of values and freedoms fundamental to our way of life.' ➤ See also ATTILA *the Hen, The* BLESSED *Margaret, The* GROCER´S *Daughter, The* LEADERENE, MAGGIE, *The* MILK *Snatcher,* TINA.

The Iron Man Emil Zatopek (1922–2000), Czech athlete, the greatest long-distance runner of his day, known for his head-rolling style of running and the contorted expression on his face. He won the 10 000m at the 1948 Olympics and four years later won gold medals in the 5 000m, 10 000m, and the marathon. His strength and endurance led him to be known as the *Iron Man*.

Iron Mike Mike (Michael Gerald) Tyson (b.1966), US boxer. When he won the WBC heavyweight title in 1986, Tyson became the youngest world heavyweight champion ever. The following year he became the first undisputed world heavyweight champion since 1978, having won the WBC, WBA, and IBF titles. In 1992 he was imprisoned for rape. After his release in 1995 he reclaimed the WBC and WBA titles in the following year.

Ironside Edmund II (*c.*980–1016), son of Ethelred the Unready, king of England 1016 (April to November). He was given the name *Edmund Ironside* either because of his courage or because of his iron armour.

Ironsides Oliver Cromwell (1599–1658), English general and statesman, Lord Protector of the Commonwealth 1653–58. Cromwell was the driving force in the revolutionary opposition to Charles I in the English Civil War, and led the Parliamentary army. His nickname *Ironsides* or *Old Ironsides* was of Royalist origin. After the battle of Marston Moor in 1644, Prince Rupert admiringly dubbed his opponent Old Ironsides in tribute to his tenacity in battle. The name Ironsides was later transferred to Cromwell's cavalry regiment. ➤ See also *The* ALMIGHTY *Nose,* COPPER *Nose,* CRUM-HELL, KING *Oliver,* OLD *Noll.*

The Irrefragable Doctor Alexander of Hales (*c.*1186–1245), English theologian and Franciscan. He studied at Paris and taught theology there. His *Summa Universae Theologiae* was considered indisputable, hence the sobriquet he earned in the later Middle Ages, the *Irrefragable Doctor* or *Doctor Irrefragabilis*. Irrefragable means 'not able to be disputed'.

The Italian Stallion   Sylvester Stallone (b.1946), Italian-born US film actor, particularly associated with action roles in such films as *Rambo* (1985) and *Demolition Man* (1993). The *Italian Stallion* was the nickname of Rocky Balboa, the Italian-American boxer Stallone played in *Rocky* (1976), the film that made his name, and in a number of sequels. The nickname subsequently transferred to the actor himself, who is also familiarly known as SLY.

The It Girl   Clara Bow (1905–65), US film actress. She was one of the most popular stars and sex symbols of the 1920s. She became known as the *It Girl* after appearing as a vivacious flapper in the silent film *It* (1927), based on an Elinor Glyn novel. The word 'it' here means sex appeal. She once said: 'Being a sex symbol is a heavy load to carry, especially when one is tired, hurt and bewildered'.

Jj

The Jackal   Carlos Martinez (born Illich Ramirez Sanchez) (b.1949), Venezuelan assassin, hired by various terrorist organizations in the 1970s. The sobriquet the *Jackal*, bestowed on him by journalists, derives from the codename of the professional assassin in Frederick Forsyth's thriller *The Day of the Jackal* (1971), about a plot to assassinate President de Gaulle.

Jack Amend-all   Jack Cade (d.1450), Irish rebel. In 1450 he led a Kentish rebellion against Henry VI, demanding the recall from Ireland of Richard Plantagenet, Duke of York. Promising an end to royal corruption and misgovernment, he gained the nickname *Jack Amend-all*. The rebels defeated the royal forces and occupied London for three days. Cade subsequently died of a wound received in an attempt to capture him.

Jackie O   Jacqueline Lee Bouvier Kennedy Onassis (1929–94), wife of US President John F. Kennedy. Her tenure as a popular and glamorous First Lady was cut short by President Kennedy's assassination in 1963. Following her subsequent marriage to the Greek shipping magnate and financier Aristotle Onassis (1906–75), she became known as *Jackie O* (short for Onassis), before being widowed for a second time in 1975.

Jacko   Michael (Joe) Jackson (b.1958), US pop singer and songwriter, informally known as *Jacko*. As a child he performed with his four older brothers in the pop group the Jackson Five. In 1979 he began his career as a solo artist, becoming the most commercially successful US star of the 1980s. His albums include *Thriller* (1982), *Bad* (1987), and *Dangerous* (1991). Accounts of his eccentric behaviour, from sleeping in an oxygen tent to keeping a pet monkey, have led newspapers to dub him Wacko and *Wacko Jacko*. There has been much speculation about the singer's appearance. Jackson himself attributes the lightening of his skin to a rare skin disorder and has repeatedly denied receiving plastic surgery to change the shape of his face.

Jack the Dripper   Jackson Pollock (1912–56), US abstract expressionist painter. From 1947 he abandoned the use of brushes and developed the style known as action painting. Laying a huge canvas flat on the studio floor, he poured, splashed, or dripped paint onto it. The works he produced became known as his 'drip paintings' and Pollock himself was dubbed *Jack the Dripper* (a clever variation of 'Jack the Ripper') by *Time* magazine.

Jack the Lad   Jack Sheppard (1702–24), English thief who was famous for his daring prison escapes. The last of these was made from a Newgate prison cell to the floor of which he had been handcuffed, manacled, and chained. He was finally executed at Tyburn on 16 November 1724, reportedly in front of a crowd of an estimated 200 000

people. Sheppard was the subject of many plays and ballads and of a novel by
W. H. Ainsworth (1839). The term 'jack-the-lad' is now used to denote a brash,
self-assured young man.

Jack the Ripper   The unidentified 19th-century English murderer. From August
to November 1888 at least six prostitutes were brutally killed in the East End of
London, the bodies being mutilated in a way that indicated a knowledge of
anatomy. The authorities received taunting notes from a person calling himself
Jack the Ripper and claiming to be the murderer, but the cases remain unsolved
despite a wide variety of names being suggested. ➤ See also JACK *the Dripper*.

Jelly Roll   Jelly Roll Morton (born Ferdinand Joseph La Menthe Morton)
(1890–1941), US jazz pianist, composer, and band-leader, one of the principal links
between ragtime and New Orleans jazz. Indeed he claimed to have invented jazz,
styling himself 'the Originator of Jazz Stomps and Blues'. In 1926 Morton formed his
own band, the Red Hot Peppers, with whom he made a series of classic recordings.
'Jelly roll' is southern black slang for the sexual act or the female genitals. He may
have acquired his nickname in recognition of his sexual prowess or his sideline
profession of pimp. According to his own account, it came from his calling
himself Sweet Papa Jelly Roll in an ad-lib when performing a vaudeville routine
on stage early in his career. Among his compositions is 'Jelly Roll Blues': 'In New
Orleans, Louisiana town,/There's the finest boy for miles around/Lord, Mister
Jelly Roll, your affection he has stole.../He's so tall and chancey,/He's the lady's
fancy./Everyone know him,/Certainly do adore him.'

Jemmy Twitcher   John Montagu, 4th Earl of Sandwich (1718–92). *Jemmy
Twitcher* is the name of a highwayman who betrays his associate Macheath in
John Gay's *The Beggar's Opera* (1728). It was used as a nickname for Lord
Sandwich who was active in collecting evidence against the radical John Wilkes
despite their past friendship.

The Jersey Lily   'Lillie' Langtry (born Emilie Charlotte le Breton) (1852–1929),
Jersey-born actress, famous for her beauty and her liaison with the Prince of Wales,
later Edward VII. The daughter of the Dean of Jersey, she made her stage debut in
1881. She was one of the first women from an aristocratic background to become an
actress. Her portrait by John Millais was entitled 'A Jersey Lily' (1878).

Jessyenormous   Jessye Norman (b.1945), US operatic soprano with a rich and
powerful voice. She made her debut in Berlin in 1969, subsequently performing in
the major European opera houses. Norman's repertoire includes both opera and
concert music and she has excelled in performances of works by Wagner, Schubert,
and Mahler. Her nickname *Jessyenormous*, punning on her full name, alludes to the
singer's statuesque figure.

The Jewel of the Adriatic   The city of Venice, Italy. ➤ See *The* BRIDE *of the Sea*.

JFK   John F(itzgerald) Kennedy (1917–63), US Democratic statesman, 35th President
of the US 1961–63. At the age of 43 he was the youngest man ever to be elected US
President. Kennedy was seen as a glamorous and popular world leader, particularly
after the Cuban Missile Crisis. He was assassinated while riding in a motorcade
through Dallas, Texas, in November 1963. Like his Democratic predecessor Franklin

D. Roosevelt, he was widely referred to by his initials. New York's main airport is known as JFK, short for John F. Kennedy International.

Jimbo   Jimmy (James Scott) Connors (b.1952), US tennis player. A left-hander who popularized the two-fisted backhand, Connors won the Wimbledon title in 1974 and 1982 and the US Open title in 1974, 1976, 1978, 1982, and 1983. He was popularly known as *Jimbo*.

Jix   William Joynson-Hicks (1865–1932), British Conservative politician, Home Secretary 1924–29. His name was originally Hicks, but he added Joynson when he married Grace Joynson, daughter of a Manchester silk-manufacturer. Contemporaries simply referred to him as *Jix*.

Joburg   The city of Johannesburg, South Africa. The common contraction *Joburg* (or *Jo'burg*) dates from the end of the 19th century.

Jockey of Norfolk   John Howard, Duke of Norfolk (*c*.1430–85), supporter of Richard III, who was killed at the Battle of Bosworth. There is a tradition (recorded in Shakespeare's play) that the night before the battle he received a written warning, 'Jockey of Norfolk be not too bold,/For Dickon thy master is bought and sold.' Jockey is a diminutive form of the name Jack (or John).

Joe Bananas   Joseph Bonanno (1905–2002), Sicilian-born US Mafia boss. At the height of his career in the 1950s and 1960s he ran one of New York's five largest crime families. He was known in the press as *Joe Bananas*, an Americanization of his name. Bonanno was involved in a Mafia power struggle in the 1960s which became known as the 'Bananas War'.

John Company   The East India Company, a trading company founded in 1600 to develop commerce in the newly colonized areas of SE Asia and India. The nickname *John Company* was taken over from the name *Jan Kompanie*, by which the Dutch East India Company and Dutch government were traditionally known in the East Indies. A translation (1785) of Sparman's *Voyage to the Cape of Good Hope* notes that the Dutch as traders in this area had represented their company as 'one individual powerful prince, by the Christian name of *Jan* or *John*', and from this the writer had told his interpreter to say 'that we were the children of *Jan Company*'.

John the Painter   James Aitken (1752–77), Edinburgh-born arsonist, originally apprenticed to a house-painter. He is said while in America to have taken part in the Boston Tea Party incident (1773). Offering his services to the Americans, he planned to attack British dockyards and shipping. He succeeded in setting fire to the rope house at Portsmouth and warehouses at Bristol. Arrested, charged, and convicted, Aitken was hanged at Portsmouth.

Jolly Jack   J(ohn) B(oynton) Priestley (1894–1984), English novelist, dramatist, and critic. His works include the novel *The Good Companions* (1929) and the plays *Time and the Conways* (1937) and *An Inspector Calls* (1947). During and after the Second World War he was a popular radio broadcaster on current affairs. The nickname is an ironic reference to the Yorkshire-born writer's reputation as something of a curmudgeon.

Joltin' Joe Joe DiMaggio (1914–99), US baseball player. A player of exceptional grace and elegance, he spent his entire career with the New York Yankees (1936–51), helping them to win nine World Series. In 1941 he hit in a record-setting 56 consecutive games. DiMaggio was famously known as *Joltin' Joe*, or the *Jolter*. There is a reference to Joltin' Joe in Simon and Garfunkel's song 'Mrs Robinson' (1968). He also attracted many nicknames alluding to his Italian ancestry, such as the *Wallopin' Wop*, the *Roamin' Roman*, the *Little Bambino*, *Big Giuseppe*, and *Dago*. ➤ See also *The* YANKEE *Clipper*.

Judge Robin Arnold Smith (b.1963), South African-born English cricketer. He was dubbed *Judge* by his fellow players, who thought that his hair resembled a judge's wig.

The Juice O(renthal) J(ames) Simpson (b.1947), former US American football player, considered to be one of the greatest running backs of all time. Simpson, who spent most of his playing career with the Buffalo Bills, was widely known as the *Juice* or ORANGE JUICE, partly because of his ability to squeeze out of tight places and partly from his initials. In 1995, after a long and controversial trial which received an enormous amount of publicity, he was acquitted of the murder of his ex-wife Nicole Brown and her friend Ronald Goodman.

The Jumbo State The US state of Texas. Until Alaska was admitted as the 49th state of the US in 1959, Texas was the largest state. With an area of 692 405 sq km (267 338 sq miles), it was sometimes known as the *Jumbo State*. ➤ See also *The* LONE *Star State*.

Kk

K   Kenneth (Mackenzie) Clark (1903–83), British art historian. ➤ See LORD *Clark of Civilisation*.

The Kaiser   Franz Beckenbauer (b.1945), German footballer who won a record 103 international caps for West Germany (1965–77). He was the first person to win the World Cup both as team captain (in 1974) and as national coach (in 1990). Beckenbauer's nickname the *Kaiser* reflects both his commanding presence as a player and his immense influence on German football.

Kaiser Bill   Wilhelm II (1859–1941), emperor of Germany and king of Prussia 1888–1918. He was unable to prevent the outbreak of the First World War (1914), and was vilified by Allied propaganda as the author of the conflict. He was titled Kaiser Wilhelm (*Kaiser* being the German form of 'Caesar'), but during the war was ridiculed in Britain as *Kaiser Bill*. In 1918 he went into exile in Holland and abdicated his throne.

Keith   Prince Philip, Duke of Edinburgh (b.1921), husband of Elizabeth II. *Keith* is the nickname used in the satirical magazine *Private Eye*. ➤ See also PHIL *the Greek*.

Ken Leninspart   Ken(neth) Livingstone (b.1945), British Labour politician. While serving as the left-wing leader of the Greater London Council (1981–86), Livingstone was dubbed *Ken Leninspart* by the satirical magazine *Private Eye*, combining the names 'Lenin' and 'Spart'. Dave Spart was the name of the fictional left-winger who regularly appeared in the magazine. ➤ See also RED *Ken*.

The Keystone State   The US state of Pennsylvania. The state is the seventh or central one of the original thirteen states, hence its nickname the *Keystone State*. Some of the most important events in the history of the United States took place in Pennsylvania, such as the signing of the Declaration of Independence at Philadelphia in 1776 and the drafting of the US Constitution in the same city in 1787. ➤ See also *The* QUAKER *State*.

The Killer   Jerry Lee Lewis (b.1935), US rock-and-roll and country singer and pianist. His hits include 'Whole Lotta Shakin' Going On' and 'Great Balls of Fire', both recorded in 1957. His nickname suited his 'wild man' image, though he acquired it in his youth.

The King[1]   (William) Clark Gable (1901–60), US film actor. Portraying a self-confident and nonchalant masculinity, Gable was one of the most popular male Hollywood stars of the 1930s and 1940s. His films include *It Happened One Night* (1934), for which he won an Oscar, and *Gone with the Wind* (1939), in which he starred as Rhett Butler. He was known as the KING OF HOLLYWOOD, or simply the

King, during the height of his celebrity. The title was dismissed by the actor himself: 'This King stuff is pure bull. I eat and drink and go to the bathroom just like anybody else. I'm just a lucky slob from Ohio who happened to be in the right place at the right time.'

The King[2]   Elvis (Aaron) Presley (1935–77), US pop and rock-and-roll singer. Influenced by black rhythm and blues, he was the dominant personality of the rock-and-roll era. He shot to fame in 1956, soon becoming the most successful popular singer in the world. His many hit records include 'Heartbreak Hotel', 'Blue Suede Shoes', 'Love Me Tender', and 'Don't Be Cruel'. After making a number of films during the 1960s, he resumed his personal appearances in the 1970s, mostly in Las Vegas. He is regarded by his many admirers as the *King of Rock 'n' Roll*, or simply the *King*. ➤ See also ELVIS *the Pelvis*.

The King[3]   Barry John (b.1945), Welsh Rugby Union player. Acclaimed as one of the great fly-halves in the history of the game, he played for Wales 25 times, scoring 90 points. In 1971 he scored a record 180 points on the British Lions' tour of New Zealand.

King Andrew the First   Andrew Jackson (1767–1845), US general and Democratic statesman, 7th President of the US 1829–37. He made wide use of his executive powers while in office, at times acting without the approval of Congress. His political enemies accused him of exceeding his constitutional authority and dubbed him *King Andrew the First*. ➤ See also OLD *Hickory*.

King Arthur   Arthur Scargill (b.1938), British trade union leader, President of the National Union of Mineworkers 1981–2002. A fervent and combative champion of the coal miners' cause, he led his union into the national miners' strike 1984–85, during which dispute the press labelled him *King Arthur*. In 1996 Scargill broke away from the Labour party to form the Socialist Labour Party.

King Billy   William III (1650–1702), king of Great Britain and Ireland 1689–1702. He is known by this name among Irish Protestants. ➤ See also DUTCH *Billy*, *The* GREAT *Deliverer*.

King Dick   Richard Cromwell (1626–1712), briefly Lord Protector of the Common-wealth on the death of his father Oliver Cromwell, KING OLIVER. He succeeded his father in September 1658 but lacked the competence to govern and was forced to abdicate by the army in May the following year. His enemies derided him as *King Dick*. ➤ See also QUEEN *Dick*, TUMBLEDOWN *Dick*.

The Kingfish   Huey (Pierce) Long (1893–1935), US Democratic politician. Long was governor of Louisiana 1928–31 and state senator 1930–35. A populist and a dema-gogue, he is reported to have said of himself, 'For the present you can just call me the Kingfish.' He declared his intention to run for the presidency in 1934, but was assassinated in the following year. A kingfish is a large sea fish.

King Kev   (Joseph) Kevin Keegan (b.1951), English football player and manager. ➤ See MIGHTY *Mouse*.

The Kingmaker   Richard Neville, Earl of Warwick (1428–71), English statesman. He fought on both sides during the Wars of the Roses, first helping the Yorkist Edward IV to become king (1461) and then briefly restoring the Lancastrian Henry VI to the throne (1470). He was killed at the battle of Barnet. Warwick was first called the *Kingmaker* by John Major in his *History of Greater Britain, both England and Scotland* (1521).

The King of Bath   Richard Nash (1674–1762). ➤ See BEAU *Nash*.

The King of Comedy   Mack Sennett (Michael Sinnott) (1880–1960), Canadian-born US film director and producer. The silent comedies made at his Keystone studios (1912–35) typically comprised chaotic slapstick and frenetic chases, featuring the Keystone Kops, Fatty Arbuckle, and early appearances by the likes of Charlie Chaplin and Buster Keaton. Sennett promoted himself as the *King of Comedy*, though he did offer this rueful comment on the title: 'I called myself king of comedy, but I was a harassed monarch. I worked most of the time. It was only in the evenings that I laughed.'

The King of Hi de Ho   Cab Calloway (Cabell Calloway III) (1907–94), US bandleader and singer, known for his exuberant showmanship and striking zoot-suited appearance. His most famous song is 'Minnie the Moocher', which contains the refrain 'hi-de hi-de hi-de-hi, hi-de hi-de hi-de-ho', echoed by the audience during live performances. He made 'hi-de-ho' a national catchphrase.

The King of Hollywood   (William) Clark Gable (1901–60), US film actor. ➤ See *The* KING.

The King of Jazz   Paul Whiteman (1890–1967), US swing-orchestra leader, associated with his own brand of 'symphonic jazz' which did much to make the form acceptable to a wide audience. He promoted the first prestige jazz concert in New York in 1924, in which he conducted the premiere of George Gershwin's *Rhapsody in Blue*. From this time on, Whiteman was widely billed as the *King of Jazz*, a promotional title he had himself created. The designation was reinforced by the Hollywood screen biography *The King of Jazz* (1930), but has proved controversial as the big band music he played, smoothly orchestrated and with no improvisation, was to some purists scarcely jazz at all. ➤ See also POPS.

The King of Swing   Benny Goodman (full name Benjamin David Goodman) (1909–86), US jazz clarinettist and band-leader, who introduced jazz to a mass audience. He formed his own big band in New York in 1934, and soon gained a mass following through radio and live performances. With the arranger Fletcher Henderson, he developed a distinctive style of big-band jazz in which an ensemble arrangement of lively rhythm and simple melody would incorporate the improvisations of fine soloists. He soon became known as the *King of Swing*. Goodman also led small ensembles that included musicians such as Gene Krupa, Teddy Wilson, and Lionel Hampton.

The King of (the) Calypso   Harry (Harold George) Belafonte (b.1927), US singer, associated particularly with the calypso form. He was born in New York City, spent five years of his childhood in Jamaica, then returned to the US aged 13. His hits included 'Mary's Boy Child' and 'Banana Boat Song' (also known as 'Day-O'). His album *Calypso* (1956) was the first to sell a million copies and spent 31 weeks at the top of the US album chart. He became a hugely successful international star, and was active in the civil rights movement in the 1960s.

The King of the Cowboys   Two US film actors were known as the *King of the Cowboys* in their day, Tom Mix and Roy Rogers. Tom (Thomas Hezikiah) Mix (1880–1940) was a popular star of over 400 silent westerns in the 1920s and 1930s. His films, which were action-packed and full of stunts, included *Riders of the Purple Sage* (1925) and *King Cowboy* (1928). Mix's character was usually dressed in white and rode a black horse. Roy Rogers (born Leonard Slye) (1912–98) was a popular singing cowboy of the 1930s and 1940s, starring mostly in B-films. His horse was called Trigger. ➤ See also *The* SINGING *Cowboy.*

King Oliver   Oliver Cromwell (1599–1658), English general and statesman, Lord Protector of the Commonwealth 1653–58. King in all but name, he refused Parliament's offer of the crown in 1657. ➤ See also *The* ALMIGHTY *Nose,* COPPER *Nose,* CRUM-HELL, IRONSIDES, OLD *Noll.*

The King o' the Commons   James V (1512–42), son of James IV, king of Scotland 1513–42. He used to wander incognito around Edinburgh and other parts of his kingdom to learn the thoughts of the ordinary people. James was popular with the poor because his sense of justice led him to protect them from oppression by the nobility.

The King over the Water   This was the Jacobite name for the exiled James II (1633–1701), 'over the water' in France, once he had been succeeded by William III. The term was later used for his son James Edward the Old Pretender (regarded by his supporters as James III) and grandson Charles Edward the Young Pretender (Charles III to the Jacobites). Jacobite sympathizers would drink a secret toast to the Stuart king by passing their glasses over a bowl of water as a signal. ➤ See also BONNIE *Prince Charlie, The* OLD *Pretender, The* POPISH *Duke, The* WARMING *Pan Baby, The* YOUNG *Chevalier, The* YOUNG *Pretender.*

Kirke's Lambs   The 2nd Foot (later the Queen's Royal Regiment (West Surrey)), a regiment of the British army. In 1661 the regiment was raised for service fighting Muslim forces in Tangier, hence the Christian emblem of the paschal lamb on the regimental badge. The ironic nickname *Kirke's Lambs* alludes not only to the badge but also to the regiment's reputation for savagery and ruthlessness in suppressing the Monmouth rebellion in the West Country in 1685, under the command of Colonel Percy Kirke (1646?–91). The regiment was also known as the *Tangerines* because of its origin.

The Knight of the Rueful Countenance   Don Quixote, the eponymous hero of a romance (1605–15) by Miguel de Cervantes, a satirical account of chivalric beliefs and conduct. Don Quixote is a poor gentleman devoted to the ideal of chivalry, who seeks adventures wearing rusty armour and riding his old horse Rosinante. Cervantes gives him the title *El Caballero de la Triste Figura,* the *Knight of the Rueful* (or *Doleful*) *Countenance.*

K of K (Horatio) Herbert Kitchener, 1st Earl Kitchener of Khartoum (1850–1916), British soldier and statesman. As head of the Egyptian army, he defeated the Mahdist forces at Omdurman and recaptured Khartoum in 1898. He was ennobled as Lord Kitchener of Khartoum, a title often shortened to *K of K*. At the outbreak of the First World War he was made Secretary of State for War, in which capacity he was responsible for organizing the large volunteer army which eventually fought the war on the Western Front. His commanding image appeared on recruiting posters urging 'Your King and Country need you'.

L1

The Lacedaemonians The 46th Foot (Duke of Cornwall's Light Infantry), a regiment of the British army, later the 2nd Battalion. The regimental nickname the *Lacedaemonians* derives from their colonel's supposed espousal of Spartan discipline during the American War of Independence. *Lacedaemonian* means Spartan, from Lacedaemon, an area of ancient Greece comprising the city of Sparta and its surroundings.

Lackland John (1165–1216), son of Henry II, king of England 1199–1216. John was the youngest of the eight children of Henry II and Eleanor of Aquitane and unlike his three elder brothers he received no territory in England or France, accounting for his nickname *Lackland*. He was known as John Lackland throughout his youth. Later the appropriateness of his nickname was confirmed by the loss of most of England's possessions in France during his reign. The phrase is recorded from the late 16th century, and translates the Latin *Sine Terra* and Anglo-Norman French *Sanz Tere* (both meaning 'without land') of earlier chroniclers. ➤ See also SOFTSWORD.

The Lad ('Imself) Tony (Anthony John) Hancock (1924–68), British comedian. Known as the *Lad* or the *Lad 'Imself*, he became a star in the 1950s with the popular radio series *Hancock's Half Hour*, in which he played a lugubrious but witty misfit who is always grumbling about suburban life. The series successfully transferred to television (1956–61). Hancock committed suicide in 1968.

Lady Bird Claudia Johnson (née Taylor) (b.1912), wife of president Lyndon Baines Johnson. She acquired her nickname *Lady Bird* in childhood after her nurse Alice Tittle remarked, 'She's as pretty as a lady bird'. The name stuck, with the result that in adult life her initials matched those of her husband.

Lady Day Billie Holiday (born Eleanora Fagan; she adopted the name Billie after the US film star Billie Dove whom she admired) (1915–59), US jazz singer. Initially a singer in Harlem clubs, she began her recording career with Benny Goodman's band in 1923, going on to perform with numerous jazz groups. Her singing was characterized by its dramatic intensity and highly individual phrasing. In a notable case of mutual nicknaming, it was the saxophonist Lester Young, who accompanied her on many of her recording sessions, who first dubbed her *Lady Day* in acknowledgement of her ladylike demeanour, which she reciprocated by calling him the PRESIDENT, later shortened to PREZ. Holiday liked to be called Lady the rest of her life. She published her autobiography *Lady Sings the Blues* in 1956.

Lady Forkbender Marcia Williams, Lady Falkender (b.1932), Prime Minister Harold Wilson's private and political secretary 1956–73. Given a life peerage in Wilson's resignation honours list in 1974, she was dubbed *Lady Forkbender* in the satirical magazine *Private Eye*. As well as playing on her name, this alluded to Uri

Geller (b.1946), the Israeli psychic performer who came to fame in the 1970s with his demonstrations of bending cutlery, stopping watches, and other feats.

Lady Lindy Amelia Earhart (1898–1937), US aviator. She was the first woman to fly the Atlantic in 1928, and the first woman to do so solo in 1932, completing the journey from Newfoundland to Londonderry in a time of 13¼ hours. Inevitably acclaimed as the female equivalent of Charles Lindbergh, she was dubbed *Lady Lindy*. The aircraft carrying Earhart and her navigator, Frederick J. Noonan, disappeared over the Pacific Ocean during a subsequent round-the-world flight in 1937.
➤ See also LUCKY *Lindy.*

The Lady of the Lamp Florence Nightingale (1820–1910), English nurse and medical reformer. In 1854, during the Crimean War, she improved sanitation and medical procedures at the army hospital at Scutari, achieving a dramatic reduction in the mortality rate. She became known as the *Lady of the Lamp* for her nightly rounds of the wards, carrying a lamp. This popular image of her in the wards at night is first alluded to by Longfellow in *The Courtship of Miles Standish* (1858): 'A Lady with a Lamp shall stand in the great history of the land, A noble type of good, Heroic womanhood.' The sobriquet is subject to a little grammatical variation: she can be the Lady 'of the Lamp', 'with the Lamp', or 'with a Lamp'. A 1951 film of Florence Nightingale's life, starring Anna Neagle, is called *The Lady with a Lamp.*

The Laird of the Halls Harry Lauder (born Hugh MacLennan) (1870–1950), Scottish music-hall comedian. He became highly popular singing Scottish songs, many of which were his own compositions, such as 'I Love a Lassie' and 'Roamin' in the Gloamin'', and entertained troops at home and abroad in both world wars. *Laird* is the Scots form of 'lord'. ➤ See also *The* QUEEN *of the Halls.*

La Lollo Gina (Luigina) Lollobrigida (b.1927), Italian film actress. Glamorous and voluptuous, her Hollywood films include *Trapeze* (1956) and *Solomon and Sheba* (1959). She was often referred to as *La Lollo.*

The Land of Cakes Scotland. The term 'Land o' Cakes', referring to Scottish oatmeal cakes, was used by the poet Robert Burns.

The Land of Enchantment The US state of New Mexico. The state's self-coined nickname is the *Land of Enchantment.* At other times it has promoted itself as the *Land of Heart's desire* and the *Land of the Delight Makers.*

The Land of Flowers The US state of Florida. The state's name means 'flowered' in Spanish, hence one of its nicknames the *Land of Flowers.* ➤ See also *The* SUNSHINE *State.*

The Land of Saints and Scholars Ireland. Its nickname the *Land of Saints and Scholars* alludes to the holiness and learning associated with the early Celtic Church.
➤ See also *The* EMERALD *Isle.*

The Land of the Free The United States. This informal epithet was taken from the poem by the American lawyer and verse-writer Francis Scott Key (1779–1843), which was adopted as the US national anthem in 1931: ''Tis the star-spangled banner; O long may it wave/O'er the land of the free, and the home of the brave!' ('The Star-Spangled Banner', 1814).

The Land of the Little Sticks   Canada. The name *Land of the Little Sticks* comes
from the Chinook word *stik* 'wood, tree, forest', the subarctic tundra region of
northern Canada, characterized by its stunted vegetation.

The Land of the Long White Cloud   New Zealand. The Maori name for New
Zealand is *Aotearoa*, literally 'land of the long white cloud'.

The Land of the Midnight Sun   Any of the most northerly European countries,
where it never gets fully dark during the summer months. The term is generally
applied to Lapland and the northern regions of Norway, Sweden, and Finland. In the
US, it is sometimes used to refer to Alaska.

The Land of the Rising Sun   Japan. The *Land of the Rising Sun* is a translation
of Japanese *Nippon*, which comes from the words *nichi* 'the sun' and *pon, hon*
'source'. *Nippon* is recorded in English from the early 17th century, but *Land of the
Rising Sun* is not found until the mid-19th century.

The Land of the Saints   The US state of Utah. The first settlers in Utah were
members of the Church of Latter-Day Saints, also known as Mormons. From this
comes the state's informal name the *Land of the Saints* (and the alternative nicknames the *Land of the Mormons* and the *Mormon State*). The first Mormon settlers
named the state Deseret (meaning 'honeybee'). ➤ See also *The* BEEHIVE *State*.

Larry   Laurence (Kerr) Olivier (1907–89), English actor and director, who made his
professional debut in 1924 and subsequently performed all the major Shakespearian
roles. He was director of the National Theatre (1963–73). Olivier directed and starred
in several film versions of Shakespeare's plays including *Henry V* (1944), *Hamlet*
(1948), and *Richard III* (1955). Other screen appearances include *Wuthering Heights*
(1939) and *Rebecca* (1940). In 1970 he was made a life peer, the first actor to be so
honoured. He was affectionately known as *Larry* and the Laurence Olivier Awards,
presented by the Society of West End Theatre, are popularly known as 'Larries'.

Larry Legend   Larry (Joe) Bird (b.1956), US basketball player. He joined the Boston
Celtics in 1979, and led his team to the NBA championship in 1981, 1984, and 1986.
He was voted NBA most valuable player three times (1984–86). Bird retired in 1992
after 13 seasons. In that year he captained the gold medal-winning US Olympic
basketball team (known as the 'Dream Team'). A greatly admired forward, he was
widely known as *Larry Legend*.

The Last Man   Charles I (1600–49), son of James I, king of England, Scotland, and
Ireland 1625–49. The Parliamentarians referred to him as *The Last Man*, that is, the
last king of England. It is a deliberate evasion, avoiding the use of the despised word
'king'. His son, Charles II, was called the SON OF THE LAST MAN by the Royalists.
➤ See also *The* MARTYR *King*.

The Last of the Cocked Hats   James Monroe (1758–1831), US Democratic
Republican statesman, 5th President of the US 1817–25. He is chiefly remembered as
the originator of the Monroe Doctrine, the US policy opposing future colonization
of the Americas by any European power. During his presidency he sometimes wore
the cocked hat of a Revolutionary army officer, a reminder that as a young man
he had served in the War of Independence, the last US president to have done so.
Monroe was accordingly nicknamed the *Last of the Cocked Hats*.

The Last of the Mohicans   Uncas, an American Indian character in James Feni-more Cooper's novel of that name (1826), the last survivor of his people. The term the *Last of the Mohicans* is sometimes used allusively for the sole survivor of a noble race or kind.

The Last of the Red Hot Mommas   Sophie Tucker (Sophia Kalish-Abuza) (1884–1966), US vaudeville and cabaret singer, the daughter of Russian parents who emigrated to the USA. Her nickname was taken from the title of the song 'I'm the Last of the Red Hot Mommas', written by Jack Yellen, and first sung by Tucker in 1928. It fitted her brassy, dynamic image and was how she would be billed for the rest of her life. Because she was plump she was also sometimes known as *Sophie Tuckshop*.

The Last of the Saxons   Harold II (*c*.1019–66), the last Anglo-Saxon king of England, reigned 1066. Harold was killed and his army defeated by William of Normandy at the Battle of Hastings. *Harold*, a historical romance by Lord Lytton published in 1848, has the subtitle 'the Last of the Saxon Kings'.

The Laughing Philosopher   Democritus (*c*.460–*c*.370 BC), Greek philosopher. He is said to have shown wry amusement at the follies of mankind, hence his sobriquet the *Laughing Philosopher*, in contrast to the gloomy Heraclitus, the WEEPING PHILOSOPHER.

LBJ   Lyndon Baines Johnson (1908–73), US Democratic statesman, 36th President of the US 1963–69. As Vice-President, he succeeded to the Presidency on Kennedy's assassination. Like his predecessor, he was known by his initials. Johnson ran for election in 1964 with the slogan 'All the way with LBJ'. Another slogan that came to be associated with him was 'Hey, hey, LBJ, how many kids did you kill today?', chanted by those demonstrating against US involvement in the Vietnam War.

The Leaderene   Margaret (Hilda) Thatcher (b.1925), British Conservative states-woman, Prime Minister 1979–90. The *Leaderene* was a humorous name for Thatcher while Leader of the Opposition, and later Prime Minister. Meaning 'a female leader', the word's female ending is based on forenames such as Marlene. It is thought to have been coined by the Conservative politician Norman St John Stevas. ➤ See also ATTILA *the Hen, The* BLESSED *Margaret, The* GROCER'S *Daughter, The* IRON *Lady*, MAGGIE, *The* MILK *Snatcher*, TINA.

The Learned Blacksmith   Elihu Burritt (1810–79), US pacifist and scholar. Born in New Britain, Connecticut, Burritt was a self-taught linguist who could read nearly 50 languages by the time he was 30. He organized a number of peace congresses in European cities from 1848. In his early life he had worked at the forge, hence his nickname the *Learned Blacksmith*.

Leatherstocking   Natty Bumppo, the tracker hero in James Fenimore Cooper's *The Pioneers* (1823) and the four other novels (the *Leatherstocking* series) of American frontier life (1823–41). One of the names Bumppo is given is *Leatherstocking*, which in North American English denotes a frontiersman. ➤ See also HAWKEYE, *The* LAST *of the Mohicans*.

The Legs   Betty Grable (1916–73), US film actress, singer, and dancer. ➤ See *The* GIRL *with the Million Dollar Legs*.

The Liberator[1] Daniel O'Connell (1775–1847), Irish nationalist leader and social reformer. O'Connell's election to Parliament in 1828 led to the passing of the Catholic Emancipation Act of 1829, repealing discriminatory laws excluding Roman Catholics from sitting in Parliament or taking public office. Although he failed in his subsequent campaign for Irish independence, he is revered in Ireland as the *Liberator*.

The Liberator[2] Simón Bolívar (1783–1830), Venezuelan patriot and statesman. He succeeded in driving the Spanish from Venezuela, Colombia, Peru, and Ecuador, although his dream of a federation of all Spanish-speaking South American states was never realized. Upper Peru was named Bolivia in his honour.

Light Horse Harry Henry Lee (1756–1818), US cavalry officer. During the War of Independence he commanded the light-armed cavalry known as the light horse, hence his nickname *Light Horse Harry*. In 1779 his men overcame the British at Paulus Hook, New Jersey. He was the father of the Confederate Commander Robert E. Lee.

Lilibet Elizabeth II. This was a childhood nickname which derived from her younger sister Princess Margaret's attempt to pronounce 'Elizabeth'. It was adopted by the rest of the royal family. ➤ See also BRENDA.

The Lion[1] William I (1143–1214), king of Scotland from 1165, who in 1189 established Scotland as independent of the overlordship of England. He adopted a red lion rampant for his crest. This is thought to be the origin of the red lion on the arms of Scotland.

The Lion[2] Titta Ruffo (1877–1953), Italian operatic baritone, noted for his rich, resonant voice. He was also known as the *Caruso of Baritones*.

The Lion[3] Willie Smith (William Henry Joseph Berthel Bonaparte Bertholoff) (1897–1973), US jazz pianist. Smith was a flamboyant showman, a braggart, and sharp dresser. His nickname was probably conferred on him by fellow-pianist James P. Johnson, though there are several other stories purporting to account for it. It may derive from bravery at the front in the First World War or from his devotion to Judaism which led to him being called 'the Lion of Judah'. Smith would announce his arrival in a club with the words 'The Lion is here!' He is the subject of Duke Ellington's composition 'Portrait of The Lion' (1940).

The Lionheart Richard I (1157–99), son of Henry II, king of England 1189–99. ➤ See COEUR de Lion.

The Lion of Judah Haile Selassie (born Ras Tafari Makonnen) (1892–1975), emperor of Ethiopia 1930–74. During the Italian occupation of Ethiopa (1936–41), he lived in exile in Britain. He reclaimed the throne in 1941 and ruled until deposed in a military coup in 1974. As a statesman he is credited with modernizing his country and making it a prominent force in Africa. He is held in reverence as the Messiah by the Rastafarian religious movement, which is named after him. Haile Selassie was known as the *Lion of Judah*, one of the titles of the emperor of Ethiopia, deriving from the reference to Christ in the Book of Revelation as 'the Lion of the tribe of Judah'. The emblem of the the the Lion of Judah, symbolizing strength, was formerly depicted on the Ethiopian national flag: a crowned lion carrying a flagstaff flying the national colours of red, gold, and green.

The Lion of Justice Henry I (1068–1135), king of England 1100–35. He earned this sobriquet for his judicial and administrative reforms, among which was the introduction of a system of travelling judges. ➤ See also BEAUCLERC.

The Lion of the North Gustavus Adolphus (1594–1632), king of Sweden 1611–32. In the early part of his reign he fought successfully against Denmark, Russia, and Poland. His victories leading a Protestant army against the Holy Roman Empire in the Thirty Years War won him the title of *Lion of the North*.

The Lion of Vienna Nat Lofthouse (b.1925), English footballer, who played for Bolton Wanderers and England. Lofthouse was dubbed the *Lion of Vienna* following his combative performance during England's 3–2 win over Austria in 1952. The *Lion of Vienna* pub in Bolton is named after him.

The Lions Millwall football club. The London club was founded in 1885 by workers at the J. T. Morton jam and marmalade factory in West Ferry Road, on the Isle of Dogs. Since many of their early players were Scots, the club adopted the Scottish flag's lion rampant for its badge and were soon known by their supporters as the *Lions*. Since 1910 the club's ground has been appropriately named The Den.

Little America Grosvenor Square, London, associated with the United States since John Adams, the first minister to Britain (1785–88) and later President, occupied No. 9. The US Embassy stands on the west side. In the centre of the square stands a bronze statue of President Franklin D. Roosevelt. No. 20 was the headquarters of General Eisenhower during the Second World War. ➤ See also EISENHOWER *Platz*.

The Little Corporal Napoleon I (known as Napoleon; full name Napoleon Bonaparte) (1769–1821), emperor of France 1804–14 and 1815. In France he was affectionally known as *le Petit Caporal*, the *Little Corporal*. This dates from the Battle of Lodi in 1796, when his courage in battle won him the admiration of the soldiers in his artillery regiment. Napoleon was noted for his small stature. ➤ See also BONEY, *The* CORSICAN *Ogre*, *The* MAN *of Destiny*, *The* VIOLET *Corporal*.

Little Cuba Miami, Florida. It is known as *Little Cuba* on account of its large Cuban immigrant population.

The Little Flower Fiorello Henry La Guardia (1882–1947), US politician and Mayor of New York City 1933–45. La Guardia's many achievements include tackling New York's poverty and housing problems and fighting corruption and organized crime. He was known as the *Little Flower*, a translation of his Italian first name. New York's La Guardia airport, the construction of which he successfully campaigned for, is named after him.

The Little Giant Stephen A(rnold) Douglas (1813–61), US lawyer and politician. During the 1858 senatorial campaign in Illinois, Douglas took part in a famous series of seven debates with Abraham Lincoln on the issue of slavery. Although he won the senatorial race, he lost to Lincoln in the presidential campaign two years later. Unlike Lincoln, Douglas was a man of short stature, barely 5ft tall and known as the *Little Giant*.

The Little Magician Martin van Buren (1782–1862), US statesman, 8th President of the US 1837–41, and one of the founders of the Democratic Party. The sobriquet the *Little Magician* derived from his diminutive stature and his reputation for political cunning and skill. John Randolph of Roanoke (1773–1833) said of him, 'he rowed to his objective with muffled oars.' ➤ See also MARTIN *van Ruin*, OLD *Kinderhook*.

The Little Master Donald George Bradman (1908–2001), Australian cricketer. ➤ See *The* DON.

Little Miss Poker Face Helen Wills Moody (1905–98), US tennis player who dominated the women's game in the 1920s and 1930s. She was Wimbledon champion eight times and US champion seven times, winning 31 grand slam titles in all. Journalists dubbed her *Little Miss Poker Face* because of her inscrutable demeanour and intense concentration on court. She was also known as the *Queen of the Courts*. ➤ See also MISS *Frigidaire*.

Little Mo Maureen Catherine Connolly (1934–69), US tennis player. She won the US singles title aged 16, losing only a further four matches throughout the rest of her career. In 1953 Connolly became the first woman to win the grand slam by taking all four major titles (British, US, French, and Australian). Her career was ended by injury when she was 19. Only 157cm (5ft 2ins) tall, she was affectionately known as *Little Mo*.

Little Rhody The US state of Rhode Island. The smallest state in the Union, it is popularly known as *Little Rhody*. ➤ See also *The* OCEAN *State*.

Little Sparrow Edith Piaf (born Edith Giovanna Gassion) (1915–63), French cabaret singer. She started her career as a street singer at the age of 15 and went on to achieve fame as the best-loved singer in France, mourned by the whole country at her death. She is remembered for the defiant emotionalism with which she sang such songs as 'La vie en rose' and 'Je ne regrette rien'. *Little Sparrow* was both her stage name and her nickname, and comes from the cabaret impresario Louis Leplee in 1935 calling her *la mome piaf* (meaning 'little sparrow') because of her small size.

Little Sure-Shot Annie Oakley (born Phoebe Anne Oakley Moses or Mozee) (1860–1926), US markswoman. In 1885 she joined Buffalo Bill's Wild West Show, of which she became a star attraction for the next 17 years. She was nicknamed *Little Sure-Shot* by the Sioux Indian chief Sitting Bull, who also appeared in Buffalo Bill's show.

Little Venice An area of London at the west end of Regent's Canal, a secluded and attractive canal basin noted for its artists. Both Robert Browning and Lord Byron compared the area to Venice, but the name *Little Venice* was not in general usage until after the Second World War.

The Little Wonder Tom Sayers (1826–65), British prizefighter. Despite being only 5ft 8in tall and weighing only 147lb, Sayers became champion of England in 1851. His fight with the American John Heenan at Farnborough, Hampshire in 1860 was the last great prizefight (an unlicensed boxing match for prize money) staged in Britain.

The Livermore Larruper Max Baer (Maximilian Adelbert Baer) (1909–59), US boxer. He was born in Omaha, Nebraska, but he was brought up in Livermore,

California. Baer was billed as the *Livermore Larruper* ('larrup' meaning to beat or thrash someone) when he turned professional in 1929. He became world heavy-weight champion in 1934, defeating Primo Carnera.

The Lizard King   Jim Morrison (James Douglas Morrison) (1943–71), US rock singer and songwriter. He was the flamboyant lead singer with the Doors, a rock group associated with the drug culture, avant-garde art, and psychedelia of the late 1960s. Their songs, broodingly performed by Morrison, included 'Light My Fire' (1967) and 'Riders on the Storm' (1971). He referred to himself as the *Lizard King*, a title first used in his poem 'The Celebration of the Lizard King', printed on the sleeve of the album *Waiting for the Sun* (1968).

The Lizard of Oz   Paul (John) Keating (b.1944), Australian Labor statesman, Prime Minister 1991–96. A vociferous republican, Keating was vilified in the British press as the *Lizard of Oz*, echoing the title of the children's book and film *The Wizard of Oz*. In 1995, on a state visit by the Queen to Australia, Keating put his arm around the Queen, a severe breach of royal protocol.

Log-Cabin Harrison   William Henry Harrison (1773–1841), US Whig statesman, 9th President of the US. He died of pneumonia one month after his inauguration in 1841, the first president to die in office. During the 1840 presidential campaign, a Demo-cratic journalist made a jibe about Harrison's supposed simple-mindedness: 'Give him a barrel of hard cider, and settle a pension of two thousand a year on him, and he will sit the remainder of his days in his log cabin.' Brilliantly turning this remark to the advantage of their candidate, the Whigs used it to promote Harrison as a man of the people, sharing the tastes of the common man. They organized Log Cabin clubs, held Log Cabin parties, and wrote Log cabin songs. They also distributed large amounts of free cider to the voters. Far from being born in a log cabin, Harrison had in fact been born in the mansion of his aristocratic family in Virginia. In American tradition, the log cabin has continued to symbolize the humblest origins from which a person might rise to the presidency. The biography of James Garfield (1831–81), US Republican statesman and 20th President of the US, was entitled *From Log-cabin to White House* (1910, by William Roscoe Thayer). ➤ See also TIPPECANOE.

Lone Eagle   Charles (Augustus) Lindbergh (1902–74), US aviator, who made the first nonstop solo transatlantic flight in 1927. Lindbergh's baby son Charles was popularly known as the *Little Eaglet*. ➤ See also LUCKY *Lindy*.

The Lone Star State   The US state of Texas. The 'lone star' is the single star on the state flag of Texas, hence the state's well-known nickname. A single star was also depicted on the flag of the Texas Republic (1836–45). ➤ See also *The* JUMBO *State*.

The Long Fellow[1]   Eamon de Valera (1882–1975), American-born Irish statesman, Taoiseach (Prime Minister) 1937–48, 1951–54, and 1957–59 and President of the Republic of Ireland 1959–73. Tall and lean, de Valera was affectionately nicknamed the *Long Fellow*, in contrast to Michael Collins, the BIG FELLOW. ➤ See also *The* CHIEF.

The Long Fellow[2]   Lester (Keith) Piggott (b.1935), English jockey. Piggott was the champion jockey nine times between 1960 and 1971 and again in 1981 and 1982. He rode 30 Classic winners and won the Derby a record nine times. Tall (5ft 9ins) for a jockey, he was known as the *Long Fellow*.

Long Hair   George Armstrong Custer (1839–76), US cavalry general. ➤ See YELLOW *Hair.*

Longshanks   Edward I (1239–1307), son of Henry III, king of England 1272–1307. He was a tall man, with long spindly legs. On his tomb in Westminster Abbey he is referred to as *Edwardus Longus*. His height was noted in early chronicles, one observing that 'the length of his legs ensured that he was never dislodged from his seat by the galloping and jumping of horses'. There is a reference to 'Great Edward Longshanks' issue' in Marlowe's *Edward II* (1593). ➤ See also *The* HAMMER *of the Scots.*

Long Tom   Thomas Jefferson (1743–1826), US Democratic Republican statesman, 3rd President of the US 1801–9. Jefferson was the principal drafter of the Declaration of Independence (1776). He was 6ft 2½ in tall, hence his nickname *Long Tom*. ➤ See also *The* SAGE *of Monticello.*

Lord Clark of Civilisation   Kenneth (Mackenzie) Clark (1903–83), British art historian and Director of the National Gallery 1934–45. His television series *Civilisation*, first broadcast in 1969, popularized the history of art. When he was made a life peer in 1969, he took the title Lord Clark of Saltwood, though the satirical magazine *Private Eye* referred to him as *Lord Clark of Civilisation*. He was also known simply as K.

Lord Cupid   Lord Palmerston (Henry John Temple, 3rd Viscount Palmerston) (1784–1865), British Whig statesman, Prime Minister 1855–58 and 1859–65. As a young man he was strikingly good-looking and known to his friends as *Cupid*. Later in life Palmerston was a notorious philanderer and was nicknamed (and depicted in cartoons as) *Lord Cupid* or simply *Cupid*. According to a probably apocryphal story, Disraeli is said to have responded to the suggestion that political capital could be made from one of Palmerston's affairs: 'Palmerston is now seventy. If he could prove evidence of his potency in his electoral address he'd sweep the country.' ➤ See also PAM.

Lord Fanny   John Hervey (1696–1743), Baron Hervey of Ickworth, politician. He was appointed Vice-Chamberlain to George II and exercised great influence over Queen Caroline. Alexander Pope resented Hervey's close friendship with Lady Mary Wortley Montagu, whom Pope himself had initially admired but later turned against. It was Pope who gave this contemptuous nickname to Lord Hervey in his 'Imitation of the First Satire of the Second Book of Horace' (1733): 'The lines are weak, another's pleased to say,/Lord Fanny spins a thousand such a day.' The name Fanny derived from Fanius, a poetaster mentioned by Horace. In his 'Epistle to Dr Arbuthnot', Pope launched a more sustained attack on Lord Hervey, there called Sporus and portrayed as an effeminate fop.

Lord Haw-Haw   William Joyce (1906–46), wartime broadcaster, born in the United States of Irish parentage. During the Second World War he made propaganda broadcasts in English from Nazi Germany. The nickname *Lord Haw-Haw* was coined by the *Daily Express* journalist Jonah Barrington, referring to Joyce's drawling nasal delivery, affecting an upper-class accent. He was hanged for treason after the war.

Lord Look-on George Charles Bingham, 3rd Earl of Lucan (1800–88), British field marshal. Lord Lucan was a cavalry commander during the Crimean War. At the Battle of the Alma on 20 September 1854, following the orders of the army Commander Lord Raglan, he held the cavalry in reserve, earning himself the nickname *Lord Look-on*. A month later, Lucan was responsible for passing on the ambiguous orders from Raglan which led to the disastrous charge of the Light Brigade of cavalry at the Battle of Balaclava.

Lord Porn Francis Aungier Pakenham, 7th Earl of Longford (1905–2001), British political reformer. In the early 1970s Lord Longford became known in the press as *Lord Porn* because of his zealous campaigning against pornography and sexual liberation. In 1972 he headed an unofficial inquiry into pornography in the UK. He was also known as a campaigner for prison reform.

The Louisville Lip Muhammad Ali (b.1942), US boxer, the first boxer to be world heavyweight champion three times. He was born Cassius Marcellus Clay (by which name he was known until changing it to Muhammad Ali in 1964) in Louisville, Kentucky. From early on in his career he was known for his extrovert braggart persona. He recited doggerel verse in which he would predict the round he would knock out his opponent and proclaimed himself 'the Greatest'. The press coined various colourful nicknames for him such as GASEOUS CASSIUS, *Cash the Brash*, and the MOUTH, but the name which really caught on was the *Louisville Lip*. In 1964, Clay (as he then still was) entered the ring for his first world heavyweight title fight against Sonny Liston with 'The Lip' stitched on the back of his white robe. ➤ See also *The* GREATEST.

The Love Goddess Rita Hayworth (born Margarita Carmen Cansino) (1918–87), US film actress and dancer. Red-headed and voluptuous, she was one of the most glamorous film stars of the 1940s. She was the vivacious star of a succession of film musicals including *Cover Girl* (1944) and also played leading roles in several films of the film noir genre, notably *Gilda* (1946) and *The Lady from Shanghai* (1948), in which she co-starred with her second husband Orson Welles. She was dubbed Hollywood's *Love Goddess* at the height of her career.

Lovell the Dog Francis, Viscount Lovell (1454–88?). A well-known rhyme of the 15th century included the lines: 'The cat, the rat, and Lovell our dog,/Rule all England under the hog.' This referred to the rule of Richard III, whose personal emblem was a white boar, and his three favourites, William Catesby ('the cat'), Richard Ratcliffe ('the rat'), and Lord Lovell, whose crest was a dog. The rhyme is attributed to the English landowner and conspirator against Richard, William Collingbourne (d.1484).

The Lucky Country Australia. This often ironic epithet for Australia as a land of opportunity was the title of a book by Donald Horne (1921–2005), published in 1964. ➤ See also OZ, YOU *Beaut Country*.

Lucky Lindy Charles (Augustus) Lindbergh (1902–74), US aviator. In May 1927 Lindbergh made the first nonstop solo transatlantic flight in his single-engined monoplane *Spirit of St Louis*, taking 33½ hours from New York to Paris. He became a national celebrity on his return home and was awarded the Congressional Medal of

Honor. His two-year-old son was kidnapped and murdered in 1932, after which Lindbergh moved to Europe. ➤ See also LADY *Lindy,* LONE *Eagle.*

Lucky Lucan   Richard John Bingham, 7th Earl of Lucan (b.1934). Lord Lucan, known as *Lucky Lucan* because of his success at gambling, was a British peer who mysteriously disappeared in November 1974 on the night that his wife was attacked and his children's nanny was murdered. He has never been found, and speculation about his survival and whereabouts continues to this day.

Lucky Luciano   Charles Luciano (born Salvatore Luciana) (1896–1962), Sicilian-born US gangster. His nickname *Lucky* stemmed from an incident in which he survived having his throat slit by a rival gangster.

Mm

Machine Gun Kelly   George R. Kelly (born George Kelly Barnes) (1895–1954), US bankrobber and kidnapper. He married Kathryn Thorne in 1927 and it is she who is said to have bought Kelly his first machine gun and given him his underworld nickname *Machine Gun Kelly*. She encouraged him to practise shooting walnuts off fence posts.

Mac the Knife[1]   (Maurice) Harold Macmillan, 1st Earl of Stockton (1894–1986), British Conservative statesman, Prime Minister 1957–63. He acquired the nickname *Mac the Knife* after sacking seven cabinet ministers in 1962 in what became known as the Night of the Long Knives. The nickname is a deliberate echo of Mack the Knife, the murderous character from Brecht and Weill's *The Threepenny Opera* (1929), himself based on Macheath the highwayman in John Gay's *The Beggar's Opera* (1728). ➤ See also SUPERMAC[1].

Mac the Knife[2]   Ian (Kinloch) MacGregor (1912–98), Scottish-born US business executive. He was chairman of British Steel (1980–83) and the British Coal Board (1983–86). MacGregor was originally dubbed *Mac the Knife* by the trade unions because of the drastic staff cuts he implemented in the steel industry in order to make it profitable. Later, the nickname was widely used during the British miners' strike of 1984–85.

Mac the Mouth   John (Patrick) McEnroe (b.1959), US tennis player who dominated the game in the early 1980s. Among his many titles are three Wimbledon singles titles (1981, 1983–84) and four US Open singles championships (1979–81, 1984). Nicknamed *Mac the Mouth* and SUPERBRAT by the press, he was a temperamental player with a fiery temper on court, his outbursts often directed against the umpire or line judges. McEnroe was regularly fined for his tantrums and at the Australian Open in 1990 he was disqualified from the tournament for verbally abusing officials.

Madame Sans-Gêne   Madame Lefebvre (born Catherine Hubscher) (1755–1820), wife of one of Napoleon Bonaparte's marshals. A former washerwoman and vivandière, she was known as *Madame Sans-Gêne* because of her lack of sophistication at court. The literal meaning of the term *sans-gêne* is 'disregard of the ordinary forms of civility or politeness'.

Madame Veto   Marie Antoinette (1755–93), French queen, wife of Louis XVI. In late 18th century France, *Madame Veto* was a nickname given to Marie Antoinette during the French Revolution. Her husband was known as MONSIEUR VETO. This alludes to the king's right of veto, which he exercised more than once in 1791–92, with respect to decrees of the Legislative Assembly. ➤ See also *The* BAKER'S *Wife*.

The Mad Cavalier   Prince Rupert (1619–82), German-born English general and admiral, son of Frederick V, the Elector Palatine, and nephew of Charles I. He made his name in the early years of the English Civil War as the Royalist cavalry leader. His reputation for reckless courage earned him his sobriquet the *Mad Cavalier*. ➤ See also *The* RUPERT *of Debate*.

Madchester   The city of Manchester, England. In the late 1980s and early 1990s the city was dubbed *Madchester* in the press in reference to its place at the centre of the UK rock music scene, dominated by such bands as the Happy Mondays, the Stone Roses, and Inspiral Carpets. ➤ See also COTTONOPOLIS.

Madge   Madonna (born Madonna Louise Ciccone) (b.1958), US pop singer and actress. She rose to international stardom in the mid-1980s through her records and accompanying videos, cultivating her image as a sex symbol and frequently courting controversy. Among her many hit singles are 'Holiday', 'Like a Virgin', and 'Material Girl'. Her films include *Desperately Seeking Susan* (1985) and *Evita* (1996). Following her marriage to the British film director Guy Ritchie, the British press dubbed her *Madge*, in a jokey attempt to cast her as a subservient housewife. The singer has expressed her dislike of the nickname; in January 2002 a front-page story in the *Daily Star* was headlined 'Don't Call Me Madge'.

The Mad Monk[1]   Grigori (Efimovich) Rasputin (1871–1916), Russian monk. He became notorious for exercising great influence over Tsar Nicholas II and his family by claiming miraculous powers to heal the heir to the throne, who suffered from haemophilia. Rasputin's abuse of power, combined with his reputation for debauchery, led him to be eventually assassinated by a group of noblemen loyal to the tsar. He is remembered as the *Mad Monk*.

The Mad Monk[2]   Keith Joseph (1918–94), British Conservative politician. Joseph was a close political adviser to Margaret Thatcher, generally credited with being the intellectual architect of her free-market ideology. His nickname the *Mad Monk*, echoing Rasputin's, derived from his austere, intense demeanour and his reputation for agonized deliberation over an issue. It was originally coined by his fellow Conservative Chris Patten.

Maga   *Blackwood's Magazine*, published 1817–1980, originally called *Edinburgh Monthly Magazine*. The familiar name *Maga* is first recorded in a letter of July 1820 from Walter Scott. It is supposedly derived from its Scottish founder William Blackwood (1776–1843) referring to it in his broad accent as 'ma maga-zine'.

Maggie   Margaret (Hilda) Thatcher (b.1925), British Conservative stateswoman, Prime Minister 1979–90. *Maggie* was the most common nickname for Margaret Thatcher used in the British popular press, especially in headlines, during her premiership. ➤ See also ATTILA *the Hen*, *The* BLESSED *Margaret*, *The* GROCER'S *Daughter*, *The* IRON *Lady*, *The* LEADERENE, *The* MILK *Snatcher*, TINA.

The Magician of the North   Walter Scott (1771–1832), Scottish novelist and poet. ➤ See *The* GREAT *Magician*.

The Magnificent Wildcat   Pola Negri (born Appolonia Chalupek) (1897–1987), Polish-born US silent film actress. She went to Hollywood in the 1920s to star in such films as *One Arabian Night* (1920) and *The Spanish Dancer* (1923). Negri, billed as the *Magnificent Wildcat*, was a tempestuous and flamboyant actress who specialized in playing exotic vamps. Her real-life lovers included Charlie Chaplin and Rudolph Valentino.

The Magnolia State   The US state of Mississippi. The emblem of the state is the magnolia flower, hence the state's nickname the *Magnolia State*. ➤ See also *The* BAYOU *State*.

The Magpies   Newcastle United football club. The black-and-white stripes the team play in earn them the nickname the *Magpies*. Notts County football club are similarly nicknamed for the same reason. ➤ See also GAZZA.

The Maiden   Malcolm IV (1141–65), grandson of David I, king of Scotland 1153–65. He was only eleven when he came to the throne. Nicknamed the *Maiden* (or the *Maiden King*) because of his gentle disposition and devotion to the Church, he is known to have taken a vow of celibacy. Malcolm died aged 23 and without an heir.

The Maid of Norway   Margaret of Norway (1283–90), granddaughter of Alexander III of Scotland, who on her grandfather's death was acknowledged queen of Scotland, aged six. Known as the *Maid of Norway* (or the FAIR MAID OF NORWAY), she was to have married Prince Edward, son of Edward I of England, but she died in the Orkneys on her way from Norway to Scotland.

The Maid of Orleans   Joan of Arc (*c*.1412–31), French national heroine. She led the French armies against the English in the Hundred Years War, relieving besieged Orleans (1429) and ensuring that Charles VII could be crowned in previously occupied Reims. Captured by the Burgundians in 1430, she was handed over to the English, convicted of heresy, and burnt at the stake. She was canonized in 1920. 'Maid' here translates French *Pucelle*, and 'Orleans' represents the support given to her by the French royal and ducal house. ➤ See also *La* PUCELLE.

The Manassa Mauler   William Harrison ('Jack') Dempsey (1895–1983), US boxer. He was world heavyweight champion 1919–26, during which time he drew extremely large audiences to boxing. His defence of the title in 1921 (against Georges Carpentier) was the first fight at which a million dollars was taken at the gate. Born in Manassa, Colorado, Dempsey adopted the name Jack after 'Nonpareil' Jack Dempsey, a famous middleweight champion from the end of the 19th century. Sports writers dubbed him the *Manassa Mauler* because of the ferocity and aggression he displayed in the ring.

Mandy   Peter (Benjamin) Mandelson (b.1953), British Labour politician. Mandelson is often regarded as one of the architects of Labour's victory in the 1997 general election. He twice held cabinet posts, but was forced to resign from each of them in controversial circumstances, first in 1998 and a second time in 2001. He is informally known as *Mandy*, an abbreviation of his surname and perhaps originally a subtle allusion to his sexuality before it was publicly revealed that he was gay. ➤ See also *The* PRINCE *of Darkness*.

The Man from Missouri   Harry S. Truman (1884–1972), US Democratic statesman, 33rd President of the US 1945–53. Raised on a farm near Independence, Missouri, Truman was sometimes known as the *Man from Missouri*. ➤ See also GIVE *'Em Hell Harry*.

The Man in Leather Breeches George Fox (1624–91), English preacher and
founder of the Society of Friends (Quakers). From 1647 he began travelling around
the country as an itinerant preacher, teaching that truth is the inner voice of God
speaking to the soul and rejecting priesthood and ritual. He habitually wore a pair of
leather breeches which apparently helped to identify him, prompting people to
announce: 'The man in leather breeches is come!'

The Man of a Thousand Faces Lon (Alonso) Chaney (1883–1930), US film actor
who specialized in playing deformed or monstrous characters in more than 150
silent films, including *The Hunchback of Notre Dame* (1923) and *The Phantom of
the Opera* (1925). He was a master of make-up and became known as the *Man of
a Thousand Faces*. This was also the title of the 1957 film biography of the actor,
starring James Cagney.

The Man of December Napoleon III (full name Charles Louis Napoleon
Bonaparte; known as Louis-Napoleon) (1808–73), emperor of France 1852–70. He
was nicknamed the *Man of December* in allusion to December 1848, when he
was elected President of the Second Republic. Other significant Decembers for
Louis-Napoleon were in 1851, when he staged his coup d'état, and in 1852, when
he became emperor. ➤ See also *The* MAN *of Sedan, The* PRISONER *of Ham*.

The Man of Destiny Napoleon I (known as Napoleon; full name Napoleon
Bonaparte) (1769–1821), emperor of France 1804–14 and 1815. The sobriquet the *Man
of Destiny*, characterizing Napoleon as an instrument of destiny, is first recorded in
English in Walter Scott's *The Life of Napoleon Buonaparte* (1827): 'The great plans
which the Man of Destiny had been called upon earth to perform.' G. B. Shaw used
the phrase for the title of a play (1897) about Napoleon. ➤ See also BONEY, *The*
CORSICAN *Ogre, The* LITTLE *Corporal, The* VIOLET *Corporal*.

The Man of Ross John Kyrle (1637–1724), English philanthropist. He lived simply
on his estates at Ross, Hertfordshire, and devoted his surplus income to charitable
works, such as supplying poor parishes with churches. Known as the *Man of Ross*, he
is celebrated by Pope in *Epistle III* of the 'Moral Essays' (1731–35): 'But all our praises
why should Lords engross?/Rise honest Muse! and sing the Man of Ross.' In the early
19th century, the nickname was passed on to Stephen Higginson (1770–1834), a
wealthy US merchant and steward of Harvard University, similarly known for his
philanthropy.

The Man of Sedan Napoleon III (full name Charles Louis Napoleon Bonaparte;
known as Louis-Napoleon) (1808–73), emperor of France 1852–70. Having
previously gloried in the title the MAN OF DECEMBER, Napoleon III was disparaged
as the *Man of Sedan* after his surrender to the Prussians at the Battle of Sedan in
1870, marking the end of the French Second Empire. ➤ See also *The* MAN *of
December, The* PRISONER *of Ham*.

The Man of Steel[1] Joseph Stalin (born Iosif Vissarionovich Dzhugashvili)
(1879–1953), Soviet statesman, General Secretary of the Communist Party of the
USSR 1922–53. The *Man of Steel* is the literal translation of his adopted name
STALIN. ➤ See also UNCLE *Joe*.

The Man of Steel[2] Superman, a US comic-book superhero having great strength, the ability to fly, and other extraordinary powers. He conceals his true nature behind the identity of mild-mannered reporter Clark Kent. Superman was created in 1938 in a comic strip by writer Jerry Siegel (1914–96) and artist Joe Shuster (1914–92).

The Man on the Wedding Cake Thomas E(dmund) Dewey (1902–71), US Republican politician, unsuccessful presidential candidate in 1944 and 1948. The disparaging nickname the *Man on the Wedding Cake* (or the *Bridegroom on the Wedding Cake*), originally coined by Grace Hodgson Flandrau in 1948, drew attention to Dewey's short stature, his black moustache, and his uncharismatic and wooden persona. It delighted Alice Roosevelt Longworth (1884–1980), daughter of Theodore Roosevelt, who widely repeated the jibe and it is often attributed to her.

The Man with the Orchid-lined Voice Enrico Caruso (1873–1921), Italian opera singer, usually considered the greatest tenor of the 20th century. His greatest successes were in operas by Verdi, Puccini, and Jules Massenet. Caruso was the first major tenor to be recorded on gramophone records; it was said that 'Caruso made the gramophone, and the gramophone made Caruso'. The baritone-like warmth and velvety smoothness of his voice earned him the sobriquet the *Man with the Orchid-lined Voice*.

The Man You Love To Hate Erich von Stroheim (assumed name of Erich Oswald Stroheim) (1885–1957), Austrian-born US actor and director. As an actor, von Stroheim usually played villainous roles, notably in the 1918 propaganda film *The Heart of Humanity*, in which he was first billed as *The Man You Love to Hate*. He went on to play a succession of sadistic Prussian or German officers in such films as *La Grande Illusion* (1937).

The March King John Philip Sousa (1854–1932), US composer and conductor. He became director of the US Marine Band in 1880, forming his own band in 1892. His compositions include more than 100 marches, for example 'Liberty Bell', 'The Stars and Stripes Forever', 'King Cotton', and 'Hands Across the Sea'. The sousaphone, invented in 1898, was named in his honour.

Marks and Sparks Marks and Spencer, a British chain of clothes and food stores. The company was originally founded as the Marks and Spencer Penny Bazaars by Michael Marks, Polish-born English retailer (1863–1907), and Thomas Spencer, English retailer (c.1852–1904). The informal and humorous name *Marks and Sparks* dates from the 1940s.

Marse Robert Robert E. Lee (1807–70), US general, Commander of the Confederate army of Northern Virginia for most of the American Civil War. His invasion of the North was repulsed at the Battle of Gettysburg (1863) and he surrendered at Appomattox in 1865. *Marse Robert* represented a southern pronunciation of 'Master Robert'.

Marshal Forwards Gebhard Leberecht von Blücher (1742–1819), Prussian field marshal. He played a crucial role in the defeat of Napoleon at Waterloo in 1815. He was known as *Marshal Forwards* ('*Marschall Vorwärts*') or *Old Forwards* ('*Alte*

Vorwärts') from the words with which he urged on his troops: '*Vorwärts! immer Vorwärts!*'

Martel   Charles Martel (*c*.688–741), Frankish ruler of the eastern part of the Frankish kingdom from 715 and the whole kingdom from 719. He earned his nickname *Martel* ('the hammer') from his crushing defeat of the numerically superior Saracens at the battle of Poitiers in 732. Charles Martel was the grandfather of Charlemagne.

Martin van Ruin   Martin van Buren (1782–1862), US statesman, 8th President of the US 1837–41, and one of the founders of the Democratic Party. His political enemies disparaged him as *Martin van Ruin*, blaming him for the depression that followed the economic panic of 1837. ➤ See also *The* LITTLE *Magician*, OLD *Kinderhook.*

The Martyr King   Two kings of England have earned the title the *Martyr King*: (i) Henry VI (1421–71), son of Henry V, king of England 1422–61 and 1470–1. Known for his piety, he was murdered at his prayers in the Tower of London on 21 May 1471, perhaps at the hands of Richard of Gloucester. There have been efforts made to have him canonized. (ii) Charles I (1600–49), son of James I, king of England, Scotland, and Ireland 1625–49. Charles was beheaded on 30 January 1649. The title the *Martyr King* has been used by those who characterize his execution as an act of religious persecution. ➤ See also *The* LAST *Man.*

Marvelous Marvin   Marvin Nathaniel Hagler (b.1952), US boxer. The shaven-skulled Hagler was world middleweight champion 1980–87. In 1982 the boxer had his name legally changed by deed poll to *Marvelous Marvin Hagler.*

The Ma State   The state of New South Wales, Australia. It was the earliest Australian colony to be founded, hence its nickname the *Ma State*. ➤ See also *The* MOTHER *of States.*

The Master[1]   W(illiam) Somerset Maugham (1874–1965), British novelist, short-story writer, and dramatist. His novels include *Of Human Bondage* (1915), *The Moon and Sixpence* (1919), and *Cakes and Ale* (1930). Maugham was an expert writer of short stories, some of which are considered among the best ever written in English. To his admirers he was the *Master.*

The Master[2]   D(avid) W(ark) Griffith (1875–1948), US film director. A pioneer in the development of cinema, he introduced the techniques of close-ups, cross-cutting, fade-out, moving-camera shots, and flashback in such films as his epic of the American Civil War *The Birth of a Nation* (1915) and *Intolerance* (1916).

The Master[3]   Jack Hobbs (full name John Berry Hobbs) (1882–1963), English cricketer. He is often regarded as the finest English batsman of the 20th century, hence his nickname the *Master*. In a career that lasted nearly 30 years, Hobbs scored 61 237 first-class runs and 197 centuries (1905–34). He first played for England in 1907 and went on to play in 61 Tests.

The Master[4]   Noël (Pierce) Coward (1899–1973), English dramatist, actor, and composer, famous for his sophistication and wit. As well as plays such as *Hay Fever* (1925) and *Private Lives* (1930), he wrote revues and musicals, including *Cavalcade* (1931). Among his many songs is 'Mad Dogs and Englishmen' (1932). Coward's films (as writer and producer) include *In Which We Serve* (1942) and *Brief Encounter*

(1945). He is said to have disliked the sobriquet the *Master*, which had also been applied to the writer Somerset Maugham (1874–1965) and the US film director D. W. Griffith (1875–1948). His own comment on the label was 'Oh, you know, jack of all trades, master of none…'

The Master of Suspense   Alfred Hitchcock, English film director. ➤ See HITCH.

The Match King   Ivar Kreuger (1880–1932), Swedish industrialist and financier. Having founded the United Swedish Match Company in 1913, he set out to control the worldwide match industry in the 1920s through a series of acquisitions. Known as the *Match King*, Kreuger eventually controlled three quarters of the world's production of matches. His empire collapsed with the Great Depression and, following the disclosure that it had been built on forgery and fraudulent deals, he committed suicide in 1932.

Maximum John   John Joseph Sirica (1904–92), US federal judge who became famous during his participation in the Watergate prosecutions of the 1970s. His nickname *Maximum John* was due to his uncompromising reputation for heavy sentencing.

The Mekon   William (Jefferson) Hague (b.1961), British Conservative politician, leader of the Conservative Party 1997–2001. During his tenure as the leader of the Opposition, Hague attracted the uncomplimentary nickname the *Mekon*, referring to his bald head. The Mekon is Dan Dare's arch-enemy in the comic strip by Frank Hampson which appeared in the *Eagle* comic between 1950 and 1967. He originates from the planet Venus, is green-skinned, and has a small body and an enormous bald head.

The Mellifluous Doctor   St Bernard of Clairvaux (1090–1153), French theologian and monastic reformer. He was the first abbot of Clairvaux and his monastery became one of the chief centres of the Cistercian order. In the *Golden Legend* (a medieval collection of saints' lives), he was given the name *Doctor Mellifluus* (or the *Mellifluous Doctor*) in recognition of his eloquence. His emblem is the beehive, similarly representing the sweetness of his writings.

The Merciless Doctor   John Haighton (1755–1826), English physician and physiologist. He became known as the *Merciless Doctor* on account of his many and ruthless physiological experiments. On one occasion when a colleague disputed some of his results, Haighton is said to have killed a favourite spaniel to prove the colleague wrong.

The Merry Millers   Rotherham football club. Their ground is called Millmoor, from whose name they derive their nickname the *Merry Millers*.

The Merry Monarch   Charles II (1630–85), son of Charles I, king of England, Scotland, and Ireland 1660–85. This enduring nickname derives originally from a poem by Rochester (1647–80): 'Restless he rolls about from Whore to Whore,/A merry Monarch, scandalous and poor' ('A Satire on King Charles'). Charles was renowned for his good humour, wit, and mistresses; his reign was joyous and relaxed in contrast to the austerity of the Puritan Commonwealth which preceded it. ➤ See also *The* BLACK *Boy*, OLD *Rowley, The* SON *of the Last Man*.

The Mersey Funnel The Roman Catholic Cathedral (Christ the King), Liverpool. Its local nickname the *Mersey Funnel* both alludes to the distinctive shape of the cathedral's central lantern tower and also puns on the Mersey Tunnel that provides a link under the River Mersey between Liverpool and Birkenhead. ➤ See also PADDY'S *Wigwam*.

The Met Two institutions are familiarly known as the *Met*; in each case this is an abbreviation of the word *Metropolitan*. In Britain, the term is used for the Metropolitan Police in London. In the US, it is used for the Metropolitan Opera House (and Company) in New York.

Mighty Mouse (Joseph) Kevin Keegan (b.1951), English football player and manager, who won the European Footballer of the Year award twice. He was a star striker for Liverpool in the 1970s, for whom he made 230 league appearances, and played for England 63 times. His managerial career at club level has included periods at Newcastle United, Fulham, and Manchester City, and he has also managed the England team (1999–2000). Relatively small in stature, Keegan became known as *Mighty Mouse* while playing in Germany for SV Hamburg. His later managerial exploits at Newcastle led him to be hailed as KING KEV by the fans.

The Mile High City The US city of Denver, Colorado. It is situated at an altitude of 1 608m (5 280 ft) near the foothills of the Rocky Mountains, hence its nickname the *Mile High City*.

The Milk Snatcher Margaret (Hilda) Thatcher (b.1925), British Conservative stateswoman, Prime Minister 1979–90. As Minister of Education in Edward Heath's government (1970–74), she abolished free school milk for children over the age of eight, earning herself the rhyming nickname *Thatcher the Milk Snatcher*. ➤ See also ATTILA *the Hen*, The BLESSED *Margaret*, The GROCER'S *Daughter*, The IRON *Lady*, The LEADERENE, MAGGIE, TINA.

The Mill Boy of the Slashes Henry Clay (1777–1852), US statesman and orator. His colourful nickname the *Mill Boy of the Slashes* is a reference to the time he spent as a boy working in a mill in 'The Slashes', an area of low, swampy ground in Harrison, Virginia. ➤ See also *The* GREAT *Compromiser*.

Ming Robert Gordon Menzies (1894–1978), Australian Liberal statesman, Prime Minister 1939–41 and 1949–66. He became Australia's longest-serving prime minister, presiding over a period of economic prosperity for his country. Known for his autocratic style of leadership, he was nicknamed *Ming* in reference to Ming the Merciless, the evil emperor who appeared in the Flash Gordon comic strip. There is also an allusion to the Scottish pronunciation of his surname, 'Ming-ies'. Menzies' long second term became known as the 'Ming Dynasty', after the Chinese dynasty founded in 1368 by Zhu Yuanzhang.

Miss Frigidaire Chris (Christine Marie) Evert (b.1954), US tennis player. She won both the US and French Open championships six times and three Wimbledon titles (1974, 1976, 1981). Evert was dubbed *Miss Frigidaire* by the British press because of her cool, unruffled manner on court. ➤ See also LITTLE *Miss Poker Face*.

Mogadon Man (Richard Edward) Geoffrey Howe (b.1926), British Conservative politician. Howe served as Chancellor of the Exchequer 1979–83, Foreign Secretary

1983–89, and deputy Prime Minister 1984–90. Parliamentary correspondents called him *Mogadon Man* because of the supposedly soporific effect of his speeches. Mogadon is the proprietary name for a tranquilizing drug used to treat insomnia.

Moll Cutpurse Mary Frith (1584–1659), English thief, on whose life Middleton and Dekker's play *The Roaring Girl* (1611) was based. Often dressing as a man, she had accumulated enough wealth from picking pockets and spending time as a 'highwayman' that, once caught, she was able to buy herself out of Newgate prison. A cutpurse is an archaic term for a pickpocket, from the practice of cutting purses suspended from a waistband.

The Monkey State The US state of Tennessee. The mocking nickname recalls the famous Monkey Trial of 1925, in which a schoolteacher called Thomas Scopes was found guilty of teaching the Darwinian theory of evolution, at that time prohibited in any Tennessee schools supported by public funds. ➤ See also *The* HOG *and Hominy State*, *The* VOLUNTEER *State*.

Monk Lewis M(atthew) G(regory) Lewis (1775–1818), novelist, playwright, and poet. His gothic novel *The Monk* (1796), concerning the descent into sexual depravity of a young monk called Ambrosio, enjoyed sensational success and led to its author being known as *Monk Lewis*.

Monsieur Veto Louis XVI (1754–93), grandson and successor of Louis XV, king of France 1774–93. In late 18th century France, *Monsieur Veto* was a nickname given to Louis XVI during the French Revolution. His wife Marie Antoinette was known as MADAME VETO. This alludes to the king's right of veto, which he exercised more than once in 1791–92, with respect to decrees of the Legislative Assembly. ➤ See also *The* BAKER.

Monty Bernard Law Montgomery (1887–1976), British field marshal. In 1942 he commanded the 8th Army in the Western Desert, where his victory at El Alamein proved the first significant Allied success in the Second World War. He was later given command of the Allied ground forces in the invasion of Normandy in 1944 and received the German surrender in 1945. He was affectionally known as *Monty*. Among various derivations that have been proposed for the expression 'the full monty' (meaning the full amount possible, 'the works') is Montgomery's apparent insistence on eating a full English breakfast.

The Monumental City The city of Baltimore, Maryland. It is nicknamed the *Monumental City* (or the *Monument City*) on account of the Washington Monument, the first erected to George Washington, and its other monuments.

The Moonrakers The 62nd Foot (later the 1st Battalion Wiltshire Regiment), a regiment of the British army. The regiment is informally known as the *Moonrakers* from the term *moonraker* denoting a native of the English county of Wiltshire. This alludes to the Wiltshire story of smugglers caught raking a pond for kegs of smuggled brandy, who fooled the revenue officials by feigning stupidity, claiming that they were raking out the moon's reflection in the water.

Mormon City Salt Lake City, capital of Utah, situated near the south-eastern shores of the Great Salt Lake. Founded by Brigham Young, the city is the world headquarters of the Church of Latter-Day Saints, also known as Mormons. ➤ See also *The* CITY *of Saints*.

The Mosquito State   The US state of New Jersey. In the 1880s and 90s New Jersey was known as the *Mosquito State* because of the swarms of insects from the New Jersey marshes that plagued New York City at that time. ➤ See also *The* FOREIGNER *State*, *The* GARDEN *State*.

Moss Bros   Moss Brothers, a British firm of tailors and outfitters, associated with the hire of formal clothes. The informal name *Moss Bros* is pronounced 'Moss Bross'.

The Mother of Presidents   The US state of Virginia. The state was the birthplace of eight US presidents, including four of the first five: Washington, Jefferson, Madison, and Monroe. The title the *Mother of Presidents* has also been claimed by the state of Ohio, birthplace of seven presidents including Grant, Garfield, and Taft. ➤ See also *The* MOTHER *of States*, *The* OLD *Dominion*.

The Mother of States   The US state of Virginia. There are two reasons why Virginia is appropriately nicknamed the *Mother of States*. Firstly, the first permanent English settlement in North America was founded at Jamestown, Virginia in 1607. More significantly, all or part of eight other states (namely, Illinois, Indiana, Kentucky, Michigan, Minnesota, Ohio, West Virginia, and Wisconsin) were formed from western territory originally claimed by Virginia. ➤ See also *The* MA *State*, *The* MOTHER *of Presidents*, *The* OLD *Dominion*.

The Mother of the Blues   Ma Rainey (Gertrude Malissa Nix Rainey née Pridgett) (1886–1939), US blues singer who is said to have taught Bessie Smith, though she only began making records herself a year after Smith did. Her recording career (mostly 1923–29) was short but prolific. Apparently she disliked the title Ma Rainey (which she acquired after marrying William 'Pa' Rainey in 1904, with whom she formed a song and dance team), preferring to be addressed as Madame Rainey.

Motor City   The city of Detroit, Michigan. ➤ See MOTOWN.

Motown   The city of Detroit, Michigan, the centre of the US automobile industry. *Motown* is an abbreviation of 'Motor Town'. The record company Tamla Motown was founded by Barry Gordy in Detroit in 1959. Detroit is also known as *Motor City*. ➤ See also *The* AUTO *State*.

The Mountain State   The US state of West Virginia. Almost 80% of the state lies in the rugged and mountainous Allegheny Plateau, hence its nickname the *Mountain State*. ➤ See also *The* PANHANDLE *State*.

The Mouth   Muhammad Ali (b. 1942), US boxer. ➤ See *The* LOUISVILLE *Lip*.

Mr Chips   Arthur Chipping, the schoolmaster hero of James Hilton's novel *Good-bye, Mr Chips* (1934). He teaches classics at a fictional English public school called Brookfield, devoting himself to teaching generations of boys at the school until his retirement. His dedication earns him the respect and affection of pupils and colleagues. The character was based partly on Hilton's headmaster father and partly on a housemaster at a Cambridge school that Hilton had attended.

Mr Five-Per-Cent Calouste Sarkis Gulbenkian (1869–1955), Turkish-born British oil magnate and philanthropist, of Armenian descent. He founded the Gulbenkian Foundation, to which he left his large fortune and art collection. Gulbenkian was known as *Mr Five-Per-Cent* because he retained a 5% interest in the Iraq Petroleum Co., a company he founded.

Mr October Reggie (Reginald Martinez) Jackson (b.1946), US baseball player. He was dubbed *Mr October* because of his heroic performances in the World Series, which takes place in October after the end of the season. In the 1977 World Series he hit three home runs in one game.

Mr Saturday Night Jackie (Herbert John) Gleason (1916–87), US comedian. In the 1950s he was an ever-present fixture on Saturday night television, first hosting the variety show *Cavalcade of Stars* and then starring in the popular television series *The Honeymooners*. The portly comedian thus came to be dubbed *Mr Saturday Night*.

Mrs Brown Victoria (1819–1901), queen of Great Britain and Ireland 1837–1901 and empress of India 1876–1901. After the death of Prince Albert, Victoria became devoted to her Scottish gillie John Brown whom she had made her personal attendant. Rumours spread that she had secretly married him, prompting jokes in the country about 'Mrs Brown'. ➤ See also *The* FAMINE *Queen, The* GRANDMOTHER *of Europe, The* WIDOW *at Windsor*.

Mrs Bull Anne (1665–1714), queen of England and Scotland (known as Great Britain from 1707) and Ireland 1702–14. In John Arbuthnot's satire *The History of John Bull* (1712), the character of John Bull represents England and that of his wife partly represents the queen. Arbuthnot was the queen's personal physician. ➤ See also BRANDY *Nan,* MRS *Morley*.

Mrs Morley Anne (1665–1714), queen of England and Scotland (known as Great Britain from 1707) and Ireland 1702–14. *Mrs Morley* was the name assumed by Queen Anne in her correspondence with her favourite Sarah Churchill, Duchess of Marlborough, likewise called *Mrs Freeman*. ➤ See also BRANDY *Nan,* MRS *Bull,* QUEEN *Sarah*.

Mr Teasie Weasie Raymond (born Raymond Pierre Carlo Bessone) (1911–92), London hairdresser. In the early 1950s he regularly demonstrated hairdressing on a television show called *Quite Contrary*. His nickname *Mr Teasie Weasie* was a reference to his catchphrase 'A teasie-weasie here, and a teasie-weasie there'.

Mr Television Milton Berle (Mendel Berlinger) (1908–2002), US television comedian. Berle was an enormous star of US television in the 1950s. Having worked in vaudeville, he made his debut in television in 1948, as the host of the variety show *Texaco Star Theater* (later *The Milton Berle Show*). The show, which helped to establish television as a popular medium, was characterized by irreverent humour, slapstick, dreadful puns, and general buffoonery. Berle became affectionately known to his audiences as *Mr Television* and UNCLE MILTIE; he also acquired the less complimentary, but ingenious, sobriquet the THIEF OF BADGAGS, punning on the title of the film *The Thief of Baghdad* (1940).

Muscles Ken(neth Robert) Rosewall (b.1934), Australian tennis player. Rosewall won 18 Grand Slam titles, including the Australian four times (1953, 1955, 1971–72), the French twice (1953, 1968), and the US twice (1956, 1970). He failed to win the Wimbledon singles title, although he played in three finals. As a teenager he was given the ironic nickname *Muscles* because he looked so skinny.

The Muscles from Brussels   Jean-Claude Van Damme (Jean-Claude Van Varenberg) (b.1961), Belgian film actor and former kickboxing champion. His action films include *Double Impact* (1991), *Universal Soldier* (1992), and *Hard Target* (1993).

The Nabob of Sob   Johnnie Ray. ➤ See *The* PRINCE *of Wails*.

Namby-Pamby   Ambrose Philips (*c.*1675–1749), English poet whose pastorals were ridiculed as insipidly sentimental by Alexander Pope and the dramatist Henry Carey. It was Philips's verses addressed to the young children of wealthy people, mocked by these writers as ludicrously infantile, that earned him his nickname, coined by Carey in his parody *Namby-Pamby, or a panegyric upon the new versification* (1726) and readily adopted by Pope. *Namby* represents a child's pronunciation of 'Ambrose', the rhyming *Pamby* standing for the initial of his surname. The term has come to mean 'lacking energy or courage; feeble'.

The Napoleon of Crime   Two literary characters have been dubbed the *Napoleon of Crime*. In Arthur Conan Doyle's stories of Sherlock Holmes, Professor James Moriarty is the fiendish criminal who is the great detective's arch-enemy. He is described thus by Holmes in *The Memoirs of Sherlock Holmes* (1894): 'He is the Napoleon of crime, Watson. He is the organizer of half that is evil and of nearly all that is undetected in this great city...He sits motionless, like a spider in the centre of its web, but that web has a thousand radiations, and he knows well every quiver of each of them.' In T. S. Eliot's collection of poems *Old Possum's Book of Practical Cats* (1939), Macavity the Mystery Cat is similarly a criminal mastermind. All other feline wrong-doers 'Are nothing more than agents for the Cat who all the time/Just controls their operations: the Napoleon of Crime!' To describe someone as a Napoleon of something is usually to attribute to them qualities of leadership and strategic genius, alluding to Napoleon Bonaparte.

Nasty   Ilie Nastase (b.1946), Romanian tennis player, winner of the US Open in 1972 and the French Open in 1973. A flamboyant and controversial player, he was known as *Nasty*, punning on his surname, because of his volatile temper and gamesmanship on court.

The Navel of the Nation   The US state of Kansas. Kansas lies in the geographical centre of the United States (or, strictly speaking, the 48 contiguous states), hence its nickname the *Navel of the Nation*. ➤ See also *The* SQUATTER *State, The* SUNFLOWER *State*.

Neddy   The National Economic Development Council, a British advisory body formed in 1962 as a forum for economic consultation between government, management, and trade unions, in order to plan ways of increasing growth and efficiency in British industry. Known informally as *Neddy* from its initials, the NEDC also set up other committees to study conditions in individual industries. These were accordingly dubbed *Little Neddies*.

Nell of Old Drury   Nell (Eleanor) Gwyn (1650–87), English actress and mistress to
Charles II. ➤ See SWEET *Nell*.

Neutral Ground   Westchester County, New York. During the American War of
Independence, it was known as *Neutral Ground* because of the divided sympathies of
its inhabitants, neither army occupying it for any length of time.

The News of the Screws   *The News of the World*, a popular British Sunday
newspaper. Its reputation for publishing lurid stories about the sex lives of celebrities
has won it the nickname the *News of the Screws*.

New Sweden   The US state of Delaware. The state's first permanent settlement Fort
Christina (now Wilmington) was established by Swedish immigrants in 1638, and for
many years the peninsula was known as Ny Sverige (*New Sweden*). ➤ See also *The*
BLUE *Hen State, The* DIAMOND *State, The* FIRST *State*.

Nine Days' Queen   Lady Jane Grey (1537–54), queen of England 1553. Following
the death of Edward VI and named by him as his successor, Jane, aged 15, was
proclaimed queen of England on 10 July 1553. She was deposed nine days later in
favour of Edward's sister Mary Tudor and executed the following year for high
treason.

The North Star State   The US state of Minnesota. At one time Minnesota was
the northernmost state in the Union, and it still retains the motto 'L'*Étoile du Nord*'
('The North Star') on the state seal and flag. Its official nickname is accordingly
the *North Star State*. ➤ See also *The* GOPHER *State*.

Nosey   Oliver Cromwell (1599–1658), English general and statesman. ➤ See *The*
ALMIGHTY *Nose*.

Nosey Parker   Matthew Parker (1504–75), English prelate. As Archbishop of
Canterbury during the early part of Elizabeth I's reign (1559–75), he guided the
Church of England on a moderate course between Roman Catholicism and
extreme Protestantism. He is associated with the nickname *Nosey Parker*, said to
refer to his reputation for being overinquisitive about ecclesiastical matters. The
term has come to be applied to any prying person or a busybody.

The Nun of Amherst   Emily (Elizabeth) Dickinson (1830–86), US poet. She was
born in Amherst, Massachusetts and spent almost all her life there. From the age of
24 she gradually withdrew from society and by the age of 30 she was living as a
virtual recluse in her father's house. She wrote nearly 2 000 poems, mystical in tone,
elliptical in language, and rich in imagery, but only a handful were published in her
lifetime. Her life of seclusion and preference for dressing entirely in white caused her
to be known as the *Nun of Amherst*.

The Nutmeg State   The US state of Connecticut. The nickname the *Nutmeg State*
stems from the popular tradition that the early settlers of Connecticut were so crafty
that they could sell nutmeg-shaped pieces of wood to the credulous. Hence, in the
US, a 'wooden nutmeg' is a false or fraudulent thing. ➤ See also *The* CONSTITUTION
State.

Oo

The Ocean State The US state of Rhode Island. Bordered by the Atlantic Ocean, Rhode Island promotes itself to tourists as the *Ocean State*. ➤ See also LITTLE *Rhody*.

Ol' Blue Eyes Frank Sinatra (full name Francis Albert Sinatra) (1915–98), US singer and film actor. He began his long career as a singer in 1938 performing with big bands on the radio, becoming a solo star in the 1940s with a large teenage following. Among his many hits are 'Night and Day' and 'My Way' and his films include *From Here to Eternity* (1953), for which he won an Oscar. Sinatra announced his retirement in 1971 but marked his comeback two years later with the album *Ol' Blue Eyes is Back*. The following year he was back performing on stage. The sobriquet is said to have been coined by publicity man Lee Solters. ➤ See also BONES, *The* CHAIRMAN *of the Board, The* VOICE.

Old Abe Abraham Lincoln (1809–65), US Republican statesman, 16th President of the US 1861–65. His election as president on an anti-slavery platform helped precipitate the American Civil War. Lincoln began to be known as *Old Abe* while still a lawyer, a reference partly to his many years at the bar and partly to his weather-beaten face. ➤ See also *The* GREAT *Emancipator*, HONEST *Abe, The* RAIL *Splitter*.

Old Big 'Ead Brian Clough (1935–2004), English football player and manager. He managed Derby County (1967–73), winning the League championship in 1972. Clough went on to manage Nottingham Forest (1975–93), with whom he won the European Cup in 1979 and 1980. Famously outspoken and opinionated, he was known as *Old Big 'Ead* or *Cloughie*. The former nickname was coined by his wife when he was awarded the OBE for services to football: she said that was what the letters stood for.

The Old Colony The US state of Massachusetts. The nickname the *Old Colony* refers to the original Plymouth Colony founded by the Pilgrim Fathers in Massachusetts in 1620. Another settlement, the Massachusetts Bay Colony, was founded in Salem in 1628. ➤ See also *The* BAY *State*.

Old Conky Arthur Wellesley, 1st Duke of Wellington (1769–1852), British soldier and Tory statesman, Prime Minister 1828–30 and 1834. Wellington's large aquiline nose earned him such nicknames as CONKY, *Old Conky, Nosey*, OLD NOSEY, and *Beaky*. Lord Byron describes him as 'Proud Wellington, with eagle beak so called,/That nose, the hook where he suspends the world' (*The Age of Bronze*, 1823). Contemporary caricatures also homed in on this feature of Wellington's profile. ➤ See also *The* ACHILLES *of England, The* IRON *Duke*.

The Old Contemptibles Veterans of the British Expeditionary Force sent to France in the First World War (1914). The German Kaiser is alleged to have told his soldiers to 'walk over General French's contemptible little army'. The intended slur was subsequently proudly adopted by the *Old Contemptibles*.

Old Crome John Crome (1768–1821), British painter, founder (with John Sell Cotman) of the Norwich School. Crome mainly painted East Anglian landscapes. He is often called *Old Crome* to distinguish him from his son John Bernay Crome (1794–1842), also a painter amd member of the Norwich School.

The Old Dart England. In Australia and New Zealand, the *Old Dart* is an informal name for England, with *Dart* representing a dialect pronunciation of *dirt*. ➤ See also BLIGHTY, PERFIDIOUS *Albion*.

The Old Dominion The US state of Virginia. In 1660 Virginia was the first British possession to accept the restored monarch Charles II as its king. He subsequently accorded the colony the status of a dominion, hence its long-standing nickname the *Old Dominion*. ➤ See also *The* MOTHER *of Presidents, The* MOTHER *of States*.

The Old Five and Three Pennies The 53rd Foot (King's Shropshire Light Infantry), a regiment of the British army. The regiment's nickname the *Old Five and Three Pennies* derives not only from the number 53 but also from the daily pay of an ensign in the 19th century. The 53rd were also known as the *Brickdusts* because of the brick-red facings on their uniform.

The Old Fogs ➤ See *The* FAUGH-A-BALAGHS.

Old Fuss and Feathers Winfield Scott (1786–1866), US general, widely regarded as the finest in the period between George Washington and Robert E. Lee. He fought in the War of 1812 and the Mexican War (1846–48). Scott was nicknamed *Old Fuss and Feathers* because he was a stickler for strict military decorum and formality. In this he contrasted sharply with the far more informal Zachary Taylor, OLD ROUGH AND READY.

Old Groaner Bing Crosby (born Harry Lillis Crosby) (1904–77), US singer and film actor. His affectionate nickname is a reference to his soft, husky baritone and the relaxed style of singing (known as crooning) he popularized. His songs include 'Pennies from Heaven' and 'White Christmas', the latter of which has sold over 30 million copies. Among his films are the 'Road' series of comedy films (1940–62), in which he co-starred with Bob Hope and Dorothy Lamour. The name Bing came from his big ears; as a child he used to read a comic book called *The Bingville Bugle* which featured a character called Bingo, a boy with large, floppy ears. ➤ See also DER *Bingle*.

Old Grog Edward Vernon (1684–1757), British admiral. Admiral Vernon was known as *Old Grog* because he wore a grogram cloak. Grogram is a coarse fabric of silk, or of mohair and wool, often stiffened with gum. In 1740 Vernon ordered watered-down rum to be served out to sailors instead of neat rum. Later the word *grog* came to be applied to the diluted rum itself.

Old Hickory Andrew Jackson (1767–1845), US general and 7th President of the US 1829–37. His nickname originates from an episode during the War of 1812 when he led his men through 500 miles of wilderness, and was said by them to be as 'tough as hickory'. He came to be nicknamed both *Tough* and *Hickory*, and later *Old Hickory*.

Jackson became a national hero after defending New Orleans against British troops in 1815. ➤ See also KING *Andrew the First*, YOUNG *Hickory*.

Old Hopalong   Ronald (Wilson) Reagan (1911–2004), US Republican statesman, 40th President of the US 1981–89. Alluding to his past career playing cowboys in westerns, the nickname *Old Hopalong*, coined by the satirical magazine *Private Eye*, was used in Britain during Reagan's presidency. Hopalong Cassidy was a fictional cowboy who had a limp and was dressed in black. He was created by the writer Clarence E. Mulford and played in films and a television series by the US actor William Boyd. ➤ See also DUTCH, *The* GIPPER, *The* GREAT *Communicator*, *The* TEFLON *President*.

The Old Immortals   ➤ See *The* IMMORTALS.

Old Kinderhook   Martin van Buren (1782–1862), US statesman, 8th President of the US 1837–41, and one of the founders of the Democratic Party. Van Buren was born in Kinderhook, New York, and became widely known as *Old Kinderhook*. A possible derivation of the expression OK is that it comes from the initials of this nickname, used as a Democratic slogan in the presidential election campaign of 1840 when van Buren was seeking re-election. ➤ See also *The* LITTLE *Magician*, MARTIN *van Ruin*.

The Old Lady of Threadneedle Street   The Bank of England, which stands in this street. The term dates from the late 18th century, as a caption to James Gillray's cartoon of 22 May 1797, 'Political Ravishment, or The Old Lady of Threadneedle-Street in danger!' showing the 'Old Lady' dressed in one-pound notes, seated on a strong-box containing her gold, with Pitt placing an arm round her waist and a hand in her pocket. He has dropped a scroll of forced 'loans'. The Old Lady is screaming, 'Murder! Murder! Rape! Murder!...Ruin, Ruin, Ruin!' In the pediment of the facade's portico there now stands a statue of the Old Lady of Threadneedle Street holding a model of the building on her knee.

The Old Line State   The US state of Maryland. In colonial times, Maryland was the dividing line between the Crown land grants of Lord Baltimore and those of William Penn, hence its nickname the *Old Line State*. ➤ See also *The* COCKADE *State*, *The* FREE *State*, *The* QUEEN *State*.

Old Man Eloquent   John Quincy Adams (1767–1848), US Republican statesman, 6th President of the US 1825–29. After serving his term as president, Adams returned to the House of Representatives (1831–48), where his oratory, particularly when attacking slavery, earned him the nickname *Old Man Eloquent*.

Old Noll   Oliver Cromwell (1599–1658), English general and statesman, Lord Protector of the Commonwealth 1653–58. Cromwell was known informally as *Old Noll*, Noll being a familiar form of Oliver. A 17th-century pamphlet was titled 'Oliver Cromwell's Ghost, or Old Noll newly revived'. ➤ See also *The* ALMIGHTY *Nose*, COPPER *Nose*, CRUM-HELL, IRONSIDES, KING *Oliver*.

The Old North State   The US state of North Carolina. It is sometimes called the *Old North State*, because of its geographical position and history. Sir Walter Raleigh tried unsuccessfully to establish a colony on Roanoke Island in the 1580s. The first permanent settlement was in 1663. ➤ See also *The* TAR *Heel State*.

Old Nosey Arthur Wellesley, 1st Duke of Wellington (1769–1852), British soldier and Tory statesman, Prime Minister 1828–30 and 1834. ➤ See OLD *Conky.*

The Old Pretender James Francis Edward Stuart (1688–1766), son of James II (James VII of Scotland), pretender to the British throne. After the death of his father in 1701 he was recognized as James III of England by the Jacobites. He had been referred to initially in anti-Jacobite circles as the *pretended Prince of Wales,* later becoming known as the *Pretender,* a usage which Bishop Burnet attributes to James's half-sister Queen Anne: 'She also fixed a new Designation on the Pretended Prince of Wales, and called him the Pretender.' (Gilbert Burnet *History of Our Own Time* (*a.*1715). The term denotes one who pretends or lays claim to a throne or title. The name *Old Pretender* developed later to distinguish James from his son, Charles Edward Stuart, the YOUNG PRETENDER. In 1715 James landed in Scotland to head a Jacobite uprising but was forced to withdraw through lack of support. He left the leadership of the 1745–46 uprising to his son. ➤ See also *The* KING *over the Water, The* WARMING *Pan Baby.*

Old Q William Douglas, 3rd Earl of March and 4th Duke of Queensberry (1724–1810), a notorious 18th-century rake. A friend of the Prince of Wales, he was famed for his lechery and dissolute life. Lord Queensberry was satirized by Burns, and is the 'degenerate Douglas' of Wordsworth's sonnet. He was also known as the *Rake of Piccadilly.*

Old Rough and Ready Zachary Taylor (1784–1850), US Whig statesman, 12th President of the US 1849–50. He became a national hero after his victories in the war with Mexico (1846–48). Earlier, during the war against the Seminole Indians in 1837, he had won from his troops his nickname *Old Rough and Ready.* This derived from his informal dress and his straightforward, pragmatic approach to military matters. The nickname is preserved in a presidential campaign song of 1848: 'I think I hear his cheerful voice,/"On column! Steady! Steady!"/So handy and so prompt was he,/We called him Rough and Ready.'

Old Rowley Charles II (1630–85), son of Charles I, king of England, Scotland, and Ireland 1660–85. Charles II had many mistresses and was the father of at least 13 illegitimate children. *Old Rowley* was the name of a stallion in the royal stud, noted for its many offspring. Rowley Mile at Newmarket racecourse was named after Charles II. ➤ See also *The* BLACK *Boy, The* MERRY *Monarch, The* SON *of the Last Man.*

Old Sink or Swim John Adams (1735–1826), American Federalist statesman, 2nd President of the US 1797–1801. He was a key figure in the drafting of the Declaration of Independence (1776). When it was put to him that he should abandon the cause of independence, Adams replied, 'Sink or swim, live or die, survive or perish, I am with my country from this day on.' ➤ See also *The* COLOSSUS *of Independence.*

Old Slowhand Eric Clapton (b.1945), English blues and rock guitarist, singer, and composer. A virtuoso of the electric guitar with a seemingly effortless technique, he played in the Yardbirds (1963–65) and then formed his own group, Cream (1966–68). London graffiti in the mid-60s announced 'Clapton is God'. He later developed a more restrained style, reflected in the nickname he acquired. *Slowhand* is the title of one of his albums (1977).

Old Squiffy Herbert Henry Asquith (1852–1928), British Liberal statesman, Prime Minister 1908–16. ➤ See SQUIFFY.

Old Stoneface Buster Keaton (born Joseph Francis Keaton) (1895–1966), US film actor and director. Noted for his deadpan expression, acrobatic skills, and elaborate stunts, he was one of the biggest stars of silent comedy. Films he directed and starred in include *Sherlock Junior* (1924), *The Navigator* (1924), and *The General* (1926). He was known as *Old Stoneface* or the *Great Stoneface*.

The Old Stubborns The Sherwood Foresters, a regiment of the British army. They earned their nickname the *Old Stubborns* from their courageous resistance in defending an outpost at Talavera against the French in 1809, during the Peninsular Wars.

Old Timber Henry (Joseph) Wood (1869–1944), English conductor. In 1895 he founded the London Promenade Concerts (known as 'the Proms') and conducted these every year until his death. During this time Wood introduced British audiences to the music of such foreign composers as Schoenberg, Janáček, and Scriabin. His nickname *Old Timber* is an affectionate pun on his surname.

Ol' Man River The river Mississippi in North America. *Ol' Man River* is the title of a song written by Jerome Kern and Oscar Hammerstein in 1927 for the musical *Showboat*: 'Dere's an ol' man called de Mississippi;/Dat's de ol' man dat I'd like to be!/...But Ol' Man River,/He jes' keeps rollin' along.' ➤ See also *The* FATHER *of Waters*.

The One and Only Phyllis Dixey (1914–64), US striptease artist, the London West End's first stripper. During the Second World War, she brought her revue to the Whitehall Theatre. A 1978 TV movie about her was titled *The One and Only Phyllis Dixey*.

One-Leg Paget Henry William Paget, 1st Marquess of Anglesey (1768–1854), British cavalry officer. In the closing moments of the Battle of Waterloo, Paget was sitting on his horse next to the Duke of Wellington, when he was shot in the knee. According to the story, the following famous but probably apocryphal exchange took place: 'By God, sir, I have lost my leg!' 'By God, sir, so you have'. Paget's leg was not in fact blown off, but the cannon-shot shattered his knee and it had to be amputated. His severed leg was buried in the garden of the house in Waterloo village where the amputation had been performed. Paget came to be known as *One-Leg Paget*.

Oom Paul Stephanus Johannes Paulus Kruger (1825–1904), South African soldier and statesman, President of Transvaal 1883–99. He led the Afrikaners to victory in the First Boer War in 1881. His refusal to allow equal rights to non-Boer immigrants was one of the causes of the Second Boer War. Forced to flee the country, he died in exile in Switzerland. *Oom* in Afrikaans, meaning 'Uncle', was a traditional form of respectful address to an older or elderly man.

The Oomph Girl Ann Sheridan (born Clara Lou Sheridan) (1915–67), US film actress. Early in her career her studio promoted her, in a conscious echo of Clara Bow's IT GIRL, as the *Oomph Girl*, with the word *oomph* similarly indicating sex appeal. Her films include *Angels with Dirty Faces* (1938) and *King's Row* (1942).

Orange Juice O(renthal) J(ames) Simpson (b.1947), former US American football player. ➤ See *The* JUICE.

Orange Peel Robert Peel (1788–1850), British Conservative statesman, Prime Minister 1834–35 and 1841–46. He was known punningly as *Orange Peel* during his time as Chief Secretary for Ireland (1812–18) because he favoured the Protestants (or Orangemen) and opposed Roman Catholic emancipation. Later, as Home Secretary, he changed this position and helped to pass the Catholic Emancipation Act of 1829. ➤ See also *The* RUNAWAY *Spartan*.

Orator Henley John Henley (1692–1756), an eccentric English preacher. From 1726 he rented rooms in London's Newport market, where each Sunday he preached a morning sermon, and each Wednesday delivered a lecture on 'some other science'. His preaching was accompanied by elaborate ritual, and his pulpit was decorated with gold and velvet. He regarded himself as one who had restored eloquence to the Church. Pope addressed him in the *Dunciad* as 'Oh great restorer of the good old Stage, preacher at once, and Zany of thy age!' He was ridiculed as *Orator Henley*.

Orator Hunt Henry Hunt (1773–1835), radical politician and agitator. In 1819 he presided over the open-air meeting in St Peter's Fields, Manchester that led to the Peterloo Massacre. He is described in the *Dictionary of National Biography* as 'a violent and stentorian, but impressive, speaker'.

Oriana Elizabeth I (1533–1603), daughter of Henry VIII, queen of England and Ireland 1558–1603. During her reign poets and musicians praised the queen as *Fair Oriana*. The name derives from a medieval Spanish or Portuguese romance *Amadis of Gaul*, in which it is the name of the princess of Britain with whom the hero Amadis of Gaul is in love. ➤ See also GLORIANA, GOOD *Queen Bess*, *The* VIRGIN *Queen*.

Our 'Enery Henry William Cooper (b.1934), British boxer. Cooper was the British heavyweight champion 1959–69 and 1970–71. He unsuccessfully challenged Muhammad Ali for the world heavyweight title in 1966, having famously knocked down the American (then still known as Cassius Clay) in 1963. His nickname reveals his popularity with the British public and his Cockney background. Cooper's powerful punch was known as ''Enery's 'Ammer'.

Our Ginny (Sarah) Virginia Wade (b.1945), English tennis player. Her singles titles include the US Open (1968), the Italian championship (1971), the Australian Open (1972), and Wimbledon (1977). This last victory, in the year of Wimbledon's centenary and of Queen Elizabeth II's silver jubilee, cemented her place in the affections of the British public, to whom Wade was *Our Ginny*.

Our Gracie Gracie Fields (born Grace Stansfield) (1898–1979), English singer and comedienne. In the 1930s she starred in a series of popular films such as *Sally in Our Alley* (1931) and *Sing as We Go* (1934). Her broad Lancashire accent, cheerfulness, and humour made her hugely popular, particularly with working-class people, and she was said to be the world's highest paid entertainer by 1939. The affection with which she was regarded by the British public is demonstrated by her nickname.

Our Marie   Marie Lloyd (born Matilda Alice Victoria Wood) (1870–1922), English music-hall entertainer, known particularly for her risqué songs and flamboyant costumes. Among her most well-known songs are 'Oh! Mr Porter' and 'A Little of What You Fancy Does You Good'. As with Gracie Fields later, Marie Lloyd's nickname reflects the enormous affection that the British public felt for her. She was also known as the QUEEN OF THE HALLS.

The Owls   Sheffield Wednesday football club. The club's ground Hillsborough was originally known as Owlerton, hence their nickname the *Owls*. An owl appears on the club badge.

The Oxford Blues   The Royal Horse Guards, a regiment of the British army. The regiment, whose blue uniforms date from 1661, were named the *Oxford Blues* in 1690 after their commanding officer Aubrey de Vere, the Earl of Oxford. This was later shortened to the *Blues*. ➤ See also *The* BLUES *and Royals*.

Oz   Australia. Recorded from the early 20th century, the informal name *Oz* is a phonetic representation of *Aus*, short for Australia. ➤ See also *The* LUCKY *Country*, YOU *Beaut Country*.

Paddy Pantsdown Paddy Ashdown (born Jeremy John Durham Ashdown) (b.1941), British politician, leader of the Liberal Democrats 1988–99. 'Paddy Pantsdown' was a *Sun* headline on 6 February 1992, referring to the disclosure of a brief affair Ashdown had had with his former secretary five years previously. The sobriquet, which Ashdown described in his diaries as 'dreadful—but brilliant', gained some currency.

Paddy's Wigwam The Roman Catholic Cathedral, Liverpool. The colourful nickname *Paddy's Wigwam* alludes both to the distinctive shape of the cathedral's central lantern tower and to the city's large Irish Catholic population, Paddy being a nickname for an Irishman. ➤ See also *The* MERSEY *Funnel*.

The Palmetto State The US state of South Carolina. The flag of South Carolina bears the figure of a cabbage palmetto tree, a fan-leafed palm. The nickname the *Palmetto State* dates from around 1843. ➤ See also *The* GAMECOCK *State, The* SANDLAPPER *State*.

Pam Lord Palmerston (1784–1865), Henry John Temple, 3rd Viscount, British Whig statesman, Prime Minister 1855–58 and 1859–65. He had earlier served for many years as Foreign Secretary (1830–34; 1835–41; 1846–51). In his foreign policy he was single-minded and forceful in his promotion of British interests, declaring the second Opium War against China in 1856, and overseeing the successful conclusion of the Crimean War in 1856 and the suppression of the Indian Mutiny in 1858. Palmerston was popular with the British people and widely known as *Pam*. ➤ See also LORD *Cupid*.

The Panhandle State The US state of West Virginia. A panhandle is a narrow strip of territory that projects into the territory of neighbouring states. The term *Panhandle State* usually refers to West Virginia but is also sometimes applied to Idaho. ➤ See also *The* MOUNTAIN *State*.

Papa Ernest (Miller) Hemingway (1899–1961), US novelist, short-story writer, and journalist, noted for his terse prose style. His novels include *A Farewell to Arms* (1929), *For Whom the Bell Tolls* (1940), and *The Old Man and the Sea* (1952), and he was awarded the Nobel Prize for literature in 1954. Hemingway, who had a tough, masculine image, was also associated with such manly pursuits as big-game hunting, bullfighting, and deep-sea fishing. He was first called *Papa* by Marlene Dietrich.

Papa Doc François Duvalier (1907–71), Haitian statesman, President 1957–71. His regime was noted for being authoritarian and oppressive. Many of his opponents were either executed without trial or forced into exile. Duvalier proclaimed himself President for life in 1964. Before entering politics he had trained as a physician, hence his nickname *Papa Doc*, the use of which he himself encouraged. ➤ See also BABY *Doc*.

The Paper King John Law (1671–1729), Scottish financier and speculator. In 1716 he established the *Banque Générale* in France, the first bank of any kind in the country, which had the authority to issue notes. A frenzy of speculative investment in Law's company for French development in the Mississippi Valley was followed in 1720 by a major collapse, known as the Mississippi Bubble. As huge fortunes had been made not in reality but only on paper, Law was given the title the *Paper King*.

Parrotface Freddie Davies (b.1937), British comedian. With his beaky features and spluttering pronunciation, *Parrotface* Davies (or *Mr Parrotface*) was a popular television performer in the 1960s and 1970s.

La Pasionaria Dolores Ibarruri (1895–1975), Spanish Communist leader. During the Spanish Civil War (1936–39), she became famous as an inspirational leader of the Republicans, her emotional oratory winning her the nickname *La Pasionaria* (Spanish for 'passion-flower'). After Franco's victory, she went into exile in Moscow, not returning to Spain until 1977. Margaret Thatcher was ironically described by the Labour politician Denis Healey as 'La Pasionaria of middle-class privilege'.

The Pathfinder John Charles Frémont (1813–90), US explorer and politician. He was responsible for exploring several viable routes to the Pacific across the Rocky Mountains in the 1840s, hence his nickname the *Pathfinder*. In 1856 Frémont stood as the first presidential candidate of the new Republican Party. Although he lost to John Buchanan, he was later referred to as the *Pathfinder for Lincoln*.

Paxo Jeremy Paxman (b.1950), British television journalist and presenter. Paxman is best known for his robust style of interviewing politicians on the BBC current affairs programme *Newsnight*. His nickname obviously derives from his surname but, since it is also the name of a brand of stuffing mix, also plays on the idea of his unfortunate interviewees being 'stuffed' by Paxman.

The Peace Garden State The US state of North Dakota. The International Peace Gardens in Bottineau are a landscaped park that crosses the northern border of the state into the Canadian province of Manitoba. These Gardens, which symbolize the friendship between Canada and the United States, give North Dakota its nickname the *Peace Garden State*. ➤ See also *The* FLICKERTAIL *State*, *The* SIOUX *State*.

The Peacemaker Edward VII (1841–1910), son of Queen Victoria, king of Great Britain and Ireland 1901–10. ➤ See EDWARD *the Peacemaker*.

The Peach State The US state of Georgia. The peach is the official state fruit of Georgia, hence its nickname the *Peach State*. ➤ See also *The* CRACKER *State*, *The* GEORGIA *Peach*, *The* GOOBER *State*.

Peasant Bruegel Pieter Bruegel the Elder (1525–69), Flemish artist. Bruegel is known for his landscapes, religious allegories, and satirical paintings of peasant life, such as *Peasant Wedding Feast* (1566). His work displays a real interest in village customs combined with a satirical view of folly, vice, and the sins of the flesh. His nickname *Peasant Bruegel* distinguishes him from his two sons, who were also painters. ➤ See also HELL *Bruegel*, VELVET *Bruegel*.

The Peasant Poet   John Clare (1793–1864), English poet. After working as a farm
labourer and gardener, he published *Poems Descriptive of Rural Life and Scenery*
(1820) to great acclaim. This was followed by *The Shepherd's Calendar* (1827). Clare's
poetry, written in the poet's own dialect and grammar, celebrates the English
countryside. The words 'Peasant Poet' are inscribed on his tombstone in Helpston,
Northamptonshire.

The Peekaboo Girl   Veronica Lake (Constance Frances Marie Ockleman) (1919–73),
US film actress who often played slinky femmes fatales in 1940s thrillers. She was
promoted as the *Peekaboo Girl*, a reference to her distinctive peek-a-boo hairstyle in
which her long blonde hair was draped over one eye. This style was much imitated
by female film-goers of the time.

The Pelican State   The US state of Louisiana. The pelican is the official state bird of
Louisiana and has been depicted on the state seal since before the Civil War. The
birds are plentiful along the state's Gulf coast.

The People's Princess   Diana, Princess of Wales (born Lady Diana Frances
Spencer) (1961–97). The *People's Princess* was an informal name for Diana popularized by Tony Blair on hearing of her death: 'She was the People's Princess, and that is
how she will stay... in our hearts and in our memories forever.' The epithet was
originally coined by the journalist Julie Burchill. ➤ See also CHERYL, *The* QUEEN *of
Hearts.*

Perdita   Mary Robinson (1758–1800), actress and mistress of George, Prince of Wales
(later George IV). She became known as *Perdita* (or *Fair Perdita*) after her success at
Drury Lane in that part in Shakespeare's *The Winter's Tale*. After seeing her on stage,
the young prince was captivated by the actress and she became his mistress. He used
to sign his letters to her 'Florizel', the name of Perdita's lover in the play, once
sending her a lock of his hair with the message, 'To the adorable Perdita—Florizel, to
be redeemed'. ➤ See also FLORIZEL.

Perfidious Albion   England or Britain, considered as treacherous in international
affairs. The epithet is a rendering of the French phrase *la perfide Albion*, said to have
been first used by the Marquis de Ximenès (1726–1817) and in widespread currency
by the end of the Napoleonic War. Both terms are recorded in English from the mid-
19th century. Albion is a poetic or literary term for England or Britain, probably of
Celtic origin and related to Latin *albus* ('white'), in allusion to the white cliffs of
Dover. ➤ See also BLIGHTY, *The* OLD *Dart.*

The Perpetual Candidate   (Stephen) Grover Cleveland (1837–1908), US
Democratic statesman, 22nd and 24th President of the US 1885–89 and 1893–97.
Cleveland was the only president to hold office for two non-consecutive terms.
He was also an unsuccessful presidential candidate in 1888.

The Philosopher of Sans Souci   Frederick II (known as Frederick the Great)
(1712–86), king of Prussia 1740–86. Sans Souci (in French, literally 'Carefree') was the
name Frederick gave to the French rococo palace he built near Berlin in 1745.

Phil the Greek   Prince Philip, Duke of Edinburgh (b.1921), husband of Elizabeth II.
The son of Prince Andrew of Greece and Denmark, Philip's ancestry is Danish rather

than Greek. Nevertheless he is sometimes disrespectfully referred to as *Phil the Greek*.
➤ See also KEITH.

Phoenix City   The US city of Chicago, Illinois. It was dubbed *Phoenix City* by
Henry Ward Beecher after its recovery from the disastrous fire of 1871. ➤ See also
The WINDY *City*.

Phoney Quid   Alfred Dudley Pickman Rogers Pound (1877–1943), British admiral.
He was Commander-in-Chief of the Mediterranean fleet (1936–39) and in 1939 he
became Admiral of the Fleet and First Sea Lord. He was generally known as Dud
Pound, which was sometimes humorously paraphrased as *Phoney Quid*.

The Phrasemaker   (Thomas) Woodrow Wilson (1856–1924), US Democratic
statesman, 28th President of the US 1913–21. Wilson brought the US into the First
World War in 1917 and was later instrumental in the formation of the League of
Nations. He had a gift for oratory and for such memorable phrases as 'The world
must be made safe for democracy', used when he addressed Congress in 1917 to ask
for a declaration of war against Germany. ➤ See also *The* PROFESSOR[1].

Pig Island   New Zealand. In the late 19th and early 20th centuries, Australians
referred to New Zealand as *Pig Island*, because of the large numbers of wild pigs in
rural parts of the country, descended from the pigs originally brought by Captain
James Cook.

Pincher   William Fanshawe Martin (1801–95), British admiral. He was a strict
disciplinarian, noted for having ratings 'pinched', or arrested, for minor offences. In
naval and military circles *Pincher* subsequently became the inevitable nickname of
any man surnamed Martin.

The Pine Tree State   The US state of Maine, known as the *Pine Tree State* since the
mid-19th century. Four-fifths of the state is forested, mainly with pine trees. A pine
tree appears on the state seal.

The Pink 'Un   *The Sporting Times*, published 1865 to 1931. From April 1876 it was
printed on pink paper, hence its nickname the *Pink 'Un*.

Pistol Pete   Pete Sampras (b.1971), US tennis player. In 2002 Sampras won the US
Open, his 14th Grand Slam tournament. He had previously won the US title four
times, the Australian twice, and Wimbledon seven times. In 1993 he became the first
player to serve over 1000 aces in a season, his powerful, often unreturnable, serves
earning him his nickname *Pistol Pete*.

Plantagenet   Geoffrey, Count of Anjou (1113–51), father of Henry II of England.
Plantagenet, the surname of the English royal dynasty which held the throne for over
three hundred years, was originally a nickname for Geoffrey, deriving from his habit
of wearing a sprig of broom in his helmet (Latin *planta genista*, 'sprig of broom').
The name is first recorded in late Middle English, in the Chronicle of Robert of
Gloucester, in a passage relating to Geoffrey's death.

The Platinum Blonde   Jean Harlow (1911–37), US film actress, who appeared in the
film *Platinum Blonde* (1931). The term can also be used to describe any woman with
pale silvery-blonde hair. ➤ See also *The* BLONDE *Bombshell*.

Plon-Plon   Prince Napoleon Joseph Charles Paul Bonaparte, cousin of Napoleon III (1822–91). He gained the derisive nickname *Plon-Plon* in the Crimean War. It is a corruption of *Craint-plon* ('Fear-bullet').

The Plymouth of the West   The US city of San Diego, California. It was one of the first settlements on the West Coast, founded in 1769 by Father Junípero Serra. Its nickname the *Plymouth of the West* is a reference to Plymouth, Massachusetts, where the Pilgrim Fathers settled in 1620.

The Poachers   The Royal Lincolnshire Regiment, a regiment of the British army. Their regimental march was the traditional song 'The Lincolnshire Poacher', hence their nickname the *Poachers*.

The Pocket Dictator   Engelbert Dollfuss (1892–1934), Austrian statesman, Chancellor of Austria 1932–34. From 1933 Dollfuss attempted to block Austrian Nazi plans to force the *Anschluss* by suppressing Parliament and governing by decree. He was known as the *Pocket Dictator* because of his small stature. Dollfuss was assassinated by Austrian Nazis.

The Poet Squab   John Dryden (1631–1700), English poet, dramatist, and critic. Dryden became fat in later life and his nickname, coined by the poet Lord Rochester (1647–80), was said to reflect his appearance, a squab being a young pigeon. ➤ See also GLORIOUS *John*.

The Pompadours   The 56th foot, a regiment of the British army. In 1764 the regiment changed the colour of its facings from crimson to rose-purple, said to be the favourite colour of Madame de Pompadour (1721–64), mistress to Louis XV of France.

Pompey   The town and dockyard of Portsmouth, England. The nickname *Pompey* appears to be naval slang, dating back to the late 19th century, but its origin remains obscure. It is also the nickname of Portsmouth Football Club, as heard in the old chant 'Play up Pompey, Pompey play up!'

The Pond   The North Atlantic Ocean. ➤ See *The* HERRING *Pond*.

Pontius Pilate's Bodyguard   The 1st Foot (later the Royal Scots (the Royal Regiment)), the oldest regiment in the British Army. They are directly descended from the Scottish Archer Guard that served in the Crusades. Their nickname *Pontius Pilate's Bodyguard* is traditionally said to have stemmed from an argument in the 15th century with the *Regiment de Picardy* as to which was the oldest regiment. When the French regiment claimed that it was descended from the Roman legion on guard over Christ's tomb after the Crucifixion, the officers of the Scots regiment countered with the observation that, had it been them on duty, they would not have slept at their posts and Christ's body would not have left the Sepulchre.

Poor Fred   Frederick Louis, son of George II and father of George III (1707–51). As heir to the throne he was popular in the country but loathed by his father. He died prematurely as the result of an injury sustained from a blow on the chest from a cricket ball.

The Poor Little Rich Girl   Barbara Hutton (1912–79), US heiress to the Woolworth fortune, who inherited $10 million when she was 21. Married seven times, she had a life beset by troubles, partly through ill health. She was dubbed the *Poor Little Rich Girl* by the press. 'Poor Little Rich Girl' is the title of a song by Noël Coward (1925). When she married the film actor Cary Grant in 1947, the couple were nicknamed *Cash and Cary.*

The Pope   Enrico Fermi (1901–54), Italian-born US atomic physicist. At the age of 25 he was appointed professor of theoretical physics at the University of Rome. His students there nicknamed him the *Pope* because they considered him infallible. He was awarded the Nobel Prize for physics in 1938. Fermi directed the first controlled nuclear chain reaction in 1942.

The Pope of Trash   John Waters (b.1946), US film director, whose films are notorious for their scatology and bad taste. His films include *Mondo Trasho* (1969), *Pink Flamingos* (1972), *Hairspray* (1988), and *Cecil B. Demented* (2000). *Pink Flamingos* was described by *Variety* as 'one of the most vile, stupid, and repulsive films ever made'. His nickname the *Pope of Trash* was coined by the writer William S. Burroughs.

The Popish Duke   James II (1633–1701), son of Charles I, king of England, Ireland, and (as James VII) Scotland 1685–88. Soon after his birth James was created Duke of York, the traditional title of an English monarch's second son. During the reign of his brother Charles II, James converted to the Roman Catholic Church. His conversion, together with his marriage to the Catholic Mary of Modena, made him unpopular in the country. James's Catholicism led to the rebellion of the Duke of Monmouth in 1685 and to his deposition in favour of William of Orange and Mary II three years later. He was forced to flee to France where he eventually died in exile, leaving the Jacobite claim to the throne in the hands of his son, James Stuart. ➤ See also *The* KING *over the Water.*

Pops   *Pops* is a term of address popular among black jazz musicians and usually (though not invariably) applied to someone older than the speaker. Louis Armstrong frequently used the term and was often affectionately addressed as such himself. The band-leader Paul Whiteman was also known as Pops by his musicians. ➤ See also DIPPERMOUTH, *The* KING *of Jazz*, SATCHMO.

Popski's Private Army   A unit of the Long-Range Desert Patrol, a British military force formed in 1942 to carry out reconnaissance and sabotage behind enemy lines in North Africa during the Second World War. They were led by Lieutenant Colonel Vladimir Peniakoff (1897–1951), a Russian-born Belgian serving with the British army and familiarly known as *Popski* for ease of pronunciation.

Posh   Victoria Beckham (born Victoria Caroline Adams) (b.1975), British pop singer. As a member of the Spice Girls pop group in the 1990s she was nicknamed *Posh Spice* (the other members of the group were known as *Baby Spice, Ginger Spice, Scary Spice,* and *Sporty Spice*). Each of these nicknames was designed to reflect the distinctive persona adopted by the singer it was applied to; in Adams's case it referred to her unsmiling, slightly haughty on-stage demeanour. Later known simply as *Posh*, she married the footballer David Beckham in 1999, the celebrity couple becoming known in the newspapers as *Posh 'n' Becks*. When in 2002–3 the football club Peterborough United, itself nicknamed the POSH, sought to register the nickname as a trademark, Victoria Beckham was reported to have contested the club's right to do so.

The Posh Peterborough United football club. When the club was formed in 1934, the fans were promised 'posh players for a posh new team'. They have been known as the *Posh* ever since.

The Pot-Hooks The 77th Foot (later the 2nd Battalion of the Duke of Cambridge's Own (Middlesex Regiment)), a regiment of the British army. Their nickname the *Pot-Hooks* comes from the similarity in shape of the two 7s to pot-hooks.

The Potters Stoke City football club. The area around Stoke-on-Trent, Staffordshire, where the English pottery industry is based, is known as the Potteries. The local football club is accordingly nicknamed the *Potters*.

The Power Phil Taylor (b.1960), English darts player. His nickname the *Power* reflects his worldwide dominance of the sport since the mid-1990s. In 2002 he won his tenth World Darts Championship title.

The Prairie State The US state of Illinois. Although the Prairie States has been used as a collective term for the states of Illinois, Wisconsin, Iowa, Minnesota, and others to the south, it is Illinois with which the nickname the *Prairie State* has generally been associated since the mid-19th century. ➤ See also *The* SUCKER *State*.

The Prefect (John) Malcolm Fraser (b.1930), Australian Liberal statesman, Prime Minister 1975–83. During his time in office he was known as the *Prefect* because of his earnest and somewhat dictatorial style of leadership. In 1985 Fraser represented Australia in a Commonwealth group formed to negotiate the peaceful dismantling of South Africa's apartheid policy.

The Premier State The state of New South Wales, Australia. It was the first state to be founded, hence its nickname the *Premier State*.

The President Lester Young. ➤ See PREZ.

The Preston Plumber Tom Finney (b.1922), English footballer. A versatile player, he was genuinely two-footed and could play anywhere in the forward line. For the whole of his career he played for his home-town club Preston North End, scoring 187 goals. He also won 76 international caps, scoring 30 goals for England. Before embarking on his football career he worked as a plumber, later running his own business. He was affectionately known as the *Preston Plumber*.

Pretty Boy Floyd Charles Arthur Floyd (1904–34), US bankrobber. He probably acquired his nickname *Pretty Boy Floyd* in a Kansas City brothel. It was a name he hated and he is said to have killed at least two fellow gangsters who so addressed him. Floyd himself was shot and killed by FBI agents in Ohio in 1934. ➤ See also BABY *Face Nelson*.

Prez Lester (Willis) Young (1909–59), US tenor saxophonist and jazz composer. An influential jazz soloist and accompanist for the singer Billie Holiday, he coined her nickname LADY DAY and she reciprocated by calling him PRESIDENT, later shortened to *Prez* (or *Pres*). They started working together in the late 1930s and she is said to have been admiringly comparing the saxophonist to the then President Franklin Roosevelt.

Prezza　John Leslie Prescott (b.1938), British Labour politician, deputy Prime Minister from 1997. He is sometimes called *Prezza*, a version of his surname styled on nicknames such as GAZZA and HEZZA. ➤ See also THUMPER, TWO *Jags*.

The Prime Minister of Mirth　George Robey (born George Edward Wade) (1869–1954), British music-hall comedian and actor. From the 1890s, he performed in music-halls, originally singing humorous songs and later developing comic characters to perform in sketches. Billed the *Prime Minister of Mirth*, Robey was typically dressed in a long black coat and bowler hat, with two thickly-painted black eyebrows. He later acted in Shakespeare, playing Falstaff on stage and appearing in Laurence Olivier's film *Henry V* (1944). ➤ See also *The* DARLING *of the Halls*.

The Prince of Darkness[1]　Johnny Carson (1925–2005), US television personality. Carson dominated late-night US television for 30 years, hence his sobriquet the *Prince of Darkness*. From 1962 he hosted *The Tonight Show*, a chat show broadcast every night from 11.30 to 12.30 and attracting huge audiences. He was noted for his quick wit and satirical commentary on current affairs.

The Prince of Darkness[2]　Peter Mandelson (b.1953), British Labour politician. His nickname the *Prince of Darkness* is a reference to his perceived mastery of the 'black art' of spin-doctoring. The phrase was originally a name for the Devil, recorded from the early 17th century. Mandelson is also known as the *Sultan of Spin*. ➤ See also MANDY.

The Prince of Showmen　Phineas Taylor Barnum (1810–91), US showman. In 1842 Barnum opened his American Museum in New York and soon became famous for his extravagant advertising and exhibition of freaks, including General Tom Thumb and the original Siamese Twins. He billed his circus, opened in 1871, as 'The Greatest Show on Earth'. Ten years later it merged with that of his great rival Anthony Bailey (1847–1906), becoming the Barnum and Bailey circus. The self-styled *Prince of Showmen* coined the phrase 'There's a sucker born every minute.'

The Prince of Wails　Johnnie Ray (1927–90), US pop singer, noted for his emotional delivery on such lachrymose songs as 'Cry' and 'The Little White Cloud That Cried', the double-sided single that was no. 1 for eleven weeks in 1952. He earned several nicknames including the *Prince of Wails*, the NABOB OF SOB, and the *Cry Guy*.

The Prince of Whales　George, Prince of Wales, later George IV (1762–1830), son of George III, reigned 1820–30. In March 1812 Leigh Hunt wrote of the Prince Regent: 'This Adonis in loveliness was a corpulent man of fifty', for which he was prosecuted and sent to prison for two years. His friend the poet Charles Lamb published an anonymous verse ridiculing the Prince: 'Not a fatter fish than he/Flounders round the polar sea . . . /By his bulk and by his size,/By his oily qualities,/This (or else my eyesight fails),/This should be the Prince of Whales.' ➤ See also *The* ADONIS *of Fifty*, *The* FIRST *Gentleman in Europe*, FLORIZEL, FUM *the Fourth*, PRINNY.

Prinny   George, Prince of Wales, later George IV (1762–1830). As Prince Regent (1811–20), George was known as *Prinny*. ➤ See also *The* ADONIS *of Fifty, The* FIRST *Gentleman in Europe,* FLORIZEL, FUM *the Fourth, The* PRINCE *of Whales*.

The Prisoner of Ham   Napoleon III (full name Charles Louis Napoleon Bonaparte; known as Louis-Napoleon) (1808–73), emperor of France 1852–70. He was nicknamed the *Prisoner of Ham* after the name of the fortress in Picardy where he was incarcerated from 1840 to 1846, following two attempted coups against the French government. In 1846 he escaped to England. ➤ See also *The* MAN *of December, The* MAN *of Sedan*.

The Prisoner of Spandau   (Walther Richard) Rudolf Hess (1894–1987), German Nazi politician, deputy leader of the Nazi Party 1934–41. In 1941, he secretly parachuted into Scotland in a bid to negotiate peace terms with Britain. He was imprisoned for the remainder of the war and, at the Nuremberg trials, sentenced to life imprisonment in Spandau prison, Berlin, for war crimes. From 1966 until his death in 1987 he was the only inmate of Spandau.

The Prof   Frederick Alexander Lindemann, later Viscount Cherwell (1886–1957), German-born British physicist. He was Professor of Experimental Philosophy at Oxford (1919–56) and director of the Clarendon Laboratory. During the Second World War, he was Winston Churchill's personal adviser on scientific and aeronautical matters. He was widely known as the *Prof*, a nickname he apparently first acquired at the house of Lord Birkenhead around 1920.

The Professor[1]   (Thomas) Woodrow Wilson (1856–1924), US Democratic statesman, 28th President of the US 1913–21. A prominent academic prior to his election victory, he had been appointed professor of jurisprudence and political economy at Princeton University in 1890. His academic background, and the scholarly manner he exhibited in political life, earned him the nicknames the *Professor* and the *Schoolmaster*. ➤ See also *The* PHRASEMAKER.

The Professor[2]   Jimmy (James Keith O'Neill) Edwards (1920–88), British comedian. With his trademark handlebar moustache, Edwards is best remembered playing the bullying, blustering headmaster of a minor public school in the British TV series *Whacko!* (1956–60, 1971–72). His character was called Professor Jimmy Edwards. It was such academic roles (and his Cambridge education) that earned him his nickname the *Professor*.

Prosperity Robinson   Frederick John Robinson, Lord Goderich (1782–1859), British politician. In 1825, as Chancellor of the Exchequer, he congratulated the House on the prosperity the country was enjoying, while proposing (and carrying) a reduction of duty on coffee, sugar, wine, and spirits. This sanguine view of the economy was followed almost immediately by a developing financial crisis. The ironic nickname *Prosperity Robinson* was coined by William Cobbett.

Prosperity's Advance Agent   William McKinley (1843–1901), US Republican statesman, 25th President of the US 1897–1901. During his campaign for re-election in 1900, he was called *Prosperity's Advance Agent* by his campaign manager Mark Hanna. This was intended to remind voters of the improvement in the economy that had followed McKinley's election as president.

The Proud Duke   Charles Seymour, 6th Duke of Somerset (1662–1748). According to Horace Walpole he was the archetype of aristocratic arrogance and parental despotism. He forbade his children to sit down in his presence and refused to speak to his servants, insisting on using signs instead.

Psycho   Stuart Pearce (b.1962), English footballer. He won 78 caps for England and played for a number of clubs including Nottingham Forest. A combative left back, his crunching tackles earned him his nickname *Psycho*.

Public Enemy No. 1   John Dillinger (1903–34), US bank robber and murderer. In 1933 he became the first notorious wanted criminal to be named the FBI's *Public Enemy No.* 1 by the US Attorney General, Homer Cummings. He was shot and killed by FBI agents in Chicago in 1934.

La Pucelle   Joan of Arc (*c.*1412–31), French national heroine. The epithet *La Pucelle*, or 'the Maid', is recorded from late Middle English. She appears in Shakespeare's 1 *Henry VI* as Joan La Pucelle, and is sometimes referred to simply as Pucelle: 'Pucelle is ent'red into Orleans/In spite of us or aught that we could do.' ➤ See also *The* MAID *of Orleans*.

The Puke State   The US state of Missouri. It has been suggested that the curious former nickname the *Puke State* may be a corruption of *Pikes*, a word used in California to refer to white migratory workers from Pike County, Missouri. ➤ See also *The* BULLION *State*, *The* SHOW Me State.

Pussyfoot Johnson   William Eugene Johnson (1862–1945), US temperance supporter. He acquired the nickname *Pussyfoot Johnson* on account of his stealthy methods pursuing criminals as a special officer in the US Indian Service (1908–11) in Indian Territory. Johnson later campaigned for the prohibitionist cause in the US and tirelessly lectured on temperance all over Europe. The term *pussyfoot*, denoting an advocate of prohibition or a teetotaller, derived from Johnson's nickname.

Qq

Quaker City The US city of Philadelphia, Pennsylvania. It was founded in 1682 by William Penn (1644–1718) as a Quaker colony. ➤ See also *The* CITY *of Brotherly Love*, *The* QUAKER *State*, *The* REBEL *Capital*.

The Quaker Poet Two poets have been known by this sobriquet, one English and one American. The English poet Bernard Barton (1784–1849) was born of Quaker parents. When Barton discussed with his friend Charles Lamb whether he should give up his job as a bank clerk in Woodbridge to pursue a full-time writing career, Lamb advised against it: 'Keep to your bank, and the bank will keep you.' Like Barton, the US poet John Greenleaf Whittier (1807–92) was a Quaker. He was a committed and energetic abolitionist, editing periodicals and writing poetry for the cause. His best known poems, though, are on rural themes, especially 'Snow-Bound' (1866).

The Quakers Darlington football club. The club became known as the *Quakers* because their ground Feethams was originally owned by the prominent local Quaker and slavery abolitionist John Beaumont Pease. A Quaker hat appears on the club's badge.

The Quaker State The US state of Pennsylvania, named after the father of its founder, William Penn (1644–1718). Penn was granted a charter to land in North America by Charles II and used it to found the colony of Pennsylvania as a sanctuary for persecuted Quakers and other Nonconformists in 1682. As a result Pennsylvania is sometimes called the *Quaker State*. ➤ See also *The* KEYSTONE *State*, QUAKER *City*.

Queen Dick Richard Cromwell (1626–1712), briefly Lord Protector of the Commonwealth on the death of his father Oliver Cromwell. He was the object of a number of derogatory contemporary nicknames, including *Queen Dick*, a disdainful variation of KING DICK that hints at effeminacy or homosexuality. There is no conclusive historical evidence that Richard Cromwell was in fact homosexual. ➤ See also KING *Dick*, TUMBLEDOWN *Dick*.

The Queen of Burlesque Gypsy Rose Lee (born Rose Louise Hovick) (1914–70), US striptease artist. In the 1930s she became famous on Broadway for her striptease act, which raised what was previously considered a disreputable form of entertainment to a stylish and sophisticated art. Billed as the *Queen of Burlesque*, she found herself fêted by the New York intellectual set, including Damon Runyon.

The Queen of Crime Two English writers of detective fiction have been hailed as the *Queen of Crime*, first Agatha Christie (1890–1976), then her successor P(hyllis) D(orothy) James (b.1920). Many of Christie's novels feature the Belgian Hercule Poirot or the resourceful Miss Marple, her two most famous creations. Among her best-known detective stories are *Murder on the Orient Express* (1934) and *Death on the Nile* (1937). James is noted for her novels featuring the poet-detective Adam Dalgleish, including *Death of an Expert Witness* (1977) and *A Taste for Death* (1986).

The Queen of Hearts Elizabeth of Bohemia (1598–1662), daughter of James I of England, who with her husband Frederick V, Elector Palatine, had briefly occupied the throne of Bohemia before being driven into exile. She earned this admiring sobriquet because of her good-natured disposition, even in the face of adversity. In the late 20th century the name was applied to Diana, Princess of Wales, following an interview she gave on the BBC TV programme *Panorama* in 1995: 'I'd like to be a queen in people's hearts but I don't see myself being Queen of this country.' The term came to be frequently used by the newspapers in connection with Diana's charity work. ➤ See also CHERYL, *The* PEOPLE'S *Princess, The* WINTER *Queen*.

The Queen of the Antilles Cuba. The Antilles are the group of islands that form the greater part of the West Indies, of which Cuba is the largest.

The Queen of the Blues[1] Elizabeth Montagu (born Elizabeth Robinson) (1720–1800). She became well known for her 'Blue Stocking' circles. These were evening gatherings held regularly about 1750 at her house in Hill Street, London for the purpose of intellectual and literary conversation. Regular participants included Hannah More, Fanny Burney, and Horace Walpole. Some of the men who attended, in particular one Benjamin Stillingfleet, wore the blue worsted stockings of ordinary daytime dress (rather than the more formal black silk). Alluding to this, Admiral Boscawen is said to have dubbed the coterie the 'Blue Stocking Society'. Mrs Montagu's intelligence and conversation were admired by Samuel Johnson, who called her *Queen of the Blues*: 'Mrs Montagu is a very extraordinary woman: she has a constant stream of conversation, and it is always impregnated; it has always meaning' (*Life of Johnson*, 15 May 1784).

The Queen of the Blues[2] Dinah Washington (born Ruth Lee Jones) (1924–63), US pianist and blues singer. Although she was not exclusively a blues singer, her feeling for that music earned her the title the *Queen of the Blues*. Noted for her husky voice and unique phrasing, she also sang gospel, jazz, rhythm and blues, and pop, having notable hits with such recordings as 'What a Diff'rence a Day Makes' and 'Our Love is Here to Stay'. ➤ See also *The* EMPRESS *of the Blues*.

The Queen of the Halls Marie Lloyd, English music-hall entertainer. ➤ See OUR *Marie*.

Queen Sarah Sarah Churchill (née Jennings), Duchess of Marlborough (1660–1744), friend of and adviser to Queen Anne. She became such a powerful influence on the Queen and on the Whig ministry that she was referred to as *Queen Sarah*, though she later fell out of royal favour. ➤ See also MRS *Morley*.

The Queen's Bays ➤ See *The* BAYS.

The Queen State The US state of Maryland. The state is named after Queen Henrietta Maria, wife of Charles I, and is sometimes known as the *Queen State*. ➤ See also *The* COCKADE *State, The* FREE *State, The* OLD *Line State*.

Queer Hardie   (James) Keir Hardie (1856–1915), Scottish Labour politician. A miner (from the age of 10) before becoming an MP in 1892, he became the first leader of both the Independent Labour Party (1893) and the Labour Party (1906). Although he remained an MP until his death, his pacifism isolated him from his Labour colleagues during the First World War. His nickname *Queer Hardie* derives from his idiosyncrasies, such as wearing a cloth cap.

Rab Richard Austen Butler (1902–82), British Conservative politician. As Minister of Education (1941–45) he was responsible for the Education Act (1944), which introduced free primary and secondary education for all. Butler was twice an unsuccessful candidate for the leadership of the Conservative Party. He was universally known as *Rab* Butler, from his initials. The team of younger Conservatives who worked under Butler to reform the party after its 1945 election defeat were known as 'Rab's Boys'.

Rabbit Harry Angstrom, the hero of a series of novels by John Updike (b.1932). Updike's quartet of novels are titled *Rabbit, Run* (1960), *Rabbit, Redux* (1971), *Rabbit is Rich* (1981), and *Rabbit at Rest* (1990). A novella-length sequel 'Rabbit Remembered' was included in a collection of short stories *Licks of Love* (2000). Angstrom's nickname derives from his early days as a former basketball player.

Radical Jack John George Lambton (1792–1840), 1st Earl of Durham, British reformist Whig politician. His sustained support for radical reforms earned him the nickname *Radical Jack*. He drew up the Reform Bill of 1832.

The Rag (and Famish) The Army and Navy Club in London, founded in 1837. The familiar name the *Rag* is first recorded in Trollope's novel *The Three Clerks* (1858). The name is said in one source to have been coined by a Captain William Duff of the 23rd Fusiliers, when he referred to the food offered when he arrived for supper late one night as a mere 'rag and famish affair'. This was an allusion to the 'Rag and Famish', a cheap local gaming-house and brothel.

The Rail Splitter Abraham Lincoln (1809–65), US Republican statesman, 16th President of the US 1861–65. In the 1860 presidential campaign, the Republicans promoted Lincoln as the *Rail Splitter*. As a young man, 30 years previously, he had built a cabin and split some rails to make a wooden fence. Two of these rails had been recovered and were presented to the Illinois state convention. Lincoln thus acquired the image of a self-made man of pioneer origins, an image that proved to be hugely popular during the campaign. ➤ See also *The* GREAT *Emancipator,* HONEST *Abe,* OLD *Abe.*

The Railway King George Hudson (1800–71), British railway financier. In 1827 he invested a large bequest in North Midland Railway shares, subsequently becoming chairman of first the York and North Midland and then a number of other railway companies. Through his financial speculations, he was responsible for the railway boom in the 1840s and dominated the market, earning the sobriquet the *Railway King*. With the fall in the value of railway property, his power declined, he lost most of his fortune, and in 1865 he was briefly imprisoned for debt.

The Rajah Rogers Hornsby (1896–1963), US baseball player, mostly with the St Louis Cardinals and Chicago Cubs (1915–37). Acknowledged as one of baseball's greatest hitters, his career batting average of 0.358 is second highest only to Ty Cobb.

The Rams Derby County football club. The club derives its nickname from the famous breed of Derbyshire rams.

The Rand Witwatersrand, a goldfield district near Johannesburg, South Africa. From its informal name the *Rand* came the name rand for the base monetary unit of South Africa. Another nickname for Witwatersrand is the *Reef*.

Ranji Kumar Shri Ranjitsinhji Vibhaji (1872–1933), Maharaja Jam Sahib of Navanagar, Indian cricketer and statesman. He made his cricketing debut for Sussex in 1895, and scored a total of 72 centuries as a batsman for Sussex and England. In 1907 he succeeded his cousin as Maharaja of the state of Navanagar.

Rare Ben Benjamin ('Ben') Jonson (1572–1637), English dramatist and poet, whose comedies include *Volpone* (1606) and *The Alchemist* (1610). When Jonson was buried in Westminster Abbey (upright to save on the cost of the grave), Sir John Young paid for the inscription 'O rare Ben Jonson' to be cut into the slab.

The Rawalpindi Express Shoaib Akhtar (b.1975), Pakistani cricketer. Born in Rawalpindi, Pakistan, he is a fast bowler of blistering speed, hence his nickname the *Rawalpindi Express*. The sobriquet has inspired many newspaper headlines on the lines of 'Aussies derailed by Rawalpindi Express'. In 2002 Shoaib bowled the first ever 100mph delivery, during a one-day international between Pakistan and New Zealand.

The Rebel Capital The US city of Philadelphia, Pennsylvania. To the British it was the *Rebel Capital* when it became the capital of the thirteen colonies in 1776. ➤ See also *The* CITY *of Brotherly Love*.

The Red Baron Manfred, Baron von Richthofen (1882–1918), German fighter pilot. He is credited with shooting down 80 enemy aircraft, making him the leading fighter ace of the First World War. His nickname the *Red Baron* derived not only from his aristocratic title but also from the distinctive bright red aircraft he flew. Richthofen was eventually shot down, either by a Canadian ace flying with the RAF or by Australian small-arms fire from the ground.

The Red Cardinal Armand Jean du Plessis, duc de Richelieu (1585–1642), French cardinal and statesman. ➤ See ÉMINENCE *Rouge*.

The Red Comyn John Comyn of Badenoch (d.1306), nephew of John de Baliol, king of Scotland, and the son of a claimant to the Scottish throne. He was red-haired and given the name *Red Comyn* to distinguish him from his father John Comyn who had black hair and was known as *Black Comyn*. He was stabbed to death in an affray with Robert Bruce in the church at Dumfries.

The Red Dean Hewlett Johnson (1874–1966), Dean of Canterbury 1931–63. Newspapers dubbed him the *Red Dean* because of his controversial Communist sympathies. He visited both the Soviet Union and China.

Redeless   Ethelred II (known as Ethelred the Unready) (*c*.969–1016), king of
England 978–1016. ➤ See *The* UNREADY.

Red Ellen   Ellen Cicely Wilkinson (1891–1947), British Labour politician. She served
as MP for Jarrow 1935–47 and was appointed Minister of Education in 1945, the first
woman to hold such a position. As a former member of the Communist Party, she
was dubbed *Red Ellen*.

The Red Eminence   Armand Jean du Plessis, duc de Richelieu (1585–1642), French
cardinal and statesman. ➤ See ÉMINENCE *Rouge*.

Red Ken   Ken(neth) Livingstone (b.1945), British Labour politician. He was the
leader of the Greater London Council 1981–86 and MP for Brent East 1987–2001. His
outspoken left-wing views as leader of the GLC earned him the nickname *Red Ken* in
the right-wing press, for whom he became something of a hate figure. Livingstone
was elected mayor of London in 2000. ➤ See also KEN *Leninspart*.

The Red Priest   Antonio (Lucio) Vivaldi (1678–1741), Italian composer and violinist.
He is chiefly remembered for his concertos, his best known work being *The Four
Seasons*. (1725). He was ordained to the priesthood in 1703 but after two years was
exempted from the duties of saying Mass because of a congenital chest complaint.
From 1703 to 1740 he taught violin at an orphanage in Venice, and he composed
many of his works for performance there. His nickname (*Il Prete Rosso* in Italian) is a
reference to his red hair.

The Reef   Witwatersrand, South Africa. ➤ See *The* RAND.

The Reformed Pugilist   William Thompson (1811–80), English prizefighter. ➤ See
BENDIGO.

The Refrigerator   William Perry (b.1962), US American football player, who played
for the Chicago Bears. Weighing 330 pounds, Perry was dubbed the *Refrigerator*
because he was said to be able to eat the contents of a fridge. The nickname may also
have alluded to his bulk.

The Resolute Doctor   John Baconthorpe (d.1346), English Carmelite and scholar.
His sobriquet the *Resolute Doctor* perhaps derives from the tenacity with which he
maintained his Averroist principles, particularly the belief that philosophical truth
comes through reason. He was also an advocate of the doctrine that the power of the
clergy was subordinate to that of the monarch.

The Robber   Edward IV (1442–83), son of Richard, Duke of York, king of England
1461–83. Edward accumulated a large amount of wealth for the Crown by ruthlessly
confiscating lands from the defeated Lancastrians. This earned him the nickname
Edward the Robber.

The Robins   Cheltenham Town football club, founded in 1892. They originally
played in deep red shirts and were nicknamed the *Rubies*. In the 1930s they changed
to a red-and-white strip and adopted the nickname the *Robins*. The nickname is
shared by Bristol City, Swindon Town, and Wrexham.

Robocop   Ray(mond) Mallon (b.1955), British senior police officer and politician.
As Detective Superintendent of Cleveland police in the 1990s he introduced

'zero-tolerance' policing, in which burglars and anti-social behaviour were vigor-
ously targeted. He was dubbed *Robocop* by the press after the remorseless crime-
fighting cyborg in the 1987 science-fiction film of that title. Mallon was elected
mayor of Middlesbrough in 2002.

The Rock   Gibraltar, a British dependency situated at the foot of the Rock of
Gibraltar, a rocky headland at the southern tip of Spain. The mixed patois of Spanish
and English spoken by its inhabitants is known as Rock English. Alcatraz, a rocky
island in San Francisco Bay, California, which was the site of a top-security Federal
prison between 1934 and 1963, was also informally known as the *Rock*.

The Rocket[1]   Rod (Rodney George) Laver (b.1938), Australian tennis player. Born in
Rockhampton, Queensland, the left-hander Laver was the only player twice to win
the four major singles championships (British, American, French, and Australian) in
one year, first in 1962 and then in 1969. In all he won 11 Grand Slam titles. He was
known as the *Rocket* or the *Rockhampton Rocket* because of the power with which he
hit the ball. When Laver was still a teenager, the tag was coined by the Australian
tennis coach Harry Hopman.

The Rocket[2]   (William) Roger Clemens (b.1962), US baseball player, a pitcher with
the Boston Red Sox. He was known as the *Rocket* because of his powerful build and
the speed of his deliveries.

Rodders   Harrods, a large and prestigious London department store which originated when Charles Henry Harrod (1800–85), English grocer and tea merchant, took
over a shop in Knightsbridge, London, in 1853. This was subsequently expanded by
his son, Charles Digby Harrod (1841–1905). From the late 1940s it was fashionably
known as *Rodders* or ROD'S. ➤ See also FRED'S

Rod's   Harrods department store. ➤ See RODDERS.

Roscius   ➤ See *The* ENGLISH *Roscius, The* YOUNG *Roscius.*

The Rose-red City   The ancient city of Petra, capital of the Nabataeans from 312 BC
until 63 BC, when they became subject to Rome. The city's extensive ruins include
temples and tombs carved in the reddish sandstone cliffs. Its famous sobriquet
comes from a poem by the English clergyman John William Burgon (1813–88), with
which he won the Newdigate Prize: 'Match me such marvel, save in Eastern
clime,—/A rose-red city—half as old as Time!' (*Petra*, 1845).

Le Rougeaud   Michel Ney (1768–1815), French marshal. He was one of Napoleon's
leading generals and commanded the French cavalry at Waterloo (1815). His soldiers
called him *Le Rougeaud* ('Ginger') because of his red hair and short temper. ➤ See
also *The* BRAVEST *of the Brave.*

The Rough Rider   Theodore Roosevelt (1858–1919), US Republican statesman, 26th
President of the US 1901–9. During the Spanish–American War of 1898, Roosevelt
had raised and commanded a volunteer cavalry force that became known as the
Rough Riders. The name later came to be applied to Roosevelt himself, celebrating
his status as a war hero. ➤ See also BULL *Moose.*

The Royal Martyr   Charles I (1600–49), son of James I, king of England, Scotland, and Ireland 1625–49. ➤ See *The* MARTYR *King*.

The Royals   ➤ See *The* BLUES *and Royals*.

Ruby Nose   Oliver Cromwell (1599–1658), English general and statesman, Lord Protector of the Commonwealth 1653–58. ➤ See COPPER *Nose*.

Rufus   William II (*c.*1060–1100), son of William I, king of England 1087–1100. William acquired his nickname *Rufus* (meaning 'red-faced') because of his ruddy complexion.

The Runaway Spartan   Robert Peel (1788–1850), British Conservative statesman, Prime Minister 1834–35 and 1841–46. Formerly known as Orange Peel because of his anti-Catholic stance when Chief Secretary for Ireland (1812–18), he later changed this position and helped to pass the Catholic Emancipation Act of 1829. He then became known as the *Runaway Spartan*. ➤ See also ORANGE *Peel*.

The Rupert of Debate   Edward Stanley, later 14th Earl of Derby (1799–1869), British statesman and brilliant parliamentary speaker. On 24 April 1844, Disraeli said of Stanley in the House of Commons: 'The noble Lord is the Prince Rupert of parliamentary discussion; his charge is resistless; but when he returns from pursuit he always finds his camp in the possession of the enemy.' He was subsequently dubbed the *Rupert of Debate* by the British novelist and politician Edward Bulwer-Lytton, who compared Stanley's parliamentary style to the dashing cavalry charges of Prince Rupert in the Civil War: 'Here Stanley meets,—how Stanley scorns the glance!/The brilliant chief, irregularly great,/Frank, haughty, rash,—the Rupert of Debate!' (*The New Timon* (1846)). In similar fashion, Macaulay called him the HOTSPUR OF DEBATE.

The Rusty Buckles   The Queen's Bays (2nd Dragoon Guards), a regiment of the British army. Their nickname the *Rusty Buckles* dates from the 18th century. On returning from the damp climate of Ireland with rusty horse irons, they found that all other cavalry regiments had in the meantime replaced their steel bits and buckles with brass ones. ➤ See also *The* BAYS.

Ss

The Sagebrush State The US state of Nevada. The sagebrush is a shrubby aromatic North American plant of the daisy family (*Artemisia tridentata* and related species) which is abundant in the arid state of Nevada. It is the state's official flower and gives Nevada its nickname the *Sagebrush State*. ➤ See also *The* BATTLE-BORN *State, The* SILVER *State*.

The Sage of Chelsea Thomas Carlyle (1795–1881), Scottish historian and political philosopher. His works, written in a complex, powerful, though sometimes obscure literary style, include the autobiographical *Sartor Resartus* (1833–34) and his history of the French Revolution (1837). One of the leading 19th-century thinkers, Carlyle had considerable influence on the development of social and political ideas in Britain. He lived at No. 24 Cheyne Row, Chelsea, London from 1834 until he died, and was visited there by almost every literary celebrity of the time.

The Sage of Monticello Thomas Jefferson (1743–1826), US Democratic Republican statesman, 3rd President of the US 1801–9. Monticello was the name of the house near Charlotteville, Virginia, that Jefferson designed for himself. ➤ See also LONG *Tom*.

The Sage of Wheatland James Buchanan (1791–1868), American Democratic statesman, 15th President of the US 1857–61. After serving as president, Buchanan retired to his home in Wheatland, Pennsylvania, where he became known as the *Sage of Wheatland*. ➤ See also *The* BACHELOR *President*.

The Sailor King William IV (1765–1837), son of George III, king of Great Britain and Ireland 1830–7. Before he came to the throne (at the age of 65) on the death of his brother George IV, his whole life had been spent in the Royal Navy. At the age of 13 he joined his first ship as a midshipman in 1779, eventually rising to the rank of Lord High Admiral in 1827. A later monarch who is sometimes given the same nickname is George V, who served 15 years in the Royal Navy and was a keen yachtsman. ➤ See also GRANDPA *England*, SILLY *Billy*.

The Saint Simon Templar, the debonair gentleman-criminal created by the thriller writer Leslie Charteris (1907–93). Nicknamed the *Saint* on account of his essential decency and perhaps also because of his initials, he first appeared in *Meet the Tiger* (1928) and *Enter the Saint* (1930). His symbol is a haloed stick-figure, which he habitually leaves behind as his calling-card. He was played in a long-running television series by the actor Roger Moore.

St Mugg (Thomas) Malcolm Muggeridge (1903–90), British journalist, writer, and broadcaster. He often explored spiritual and religious issues on television, at first from a sceptical perspective. Following his conversion to Roman Catholicism in 1982, he earned his somewhat ironic nickname *St Mugg*.

The Saints Southampton football club. The nickname the *Saints* stems from the club's formation in 1885. The team was originally named Southampton St Mary's, since many of the founding players were members of St Mary's Church YMCA. The connection with the church remained strong in the club's early years; indeed, its first president was the Reverend A. B. Sole, curate of St Mary's. This link has been re-established in recent years with the club's move to its new stadium, St Mary's.

The Sally Ann The Salvation Army. ➤ See *The* SALLY *Army*.

Sally Army The Salvation Army, an international Christian organization for evangelistic and social work among the poor and destitute, founded in 1865 by William Booth and given its present name in 1878. It is organized along quasi-military lines. The organization is also sometimes referred to as the SALLY ANN. The use of *Sally* as an affectionate name for the Salvation Army dates back to the early 20th century.

The Sandlapper State The US state of South Carolina. The nickname the *Sandlapper State* is said to allude to some of its early settlers who lived on barren sand ridges in such poverty and hardship that they were forced to eat sand in order to survive. ➤ See also *The* GAMECOCK *State*, *The* PALMETTO *State*.

Sankey's Horse The 39th Foot (later the 1st Battalion Dorset Regiment), a regiment of the British army. Their nickname *Sankey's Horse* is attributed to an episode in 1707 when Colonel Sankey is said to have ordered his men to ride on mules in order to get to the scene of the Battle of Almanza in time to take part in it.

Sarah Heartburn Sarah Bernhardt (1844–1923), French actress. She was humorously known as *Sarah Heartburn*, a playful reversal of her surname. ➤ See also *The* DIVINE *Sarah*.

Satchmo (Daniel) Louis Armstrong (1900–71), US jazz musician, celebrated for his brilliant improvisatory trumpet playing and distinctive gravelly voice. In the 1920s he made over 60 recordings with the Hot Five and Hot Seven, later leading various bands such as the Louis Armstrong All-Stars. Armstrong's most popular nickname derived from the slang term *satchel-mouth*, denoting a person with a big mouth. He sometimes referred to his trumpet too as Satchelmouth. The abbreviated form *Satchmo*, later itself shortened to *Satch*, seems to date from around 1932. According to Armstrong, the first occasion he was addressed as Satchmo was in England by the then editor of *Melody Maker*, Percy Mathison Brooks. ➤ See also DIPPERMOUTH, POPS.

The Say Hey Kid Willie (Howard) Mays (b.1931), US baseball player, mostly for the New York Giants and San Francisco Giants. A great centerfielder, he hit 660 home runs during his 22-year career (1951–73). Mays acquired the nickname the *Say Hey Kid* at the start of his career because of his difficulty remembering other players' names. To catch their attention he would shout 'Say, hey!'

Scarface Al(phonse) Capone (1899–1947), US gangster, of Italian descent, who was heavily involved in organized crime in Chicago in the 1920s and controlled a vast bootlegging empire. His nickname *Scarface*, or *Scarface Al*, which Capone himself detested, derived from a huge scar on his left cheek. This was the result of a razor slash he received in a Brooklyn gang fight in his youth. He was eventually imprisoned in 1931 for federal income tax evasion.

The Scarlet Lancers   The 16th Lancers (later the 16th/5th (the Queen's Royal) Lancers), a regiment of the British army. After 1846 the 16th were the only light cavalry regiment permitted to retain the dragoon's scarlet tunic. As a result the regiment became known thereafter as the *Scarlet Lancers*.

The Scarlet Pimpernel   Sir Percy Blakeney, the hero of a series of novels by Baroness Orczy (1865–1947), including *The Scarlet Pimpernel* (1905). A dashing but elusive Englishman who daringly rescues aristocrats from the guillotine during the French Reign of Terror, he hides his true nature beneath a lazy and foppish exterior. His calling-card is the sign of the red flower from which he takes his assumed name.

Schnozzola   Jimmy (James Francis) Durante (1893–1980), US comedian and entertainer. After a long career in vaudeville, night clubs, and films, he made a successful move into television in the 1950s. He was popularly known as *Schnozzola* (or *Schnozzle*) because of his big nose. *Schnozz* or *schnozzle* is US slang for the nose, from a Yiddish word deriving from the German word *Schnauze* meaning a snout.

The Scottish Orpheus   James I (1394–1437), king of Scotland (1406–37). For the first 18 years of his reign, James was a prisoner of the English. A talented poet and musician, he composed his poem *The Kingis Quair* ('The King's Book') (1423–24) while a captive in England. In Greek mythology, Orpheus was a poet said to be able to entrance wild beasts with the beauty of his singing and lyre playing.

The Scourge of God   Attila (406–53), king of the Huns 434–53. He ravaged vast areas between the Rhine and the Caspian Sea, inflicting great devastation on the eastern Roman Empire, before being defeated by the joint forces of the Roman army and the Visigoths at Châlons in 451. His title the *Scourge of God* is a translation of the Latin term *flagellum Dei*, applied by historians to Attila. The term is recorded in English from the 14th century.

Scu   Peter (Michael) Scudamore (b.1958), English National Hunt jockey. He was champion jockey from 1986 to 1992 and in the 1988–89 season he rode a record 221 winners. By his retirement in 1993 he had ridden a total of 1 678 winners. He was known as *Scu*, a shortening of his surname.

The Scud   Mark Philippoussis (b.1976), Australian tennis player. Noted for his blistering serve, he is nicknamed the *Scud*, after a type of long-range guided missile. The nickname has been useful to headline-writers who are able to avoid using the player's long surname in headlines such as 'Scud grounded ' or 'Scud launches at Wimbledon'.

The Sea-born City   The city of Venice, Italy. In his poem *Beppo* (1817), Byron says of Venice: 'That sea-born city was in all her glory'. ➤ See also *The* BRIDE *of the Sea*.

The Sea-green Incorruptible   Maximilien François Marie Isidore de Robespierre (1758–94), French revolutionary. As leader of the radical Jacobins in the National Assembly he backed the execution of Louis XVI, implemented a purge on the Girondists, and initiated the Terror, but the following year he fell from power and was guillotined. Thomas Carlyle described him as the *Sea-green Incorruptible* in his *History of the French Revolution* (1837). One contemporary description of Robespierre refers to the prominent veins in his forehead that showed greenish-blue against his pale skin. His 'incorruptibility' stemmed from his impartiality and upholding of democratic principles.

The Senior   The United Service Club in London, founded in 1815 by veterans of the Napoleonic wars. It was known as the *Senior* since its membership was largely drawn from the senior ranks of the Army and Navy.

The Seraphic Doctor   St Bonaventura (1221–74), Franciscan theologian. Appointed minister general of his order in 1257, he was made cardinal bishop of Albano in 1273. He wrote the official biography of St Francis and had a lasting influence as a spiritual writer. His sobriquet the *Seraphic Doctor* is in Spain applied to St Teresa of Ávila (1515–82), the Spanish Carmelite nun and mystic.

Shagger Norris   Steven (John) Norris (b.1945), British Conservative politician. He acquired the tabloid nickname *Shagger Norris* in 1993 while he was a transport minister, following revelations in the press of several mistresses. Norris was an unsuccessful candidate in the 2000 election for mayor of London.

The Shakers   Bury football club. One of the club's first chairmen once predicted that his team would give a rival team 'a good shaking', hence the nickname they acquired, the *Shakers*.

Shanks   Bill Shankly (1913–81), Scottish footballer and manager. He managed Liverpool FC for 15 years (1959–74), during which period the club won three league championships, two FA Cup finals, and one UEFA Cup. He was affectionally known as *Shanks*.

Shaq   Shaquille (Rashaun) O'Neal (b.1972), US basketball player. At 7ft 1in, *Shaq* O'Neal is a towering presence on a basketball court and generally held to be the most dominant player in the game since Michael Jordan. He led his team the Los Angeles Lakers to NBA Finals victories in 2000, 2001, and 2002.

The Shepherd Lord   Henry de Clifford, 14th Baron Clifford (?1455–1523). During the Wars of the Roses, his father was killed fighting for the Lancastrians and his estates forfeited (1461). Henry de Clifford was brought up as a shepherd, and his estates and title restored to him on the accession to the throne of Henry VII. His nickname the *Shepherd Lord* is used by Wordsworth in 'Song at the Feast at Brougham Castle' (1807).

The Shepherd of the Ocean   Walter Raleigh (*c*.1552–1618), English explorer, courtier, and writer. Raleigh organized several voyages of exploration and colonization to the Americas. The title the *Shepherd of the Ocean* was coined by the poet Edmund Spenser (1552–99): 'Whom when I asked from what place he came,/ And how he hight, himselfe he did ycleepe,/The shepheard of the Ocean by name,/And said he came far from the main-sea deepe.' ('Colin Clout's Come Home Againe', 1595). The sobriquet was subsequently used by Raleigh himself.

Sherry   Richard Brinsley Sheridan (1751–1816), Irish dramatist and Whig politician. He is best known for his comedies of manners such as *The Rivals* (1775) and *The*

School for Scandal (1777). In the House of Commons Sheridan was a celebrated orator and a frequent adversary of the prime minister William Pitt the Younger. A Gillray cartoon of 1805 entitled 'Uncorking Old Sherry' depicts Pitt pulling out the cork from a bottle-shaped Sheridan to release a torrent of insults, lies, and stolen jests.

The She-Wolf of France   Isabella of France (1292–1358), daughter of Philip IV of France (*Philip the Fair*). She was queen consort of Edward II of England from 1308, but returned to France in 1325. She plotted with her lover Roger de Mortimer to overthrow her husband and order his murder at Berkeley Castle, by having a red-hot iron thrust into his bowels. Thomas Gray's poem 'The Bard' (1757) includes these lines: 'She-wolf of France, with unrelenting fangs,/That tear'st the bowels of thy mangled mate'.

The Shoe   Willie (William Lee) Shoemaker (1931–2003), US jockey. During his long career, which lasted from 1949 to 1990, Shoemaker, universally known as the *Shoe*, rode 8 833 winners. In 1986, at the age of 54, he became the oldest jockey to win the Kentucky Derby, a race he first won 32 years previously. He was the first jockey to reach $100 million in earnings.

Shoeless Joe   Joe (Joseph Jefferson) Jackson (1889–1951), US baseball player, one of the great hitters in the history of the game. He was banned from baseball for his involvement in the 1919 'Black Sox' scandal, in which Jackson and seven other Chicago White Sox players were bribed to throw the 1919 World Series. After Jackson gave his testimony at the ensuing trial, a tearful boy is said to have approached his idol and implored him to 'Say it ain't so, Joe'.

The Shop   The former Royal Military Academy at Woolwich in London. Founded in 1741, it was familiarly known among the military as the *Shop*. In 1946 the academy was merged with the Royal Military College at Sandhurst in Berkshire.

The Show Me State   The US state of Missouri. 'Show Me' here refers to what was regarded as the characteristically sceptical approach of the people of Missouri. In 1902 Willard D. Vandiner, a former Congressman from Columbia, Missouri, is reputed to have said 'I'm from Missouri, and you've got to show me.' ➤ See also *The* BULLION *State, The* PUKE *State.*

The Shrimp   Jean (Rosemary) Shrimpton (b.1942), English fashion model of the 1960s who helped introduce the miniskirt. She was nicknamed the *Shrimp*, an abbreviation of her surname that fitted her slight figure.

The Sick Man of Europe   Ottoman Turkey, during its 19th-century decline. The nickname the *Sick Man of Europe* derives from a reported conversation between Tsar Nicholas I of Russia and Sir George Seymour at St Petersburg on 21 February 1853. In the Annual Register for 1853, the Tsar is quoted as saying, 'I am not so eager about what shall be done when the sick man dies, as I am to determine with England what shall not be done upon that event taking place.'

Sicknote   Darren Anderton (b.1972), English footballer. Anderton has been injury-prone during his career, missing many games for his club, hence the nickname conferred on him by exasperated Tottenham Hotspur supporters. A sick note is a note given to an employer or teacher explaining a person's absence due to illness.

Silent Cal (John) Calvin Coolidge (1872–1933), US Republican statesman, 30th President of the US 1923–29. His utterances were famously laconic, his economy with words earning him the sobriquet *Silent Cal*. In the summer of 1927 he announced abruptly 'I do not choose to run for president in 1928.' When his death was announced, humorist Dorothy Parker is said to have remarked, 'How could they tell?'

Silicon Alley ➤See SILICON *Valley*.

Silicon Fen ➤See SILICON *Valley*.

Silicon Glen ➤See SILICON *Valley*.

Silicon Prairie ➤See SILICON *Valley*.

Silicon Valley An area with a high concentration of computing and electronics companies or industries, originally referring specifically to an area between San José and Palo Alto in Santa Clara County south-east of San Francisco, California. The term derives from the silicon chip. On the same model, there is a so-called SILICON GLEN in central lowland Scotland, a SILICON FEN in Cambridge, a SILICON PRAIRIE near Dallas, Texas, and a SILICON ALLEY in New York.

Silly Billy William IV (1765–1837), son of George III, king of Great Britain and Ireland 1830–7. According to one story, William was visiting the Bedlam asylum for the insane when one of the inmates pointed at him and called out 'Silly Billy! Silly Billy!' The nickname *Silly Billy* stuck as he had a reputation for being somewhat foolish. It was also applied to William Frederick, 2nd Duke of Gloucester (1776–1834). ➤See also *The* SAILOR *King*.

The Silver State The US state of Nevada. The discovery of silver in 1858 led to the rapid growth of silver mining in Nevada, hence its nickname the *Silver State*. ➤See also *The* BATTLE-BORN *State*, *The* SAGEBRUSH *State*.

The Singer's Singer This coveted sobriquet has been bestowed on two US singers, Tony Bennett and Mel Tormé. Tony Bennett (Antonio Dominick Benedetto) (b.1926) is the jazz-influenced singer of pop ballads such as 'I Left My Heart in San Francisco' (1962) who Frank Sinatra called 'the best singer in the business'. Mel Tormé (Melvin Howard Tormé) (1925–99) was the much-admired crooner of the late 1940s and 1950s. ➤See also *The* VELVET *Fog*.

The Singing Capon Nelson Eddy (1901–67), US singer and film star. ➤See *The* IRON *Butterfly*.

The Singing Cowboy Two US film actors were known as the *Singing Cowboy*, Roy Rogers and Gene Autry. Roy Rogers (born Leonard Slye) (1912–98) starred and sang in numerous B-film westerns of the 1930s and 1940s, accompanied by his horse Trigger. (Orvan) Gene Autry (1907–98), with his horse Champion, replaced Rogers as cinema's most popular singing cowboy, before moving to television in the 1950s. ➤See also *The* KING *of the Cowboys*.

Singing Indurain   Miguel Indurain (b.1964), Spanish cyclist. He became only the fourth cyclist to win five Tours de France (1991–95). His nickname is *Singing Indurain*, a delightful pun on the title of the Gene Kelly musical *Singin' in the Rain* (1952).

Single-speech Hamilton   William Gerard Hamilton (1729–96), politician. On 13 November 1755 he made a celebrated and eloquent maiden speech in the House of Commons, of which Horace Walpole enthused, 'You will ask, what could be beyond this? Nothing but what was beyond what ever was, and that was Pitt!' It has been suggested that Hamilton's speech may have been drafted for him by his friend Samuel Johnson. Although Hamilton was to make other speeches in the House, the nickname he acquired derived from the reputation of this first one.

The Sioux State   The US state of North Dakota. It is sometimes called the *Sioux State* in reference to the Sioux, a North American Indian people, also known as the Dakota (meaning 'allies'), who once occupied the plains and prairies of the territory. ➤ See also *The* FLICKERTAIL *State, The* PEACE *Garden State*.

Sir Geoffrey   Geoffrey Boycott (b.1940), English cricketer. ➤ See BOYCS.

Sir Reverse   Sir Redvers Henry Buller (1839–1908), British general. After a highly successful military career he served as Commander-in-Chief during the Second Boer War (1899–1900). When the Boers inflicted a succession of humiliating defeats on the British army, Buller found himself mocked by the public as *Sir Reverse*.

Sir Shortly Floorcross   Sir Hartley (William) Shawcross (1902–2003), British politician. He served as Attorney-General 1945–51 in the Labour government, but resigned from the party in 1958, earning himself the ingenious nickname *Sir Shortly Floorcross*. In the British House of Commons, to 'cross the floor' is to change one's party allegiance, literally by moving across the *floor* or open space which divides the Government and the Opposition benches.

Sir Veto   Andrew Johnson (1808–75), US Democratic statesman, 17th President of the US 1865–69. Johnson was elected vice-president in 1864 and succeeded the assassinated Abraham Lincoln. His policy of conciliation towards the defeated southern states after the Civil War was bitterly opposed by the radical Republicans in Congress. They called him *Sir Veto* because he repeatedly tried to use his presidential veto to block a series of bills laying down harsh conditions for the readmission of the ex-Confederate states to the Union. ➤ See also *The* ACCIDENTAL *President*.

Sixteen-string Jack   John Rann (d.1774), English highwayman. A foppish dandy, he was known as *Sixteen-string Jack*. According to the New Newgate Calendar (1780), this was on account of his 'wearing breeches with eight strings at each knee'. Rann was executed at Tyburn in 1774.

Skeeter   Wilma (Glodean) Rudolph (1940–94), US athlete. She won three sprint gold medals at the 1960 Olympics, in the 100m, 200m and relay. Her nickname *Skeeter* (US slang for a mosquito) was coined by her high school basketball coach Clinton Gray who told her, 'You're little and fast and you always get in my way'. Rudolph was born with polio and at the age of four she contracted double pneumonia and scarlet fever simultaneously. For a time she was unable to use her left leg and she had to wear a leg brace until she was eight.

Skeets Renaldo Nehemiah (b.1959), US athlete. Between 1978 and 1981 he was the finest high hurdler in the world, but in 1982 joined the San Francisco 49ers to begin a career in professional football. He returned to the track in 1986.

The Skins The 5th Royal Inniskilling Dragoon Guards, a regiment of the British army. Their nickname the *Skins* is derived from 'Inniskilling'.

The Slashers The 28th Foot (later the Gloucestershire Regiment), a regiment of the British army. There are two possible explanations for their nickname the *Slashers*. According to one story, soldiers from the regiment sliced off the ear of a troublesome magistrate called Thomas Walker in Canada in 1764. The other story relates to an episode at the Battle for White Plains during the American War of Independence. Although under fire, the 28th defeated the Americans using their swords rather than their muskets.

Slick Willy Bill (William Jefferson) Clinton (b.1946), US Democratic statesman, 42nd President of the US 1993–2001. Having become Attorney-General of Arkansas in 1976, he was elected state Governor in 1978 and served five terms 1979–81 and 1983–92. Clinton's enemies in Arkansas, who accused him of dubious political tactics and evasiveness, gave him the nickname *Slick Willy*. The label is thought to have been coined by John Robert Starr, editor of the *Arkansas Democrat*. ➤ See also *The* COMEBACK *Kid*.

Sly Sylvester Stallone, Italian-born US film actor. ➤ See *The* ITALIAN *Stallion*.

Smack Fletcher Hamilton Henderson (1898–1952), US jazz pianist, composer, arranger, and bandleader. Henderson's arrangements for big bands, many of which were used by Benny Goodman's band, were enormously influential on the sound of the swing era. His nickname was apparently from the smacking sound he made with his lips. There does not seem to be any connection with the slang use of the term to mean heroin.

The Smith of Smiths Sydney Smith (1771–1845), English clergyman, essayist, and wit. He was a co-founder in 1802 of the periodical the *Edinburgh Review*, to which he subsequently became a witty contributor. His nickname was coined by Lord Macaulay in a letter to his father in 1826: 'Down I went, and to my utter amazement beheld the Smith of Smiths, Sydney Smith.' In 1831 Smith was made a canon of St Paul's.

The Smoke London, and other large cities. ➤ See *The* BIG *Smoke*.

Smokey Viv Richards (full name Isaac Vivian Alexander Richards) (b.1952), West Indian cricketer. Born in Antigua, he made his debut for the West Indies in 1974, captaining the team from 1985 to 1991. During his Test career Richards scored over 6 000 runs. He was nicknamed *Smokey* because of his resemblance to the boxer SMOKIN' JOE Frazier. ➤ See also SMOKIN' *Joe*.

Smokin' Joe Joe (Joseph) Frazier (b.1944), US boxer, world heavyweight champion 1970–73. The non-stop fiery aggression with which Frazier threw his left hooks earned him his nickname *Smokin' Joe*. He fought Muhammad Ali in the famous 'Thrilla in Manila' in 1975.

The Snappers   The 15th Foot (later the East Yorkshires), a regiment of the British army. During the Battle of Brandywine in 1777 the regiment ran low of ammunition. What remained was allocated to the marksmen, while the rest of the men were given orders to snap their firelocks at the enemy to imitate the sound of gunfire. The 15th Foot subsequently became known as the *Snappers*.

Sniffer   Allan Clarke (b.1946), English footballer. He played for Leeds United 1969–78 and won 19 caps for England. He was known as *Sniffer* because of his ability to sniff out goal-scoring opportunities.

The Snow King   Frederick of Bohemia (1596–1632). ➤ See *The* WINTER *King*.

The Snow Queen   Elizabeth of Bohemia (1596–1662). ➤ See *The* WINTER *Queen*.

Soapy Sam   Samuel Wilberforce, (1805–73), Bishop of Oxford. The nickname *Soapy Sam* was first applied to him after Lord Westbury in the House of Lords had described Wilberforce's synodical judgement on 'Essays and Reviews' as 'a well-lubricated set of words, a sentence so oily and saponaceous that no one can grasp it'. Wilberforce himself declared that he owed his nickname to the fact that 'though often in hot water, he always came out with clean hands'.

Softsword   John (1165–1216), son of Henry II, king of England 1199–1216. John earned the epithet *Softsword* after making peace with Philip II of France by the Treaty of Goulet in 1200. By 1205 John had humiliatingly lost Normandy and most of his French territories to Philip. ➤ See also LACKLAND.

Son of Sam   David Richard Berkowitz (b.1953), mass murderer. He terrorized New York City from July 1976 to August 1977, killing six young women in attacks on courting couples before he was caught. Berkowitz called himself *Son of Sam* in letters he wrote to the press and the police department, a name he took from that of his neighbour Sam Carr.

The Son of the Last Man   Charles II (1630–85), king of England, Scotland, and Ireland 1660–85. The Parliamentarians referred to his father Charles I as the LAST MAN, that is, the last king of England. Charles II was defiantly dubbed the *Son of the Last Man* by the Royalists. ➤ See also *The* BLACK *Boy*, *The* LAST *Man*, *The* MERRY *Monarch*, OLD *Rowley*.

The Sooner State   The US state of Oklahoma. *Sooner* here is in the sense 'one who acts prematurely', alluding to those who tried to get into the frontier territory of Oklahoma before the US government formally opened it to settlers in 1889. Oklahoma City was settled virtually overnight in a land rush. A Sooner is colloquially a native of Oklahoma.

Spaghetti Junction   Gravelly Hill interchange on the M6 near Birmingham in the UK, opened in 1971. The term *spaghetti junction* can be applied to any similarly complex multi-level junction of intersecting roads, especially one on a motorway.

Sparky   Mark Hughes (b.1962), Welsh footballer. In the 1980s and 1990s he made 345 league appearances for Manchester United and 108 for Chelsea, also playing for such clubs as Barcelona, Bayern Munich, and Southampton. Hughes was known as *Sparky* on account of his fiery, combative temperament on the pitch. He has gone on to manage the Welsh national team.

The Speck Tasmania. The island is sometimes referred to by the derogatory nickname the *Speck* on account of its tiny size compared to continental Australia. ➤ See also APPLE *Island*, TASSIE.

The Sphinx Franklin Delano Roosevelt (1882–1945), US Democratic statesman, 32nd President of the US 1933–45. In 1939, having served two terms as president, Roosevelt's inscrutabilty regarding his intentions about seeking a third term caused the press to refer to him as the *Sphinx*. ➤ See also FDR.

Spider Althea Gibson (1927–2003), US tennis player, the first black player to win a major tennis championship. Gibson's titles included the French and Italian championships (1956) and the British and American titles (1957 and 1958).

The Spireites Chesterfield football club. Their nickname the *Spireites* stems from the famous crooked spire of St Mary's All Saints Church in Chesterfield.

The Splendid Splinter Ted (Theodore Samuel) Williams (1918–2002), US baseball player. He played for 19 years with the Boston Red Sox (1939–60), during which he had 2654 hits and hit 521 home runs. Williams was known as the *Splendid Splinter* and TEDDY BALLGAME.

Spurs Tottenham Hotspur football club. In 1882 a group of London schoolboys formed a football team which they named Hotspur FC. This alluded to Harry Hotspur, the Shakespearean character and member of the Northumberland family, whose ancestral home was near Tottenham Marshes where their first matches were played. A few years later the club's name was changed to Tottenham Hotspur. Its nickname *Spurs* is an abbreviation of *Hotspur*. ➤ See also HOTSPUR.

The Square Mile The City of London, the part of London governed by the Lord Mayor and the Corporation. An important commercial and financial centre, its precise area is 677 acres, slightly over one square mile.

The Squatter State The US state of Kansas. Immediately before the Civil War, both pro-slavery and anti-slavery groups endeavoured to rush settlers into the territory of Kansas, hence one of its nicknames the *Squatter State*. ➤ See also *The* NAVEL *of the Nation*, *The* SUNFLOWER *State*.

Squiffy Herbert Henry Asquith (1852–1928), British Liberal statesman, Prime Minister 1908–16. Asquith had a reputation as a heavy drinker, which earned him his nickname *Squiffy* or OLD SQUIFFY. After he had been displaced as Prime Minister by Lloyd George in December 1916, his followers became known as 'Squiffites'.

Stalin Joseph Stalin, born Iosif Vissarionovich Dzhugashvili (1879–1953). Soviet statesman, General Secretary of the Communist Party of the USSR 1922–53. By 1913 he had adopted the name *Stalin*, meaning 'man of steel'. This may have been intended to reflect his steely resilience throughout the preceding ten-year period in which he had been repeatedly arrested, imprisoned, and exiled to Siberia. ➤ See also UNCLE *Joe*.

Stalky Lionel Corkran, the leader of three schoolboys in Rudyard Kipling's collection of short stories *Stalky & Co* (1899). The nickname *Stalky*, meaning clever, cunning, and stealthy (i.e. good at stalking), had originally belonged to Lionel 'Stalky' Dunsterville, Kipling's schoolfriend at the United Services College at Westward Ho! in Devon.

The Stammerer Lambert, 12th-century priest of Liège. ➤ See *Le* BÈGUE.

Stan the Man Stan (Stanley Frank) Musial (b.1920), US baseball player. One of the most consistent performers in the history of the game, he played his entire career with the St Louis Cardinals (1941–63). In British sport, the nickname is usually applied to the English footballer Stan Collymore (b.1971), whose clubs included Crystal Palace, Nottingham Forest, Liverpool, and Aston Villa.

Starvation Dundas Henry Dundas, 1st Viscount Melville (1742–1811), British Tory politician. His nickname *Starvation Dundas* alludes to a parliamentary speech he made about the prospect of famine in the American colonies resulting from a 1775 bill restricting trade with the New England colonies. He had said in a debate on 6 March 1775 that he was 'afraid' that the famine spoken of 'would not be produced by this Act'. This was said to be the first use of the word *starvation* in English, although it does not occur in Dundas's actual speech.

Steel Magnolia Rosalynn Carter (born Eleanor Rosalynn Smith) (b.1927), US First Lady 1977–81, married to President Jimmy Carter. The term 'steel magnolia' is used in the US to describe a woman from the southern states who has a tough character beneath a feminine and apparently fragile exterior. Together with *Iron Magnolia*, it was often applied to Rosalynn Carter.

Steenie George Villiers, Duke of Buckingham (1592–1628), English courtier and royal favourite. James I's pet name for the good-looking Villiers was *Steenie*, a Scotticism for Stephen. It was an allusion to a passage from Acts 6:15, in which those who gazed at St Stephen 'saw his face as it had been the face of an angel'.

Sticks Twiggy (born Lesley Hornby) (b.1949), English fashion model of the 1960s. She began her modelling career in 1966, becoming famous for her thin-bodied boyish look. Her professional name was a nickname given her by the photographer Justin de Villeneuve, and was itself based on her schoolgirl nickname of *Sticks*.

Stonewall Thomas Jonathan Jackson (1824–63), US Confederate general. During the American Civil War he made his mark as a commander at the first battle of Bull Run in 1861 and later became the deputy of Robert E. Lee. His nickname derives from a comment by his fellow Confederate general Barnard Elliott Bee (1823–61) at the battle of Bull Run, in which Bee himself was killed: 'There is Jackson with his Virginians, standing like a stone wall. Let us determine to die here, and we will conquer' (21 July 1861). It is not entirely clear whether Bee was praising Jackson's stubborn resistance or denouncing his failure to come to Bee's support. Whatever Bee meant by his words (and he died before he could clarify the matter), Jackson became thereafter known by the unambiguously heroic nickname *Stonewall Jackson*.

Stormin' Norman H. Norman Schwarzkopf (b.1935), US general. Before entering the US military academy at West Point in 1952, he dropped the name Herbert, which he disliked, and legally changed it to the initial H. Early in his army career he was dubbed *Stormin' Norman* in reference to his forceful personality and volatile temper. Schwarzkopf was Commander-in-Chief of the Allied forces during the Gulf War (1991), when the nickname seemed to fit well with his purposeful, dynamic image. He became a national hero overnight and retired later in 1991. ➤ See also *The* BEAR.

Stroller   George Graham (b.1944), Scottish football player and manager. As a player he was a member of the 1970–71 Arsenal side that won the League and Cup double. He repeated this feat as a manager with the same club in 1993. Graham was dubbed *Stroller* during his playing days at Arsenal, because of his unhurried calm in midfield.

The Stub-toe State   The US state of Montana. One of Montana's early nicknames was the *Stub-toe State* because of its steep mountain slopes. ➤ See also *The* TREASURE *State*.

La Stupenda   Joan Sutherland (b.1926), Australian operatic soprano, noted for her dramatic coloratura roles. She was acclaimed for her performance of the title role in Donizetti's *Lucia di Lammermoor* at Covent Garden in 1959, and following her Italian debut in the same role two years later, the Milanese press accorded her the title *La Stupenda*.

Stupor Mundi   Frederick II (1194–1250), Holy Roman Emperor (1220–50). The term *Stupor Mundi* (Latin 'Wonder of the World') was applied to Frederick II in recognition of his extraordinary versatility. Not only a formidable statesman and soldier, he was highly cultured and a great patron of the arts and science. The title was originally used by the 13th-century chronicler Matthew Paris.

The Subtle Doctor   John Duns Scotus (*c.*1265–1308), Scottish theologian and scholar. He was the first major theologian to defend the theory of the Immaculate Conception, and opposed St Thomas Aquinas in arguing that faith was a matter of will rather than something dependent on logical proofs. His debating skill earned him his nickname the *Subtle Doctor* (a translation of the Latin DOCTOR SUBTILIS). In the 16th century his name, through his followers the Scotists, became associated with a scholasticism characterized by hair-splitting and useless distinctions, which was seen as inimical to the new learning. From this developed the word *dunce*.

The Sucker State   The US state of Illinois. Its nickname the *Sucker State* may derive from the fact that the local miners went to the mines in the spring and returned in the autumn, just as the sucker fish did in the rivers. ➤ See also *The* PRAIRIE *State*.

Sugar   Ray Robinson (born Walker Smith) (1920–89), US boxer, world welterweight champion 1946–51 and middleweight champion 1951–60. He acquired the name Ray Robinson in 1940 when he turned up for an amateur fight without having registered with the authorities and borrowed the card of another boxer. He decided to keep his adopted name. On a later occasion his manager George Gainford is said to have replied to a reporter's remark that Robinson was a 'sweet' fighter, 'Yes, he's as sweet as sugar.' From then on the boxer was known as Sugar Ray Robinson. The epithet was adopted by a later boxer Sugar Ray Leonard (b.1956).

The Sultan of Spin[1] Peter Mandelson (b.1953), British Labour politician. ➤ See *The* PRINCE *of Darkness.*

The Sultan of Spin[2] Shane Warne (b.1969), Australian cricketer. ➤ See HOLLYWOOD.

The Sultan of Swat Babe (George Herman) Ruth (1895–1948), US baseball player. He became known as the *Sultan of Swat* because of the force with which he hit (or 'swatted') the ball. The historical Sultan of Swat, or more properly the Akond of Swat, was Saidu Baba (d.1877), the ruler and high priest of Swat, a region of the northwestern part of the Indian subcontinent. The Akond of Swat was the subject of a piece of nonsense verse by the poet Edward Lear in 1873. ➤ See also *The* BABE.

The Sundance Kid Harry Longbaugh (1870–*c.*1909), US outlaw, member of the Wild Bunch gang and partner of Butch Cassidy. His nickname stems from Sundance, Wyoming Territory, where he served an 18-month term of imprisonment for horse-stealing. ➤ See also BUTCH *Cassidy.*

The Sunflower State The US state of Kansas. The sunflower is the state flower of Kansas, where they grow abundantly. ➤ See also *The* NAVEL *of the Nation, The* SQUATTER *State.*

The Sun King Louis XIV (1638–1715), son of Louis XIII, king of France 1643–1715. He is widely known as the *Sun King*, a translation of French *Le Roi Soleil.* The term derives from a heraldic device used by him and was intended to convey his pre-eminence as a ruler. His long reign represented the high point of the Bourbon dynasty and of French power in Europe, during which French art and literature flourished. ➤ See also *Le* GRAND *Monarque.*

Sunny Jim (Leonard) James Callaghan (1912–2005), British Labour statesman, Prime Minister 1976–79. Noted for his affable disposition, Jim Callaghan was widely known as *Sunny Jim*, a name which can be applied to any cheerful person. It comes from the name of a character used to advertise Force breakfast cereal early in the 20th century: 'High o'er the fence leaps Sunny Jim/"Force" is the food that raises him.'

The Sunshine State The US state of Florida. The nickname the *Sunshine State* is most closely associated with Florida, famous for its hot climate. The sobriquet has also been applied to New Mexico, South Dakota, and California. In 1992 the motto around the state seal of South Dakota was changed from 'The Sunshine State' to 'The Mount Rushmore State'. ➤ See also *The* LAND *of Flowers.*

Superbrat John (Patrick) McEnroe (b.1959), US tennis player. ➤ See MAC *the Mouth.*

Supermac[1] (Maurice) Harold Macmillan, 1st Earl of Stockton (1894–1986), British Conservative statesman, Prime Minister 1957–63. The *London Evening Standard* cartoonist Vicky (Victor Weisz (1913–66)) first depicted Macmillan as *Supermac* on 6 November 1958. He caricatured the prime minister as an elderly Superman, the US comic strip character created in 1938 by writer Jerry Siegel (1914–96) and artist Joe Shuster (1914–92). The nickname, intended to be mockingly satirical, came to be used instead as a term of admiration and affection. ➤ See also MAC *the Knife.*

Supermac² Malcolm Macdonald (b.1950), English footballer. A star player for Newcastle United in the 1970s, he was known as *Supermac* by the fans. Macdonald won 14 international caps, scoring five goals for England against Cyprus on 16 April 1975.

Supermex Lee (Buck) Trevino (b.1939), US golfer. Born in Dallas, Texas, of Mexican parentage, Trevino won three of the Majors twice: the US Open (1968, 1971), the British Open (1971, 1972), and the PGA (1974, 1984). Famous for his wise-cracking exuberance on the course, he was popularly known as *Supermex*.

The Supremo Louis (Francis Albert Victor Nicholas) Mountbatten, 1st Earl Mountbatten of Burma (1900–79), British admiral and adminstrator. Mountbatten served in the Royal Navy before rising to become Supreme Allied Commander in South-East Asia (1943–45), hence his nickname the *Supremo*. As the last viceroy (1947) and first Governor-General of India (1947–48), he oversaw the independence of India and Pakistan.

Swaddling John John Cennick (1718–55), Protestant divine. According to John Wesley, Cennick made frequent references when he preached to 'the babe that lay in the manger, the babe that lay in Mary's lap, the babe that lay in swaddling clouts'. From this he is supposed to have acquired the nickname *Swaddling John*, and the word *Swaddler* came to be applied by Roman Catholics to Wesleyans generally, especially preachers, and later to any Protestant.

The Swamp Fox Francis Marion (1732–95), US soldier and guerrilla fighter against the British in the American War of Independence. He was given the name the *Swamp Fox* by the British in reference to his hit-and-run tactics in the swamps of South Carolina. The British colonel Banastre Tarleton was provoked to comment of his elusive adversary: 'But as for this damned old fox, the devil himself could not catch him'.

The Swan of Avon William Shakespeare (1564–1616), English dramatist and poet, so called by Ben Jonson (in 'To the Memory of My Beloved, the Author, Mr William Shakespeare', a verse used to preface the First Folio of plays, 1623): 'Sweet Swan of Avon! What a sight it were/To see thee in our waters yet appear,/And make those flights upon the banks of Thames/That so did take Eliza, and our James!' The identification of poets and musicians with swans comes from a legend that the souls of the finest poets passed into swans. The name specified in the poet's title is often, as with Shakespeare, the river running through their birthplace. Accordingly, Homer was known as the *Swan of Meander* and Henry Vaughan the *Swan of Usk*. Sometimes the place most closely associated with the poet is specified, as in the *Mantuan Swan* (Virgil) and the SWAN OF LICHFIELD (Anna Seward). ➤ See also AVONIAN *Willy, The* BARD *of Avon.*

The Swan of Lichfield Anna Seward (1747–1809), English poet who, though born in Eyam in Derbyshire, spent most of her life in Lichfield, Staffordshire. A popular poet in her day, she was a leading figure of a literary circle and frequently met

Dr Johnson on his visits to his birthplace. She was known as the *Swan of Lichfield* by her contemporaries.

The Swan of Pesaro   Gioacchino Antonio Rossini (1792–1868), Italian composer. He wrote over thirty operas, including the comic opera *The Barber of Seville* (1816) and the grand opera *William Tell* (1829). He was one of the creators of the Italian bel canto style of singing, along with Bellini and Donizetti. Rossini was known as *Le Cygne de Pesaro* ('the *Swan of Pesaro*') after his birthplace. The burghers of Pesaro once approached Rossini to help pay for a statue to be erected in his honour in his native town, telling him that, although they had sufficient funds for the pedestal, they were looking for a donation of 10 000 francs to meet the cost of the statue itself. Rossini is said to have replied, 'For 10 000 francs I'd stand on the pedestal myself'.

The Sweater Girl   Lana Turner (Julia Jean Mildred Frances Turner) (1920–95), US film actress whose films include *The Postman Always Rings Twice* (1946), *The Bad and the Beautiful* (1952), and *Imitation of Life* (1959). She was promoted as the *Sweater Girl* at the start of her career, when she was encouraged to wear tight-fitting sweaters to accentuate her bust.

The Swedish Nightingale   Jenny Lind (born Johanna Maria Lind Goldschmidt) (1820–87), Swedish soprano, acclaimed for the purity and agility of her voice. Born in Stockholm, she became an international star with her performances in opera, oratorio, and concerts. She toured the US in 1850–52 with the showman P. T. Barnum. The *Swedish Nightingale*, as she was known, was very popular in England and eventually settled there.

Swee' Pea   Billy Strayhorn (William Thomas Strayhorn) (1915–67), US jazz pianist who worked closely with Duke Ellington as an arranger and composer. Among his compositions is 'Take the "A" Train', which became Ellington's signature tune. It was Ellington who gave his young collaborator the nickname *Swee' Pea*, naming him after the hyperactive baby in the Popeye comic strip cartoon, created by Elzie Segar in 1926.

The Sweeps   The Rifle Brigade, a regiment of the British army. The regimental nickname the *Sweeps* refers to its dark-coloured uniform and facings, reminiscent of chimney sweeps. It dates back to 1850.

Sweet Nell   Nell (Eleanor) Gwyn (1650–87), English actress and mistress to Charles II. She enjoyed great public popularity and was known as *Sweet Nell* and, because she used to sell oranges at the Drury Lane Theatre, NELL OF OLD DRURY. Samuel Pepys called her *Pretty Witty Nell*. Charles himself in his last illness is said to have requested, 'Let not poor Nelly starve.'

Sweetness   Walter (Jerry) Payton (1954–99), US footballer. He joined the Chicago Bears as a running back in 1975, spending his entire career with them until he retired in 1987. At the end of his 13-year career, he had set an NFL rushing record of 16 726yds (finally broken in 2002 by Emmitt Smith). In a game against Minnesota in 1977 he rushed for 275yds, a record for a single game that stood for nearly 23 years. Payton was known as *Sweetness*, a nickname he first acquired at Jackson State, both for the smoothness of his running style and for his temperament. In 1999 he died of a rare liver disease aged 45.

Sweet Swan of Avon ➤ See *The* SWAN *of Avon*.

The Sword of Rome Marcus Claudius Marcellus (*c.*268–208 BC), Roman general of the Second Punic War. Known as the *Sword of Rome*, he captured Syracuse in 212 BC after a two-year siege.

Tt

The Tangerines The 2nd Foot (later the Queen's Royal Regiment (West Surrey)), a regiment of the British army. ➤ See KIRKE's *Lambs*.

The Tar Heel State The US state of North Carolina. Its official nickname alludes to tar as a principal product of that state. The term Tarheel for a native or inhabitant of North Carolina dates back to the mid 19th century and is thought to have originated as a derogatory reference to a brigade of North Carolinians. Their failure to hold a position during a Civil War battle was blamed by Mississippians on the fact that they had failed to tar their heels that morning. ➤ See also *The* OLD *North State*.

Tarzan Michael Heseltine (b.1933), British Conservative politician. In the late 1980s and 1990s, *Tarzan* caught on in the popular press as a nickname for Heseltine. It was coined by the Labour MP Stanley Clinton-Davis who said that Heseltine reminded him of Johnny Weissmuller, an actor who had played Tarzan in a series of films. Clinton-Davis later explained that he had in fact meant Lex Barker, another screen Tarzan. Certainly the nickname well suited Heseltine's mane of blond hair and somewhat dynamic, virile image. ➤ See also HEZZA.

Tassie Tasmania. *Tassie* is an abbreviation of Tasmania. ➤ See also APPLE *Isle*, *The* SPECK.

Teddy Ballgame Ted Williams (1918–2002), US baseball player. ➤ See *The* SPLENDID *Splinter*.

The Teflon Don John Gotti (1940–2002), US crime boss. ➤ See *The* DAPPER *Don*.

The Teflon President Ronald (Wilson) Reagan (1911–2004), US Republican statesman, 40th President of the US 1981–89. The word Teflon can be applied to a politician whose reputation remains untarnished in spite of scandal or misjudgement. In other words, nothing sticks to them. The label the *Teflon President* is most closely associated with Ronald Reagan, who managed to shrug off a number of blunders and scandals during his presidency. ➤ See also DUTCH, *The* GIPPER, *The* GREAT *Communicator*, OLD *Hopalong*.

The Thief of Badgags Milton Berle (Mendel Berlinger) (b.1908), US television comedian. ➤ See MR *Television*.

The Thimble and Bodkin Army The Parliamentary army in the English Civil War. The pejorative contemporary name the *Thimble and Bodkin Army* referred to the fact that even silver thimbles and similarly modest items had been offered and accepted as contributions to the cause. This was in marked contrast to the substantial donations made by the more wealthy Royalist supporters.

The Thinking Man's Crumpet   Joan (Dawson) Bakewell (b.1933), British broadcaster. In the late 1960s she presented the arts magazine programme *Late Night Line-
Up*. Intelligent and attractive, she was dubbed the *Thinking Man's Crumpet* by the
humorist Frank Muir.

The Thin Man   Nick Charles, the private detective hero of US crime novelist Dashiell
Hammett's thriller *The Thin Man* (1932), the film of the same title (1934), and five
film sequels (1936–47). He was played in the films by William Powell, to whose
character the phrase *Thin Man* became attached. In fact the thin man of the title
is a murder victim called Clyde Wynant, an inventor described by Nick Charles in
the novel as: 'Tall—over six feet—and one of the thinnest men I've ever seen.'

The Thorpedo   Ian (James) Thorpe (b.1982), Australian swimmer. Famously having
a shoe size of 17, he is the dominant figure in world swimming at the start of the new
millennium. He won three gold medals at the 2000 Olympic Games, six golds in the
2002 Commonwealth Games, and has broken numerous world records. Thorpe's
nickname is a pun on his surname and the word *torpedo*. In Australia he is generally
known simply as *Thorpey*.

Three-Fingered Brown   Mordecai (Peter Centennial) Brown (1876–1948), US
baseball player, a pitcher in the early 1900s. When he was a boy he lost half the index
finger of his right hand, and had his small finger paralysed, in a farming accident.
Accordingly known as *Three-Fingered Brown*, he learned to use the stump of the
missing finger to impart extra spin on his curve ball.

The Throstles   West Bromwich Albion football club. They are known as the
Throstles because of the thrushes, or throstles, that used to be seen around the hedges
in the Hawthorns area of West Bromwich. In 1900 the club moved here to a new
ground which was named The Hawthorns. Although this is their official nickname,
most supporters prefer to call them the BAGGIES. ➤ See also *The* BAGGIES.

Thumper   John Leslie Prescott (b.1938), British Labour politician, deputy prime
minister from 1997. In the early days of Tony Blair's leadership of the Labour Party,
deputy leader Prescott was portrayed as *Thumper* to Blair's BAMBI. In the Disney
cartoon film *Bambi* (1942), based on Felix Salten's story for children (1923), the
rabbit Thumper is the young deer Bambi's best friend. The nickname fitted well with
Prescott's pugnacious image as one of the 'bruisers' of British politics. ➤ See also
BAMBI, PREZZA, TWO *Jags*.

The Thunderer   *The Times* newspaper. Originally the *Thunderer* was a title given to
Edward Sterling (1773–1847), a contributor of robust columns to the newspaper who
later became its assistant editor. It probably alludes to one of his leading articles, in
which he wrote: 'We thundered forth the other day an article on social and political
reform'. The title was also sometimes applied to Sterling's editor Thomas Barnes. By
the middle of the 19th century the nickname had transferred to *The Times* itself,
befitting the magisterial tone of its editorial pronouncements. ➤ See also ALL *Souls'*
Parish Magazine.

The Tiger[1]   Tipu Sultan (*c*.1750–99), sultan of Mysore (now Karnataka), India. He
said that he would rather live two days like a tiger, than two hundred years like a
sheep.

The Tiger[2] Georges (Eugéne Benjamin) Clemenceau (1841–1929), French statesman, Prime Minister 1906–9 and 1917–20. He negotiated the Treaty of Versailles in 1919. His determination, intransigence, and polemical style earned him the nickname the *Tiger*.

The Tigers Hull City football club. Their nickname the *Tigers* derives from the team's amber and black strip.

Tina Margaret (Hilda) Thatcher (b.1925), British Conservative stateswoman, Prime Minister 1979–90. *Tina*, or TINA, is an acronym for the phrase *There is No Alternative* and was sometimes used, especially by Young Conservatives, as a nickname for Thatcher while prime minister. The phrase originally came from a speech of Margaret Thatcher's to the Conservative Women's Conference, 21 May 1980, when she asserted, in reference to the necessity of tough economic measures, 'I believe people accept there is no alternative.' ➤ See also ATTILA *the Hen*, *The* BLESSED *Margaret*, *The* GROCER's *Daughter*, *The* IRON *Lady*, *The* LEADERENE, MAGGIE, *The* MILK *Snatcher*.

Tin Pan Alley A district in New York (28th Street, between 5th Avenue and Broadway) where many songwriters, arrangers, and publishers of popular music were formerly based. The district gave its nickname *Tin Pan Alley* to the American popular music industry between the late 1880s and the mid-20th century. In London, the name was popularly applied to Denmark Street, off Charing Cross Road, where music publishers, recording studios, and musical instrument dealers congregated.

The Tins The Household Cavalry (Life Guards). Their nickname the *Tins* (or the *Tin-Bellies*) derives from the cuirass (a piece of armour consisting of a breastplate and backplate fastened together) forming part of their uniform.

Tintoretto Jacopo Robusti (1518–94), Italian painter. He acquired his name *Il Tintoretto* (meaning 'the little dyer') from his father's trade as a silk dyer or *tintore*. Primarily a religious painter, he is best known for the huge canvas *Paradiso* (after 1577) in the Doges' Palace in Venice, and for his paintings (1576–88) in the Scuola di San Rocco in Venice. Tintoretto's work is typified by a mannerist style, including unusual viewpoints and chiaroscuro effects.

Tippecanoe William Henry Harrison (1773–1841), US Whig statesman, 9th President of the US (1841). Harrison was appointed governor of Indiana Territory in 1800. On 7 November 1811 he defeated Shawnee Indians in a battle at Tippecanoe Creek, Indiana. Harrison subsequently became a national hero and acquired the sobriquet *Tippecanoe*. In 1840 he and his running mate John Tyler ran a successful presidential campaign under the slogan 'Tippecanoe and Tyler, Too'. ➤ See also LOG-CABIN *Harrison*.

The Toffees Everton football club. In the early years of the club, a sweet shop called *Ye Anciente Everton Toffee House* was situated opposite the ground and the owner used to throw toffees to the crowd before kick-off. The club accordingly became known as the *Toffees* or the *Toffeemen*. An Everton mint is a black-and-white sweet, so named because the team formerly wore black shirts with a white sash and were then nicknamed the *Black Watch*. Everton adopted its current royal blue strip in 1901.

Tokyo Rose Iva Ikuko Toguri D'Aquino (b.1916), Japanese-American propagandist broadcaster. Born in California of Japanese descent, her broadcasts on Tokyo Radio to American servicemen in the Second World War were intended to undermine morale. She was dubbed *Tokyo Rose* by the GIs, though the name also covered a number of other women broadcasting Japanese propaganda. After the war she was convicted of treason and spent six years in prison. In 1977 she was pardoned by President Ford. ➤ See also HANOI *Jane*.

Tom Terrific Tom (George Thomas) Seaver (b.1944), US baseball player. He pitched for 20 years in the major leagues, mainly with the New York Mets and the Cincinatti Reds. The power and technique of his pitching earned him his nickname *Tom Terrific*.

Tony Antoinette Perry (1888–1946), US actress, director, and producer, nicknamed *Tony*. The Tony awards, given annually for outstanding achievement in the US theatre in various categories, are named after her.

The Tonypandy Terror Tommy Farr (1913–86), British boxer. Born in Tonypandy, Wales, Farr was British heavyweight champion 1937–38. In 1937 he challenged Joe Louis for the heavyweight title, taking the champion the distance (15 rounds) but losing on points.

Toom Tabard John de Baliol, titular king of Scotland (1249–1315). He was crowned at Scone in November 1292, and the next month did homage to Edward I of England. In 1296, Edward invaded Scotland; Baliol, who had attempted to renounce his fealty, was taken prisoner to England. On his release, he went to France, where he spent the rest of his life, without any attempt to recover Scotland. His ineffectiveness led him to be known disparagingly by the Scots as *Toom Tabard* (meaning 'Empty Jacket') or TYNE TABARD (meaning 'Lose Coat').

The Toothpick State The US state of Arkansas. Its nickname the *Toothpick State* alludes to the bowie knife, also sometimes called a 'toothpick knife'. Many of the state's early settlers carried this long hunting knife, named after the American frontiersman Jim Bowie (1796–1836). The state has also been known as the *Bowie State*. ➤ See also *The* GUINEA *Pig State*.

The Torygraph *The Daily Telegraph* newspaper. Its nickname the *Torygraph* reflects the paper's traditional support of the British Conservative (or Tory) Party.

The Toy Bulldog Mickey Walker (Edward Patrick Walker) (1901–81), US boxer. He was world welterweight champion 1922–26 and world middleweight champion 1926–31. His nickname alluded to his small stature, his looks, and his tenacity in the ring.

The Toyshop of Europe The city of Birmingham, England. The epithet the *Toyshop of Europe* was coined by Edmund Burke, in reference to the knick-knacks, trinkets, and imitation jewellery once manufactured there. ➤ See also BRUM.

The Tractor Boys   Ipswich Town football club. The affectionate nickname the *Tractor Boys* is inspired by East Anglia's agricultural tradition.

Trane   John (William) Coltrane (1926–67), US jazz saxophonist. After playing in groups led by Dizzy Gillespie and Miles Davis, he formed his own quartet in 1960 and became a leading figure of the jazz avante-garde. It was during his time as a member of the Miles Davis quintet in the mid-1950s that he acquired his nickname *Trane*, an abbreviation of his surname.

The Treasure State   The US state of Montana. It is noted for its gold, silver, copper, and coal mines, hence its official nickname the *Treasure State*. ➤ See also *The* STUB-TOE *State*.

Tricky Dick   Richard Nixon (1913–94), US Republican statesman, 37th President of the US 1969–74, who resigned after the Watergate scandal. Nixon was known as *Tricky Dick* in the US and *Tricky Dicky* in Britain. The sobriquet was first used by Helen Gahagan Douglas, his Democratic opponent in the 1950 senatorial election in California. Nixon ran a dirty campaign in which he tried to smear the liberal Douglas as a Communist sympathizer, labelling her the *Pink Lady*. Alluding to his reputation for political chicanery, cunning, and evasiveness, Nixon's nickname was revived during the investigation into his involvement in the Watergate conspiracy during his 1972 re-election campaign and its attempted cover-up.

The Trimmer   George Savile, 1st Marquess of Halifax (1633–95), English politician and essayist. When he switched his support from James II to William III, Lord Halifax was given the uncomplimentary nickname the *Trimmer*, in the sense of one who inclines to each of two opposite political sides as interest dictates. Halifax himself, however, accepted the term in the sense of one who keeps the ship of state on an even keel, striving to steer a middle course between party extremes: 'This innocent word *Trimmer* signifieth no more than this, that if men are together in a boat, and one part of the company would weigh it down on one side, another would make it lean as much to the contrary' (Lord Halifax, *Character of a Trimmer* (1685, printed 1688)).

The Tripe Shop   Broadcasting House, London, the headquarters of the BBC. London taxi-drivers used to refer to the building as the *Tripe Shop*, an ironic comment on the quality of the broadcaster's output. ➤ See also ALLY *Pally*.

Tuckahoe   The lowlands of the US state of Virginia, east of the Blue Ridge Mountains. The local nickname *Tuckahoe* (which can also be applied to an inhabitant of this district) derives from the Algonquian word *tockawhoughe*, the name of a root or other underground plant part formerly eaten by North American Indians.

Tugga   Steve Waugh (full name Stephen Rodger Waugh) (b.1965), Australian cricketer. He made his Test debut in 1985–86 and has been captain of Australia since 1999. His nickname *Tugga* derives from a pun on 'tug-of-war'. ➤ See also AFGHAN.

Tumbledown Dick   Richard Cromwell (1626–1712), son of Oliver Cromwell. He succeeded his father briefly as Lord Protector (1658–59) before the restoration of the monarchy under Charles II. According to the *Verney Memoirs* for 1659, he 'retired

into complete obscurity...with the people's nickname of Tumbledown Dick.'
Tumbledown meant 'falling into ruin, ramshackle'. ➤ See also KING *Dick*, QUEEN
Dick.

Tum-Tum Edward VII (1841–1910), king of Great Britain and Ireland 1901–10. As
Prince of Wales, he acquired the nickname *Tum-Tum* because of his corpulence. On
one occasion he gently admonished Sir Frederick Johnstone, one of his guests at
Sandringham, with the words 'Freddy, Freddy, you're very drunk!' Johnstone's over-
familiar reply, 'Tum-Tum, you're very fat!', was poorly received by the prince. ➤ See
also BERTIE, EDWARD *the Caresser*, EDWARD *the Peacemaker*, The UNCLE *of Europe*.

The Turnip-Hoer George I (1660–1727), great-grandson of James I, king of Great
Britain and Ireland 1714–27. Shortly after coming to the throne, he enquired about
the cost of closing St James's Park to the public and planting it with turnips, so
gaining the nickname the *Turnip-Hoer*.

Turnip Townshend Charles Townshend, 2nd Viscount Townshend (1674–1738),
English statesman and agriculturalist. Following his career in politics, he conducted
large-scale agricultural experiments at his estate at Raynham, Norfolk, earning
himself his nickname *Turnip Townshend*. He developed crop rotation and the
cultivation of turnips as winter feeds for cattle. Alexander Pope, in his 'Imitations of
Horace' refers to Townshend's turnips, stating in a footnote that 'that kind of rural
improvement which arises from turnips' was 'the favourite subject of Townshend's
conversation'. ➤ See also *The* TURNIP-HOER.

Tusitala Robert Louis (Balfour) Stevenson (1850–94), Scottish novelist, poet, and
travel writer. Stevenson made his name with the adventure story *Treasure Island*
(1883). His other works include the novel *The Strange Case of Dr Jekyll and Mr Hyde*
(1886) and a series of Scottish romances including *Kidnapped* (1886) and *The Master
of Ballantrae* (1889). A lifelong sufferer from a chronic bronchial condition, he spent
most of his life abroad. In 1889 he settled in Samoa, where he bought the Vailima
estate. The nickname *Tusitala* (meaning 'teller of tales') was given to the writer by
the Samoans.

Twiggy Lesley Hornby (b.1949), English fashion model of the 1960s. ➤ See STICKS.

Two Brains David (Lindsay) Willetts (b.1956), British Conservative politician. After
working at the Treasury, Margaret Thatcher's Policy Unit, and as Director of Studies
at the Centre for Policy Studies, he became an MP in 1992. His nickname *Two Brains*,
referring to his reputation as an intellectual and a policy expert, was coined by the
Guardian journalist Michael White.

Two Dinners Arnold Abraham Goodman (1914–95), British lawyer. Lord Goodman
was a prominent figure in British legal and political life in the 1960s, acting as legal
adviser to the prime ministers Harold Wilson and Edward Heath. His girth earned
him the nickname *Two Dinners*.

Two-Gun Patton George Smith Patton (1885–1945), US general, Commander of the
3rd Army in the Second World War. A flamboyant larger-than-life character, he
always wore two pearl-handled revolvers, hence his nickname *Two-Gun Patton*.
➤ See also BLOOD *and Guts*.

Two Jags John Leslie Prescott (b.1938), British Labour politician, Deputy Prime Minister from 1997. Prescott was responsible for the transport portfolio. At the Labour party conference in 1999, he used two cars to make the 300-yard journey from his hotel to the conference centre in order to deliver a speech urging less car use. This prompted William Hague, leader of the Conservative party, to remark: 'People work hard and save hard to own a car. They do not want to be told that they cannot drive it by a Deputy Prime Minister whose idea of a park and ride scheme is to park one Jaguar and drive away in another.' On 16 May 2001, during the General Election campaign, Prescott punched egg-throwing protester Craig Evans in Rhyl. His nickname was neatly converted to *Two Jabs* on the front page of the following morning's *Sun* newspaper. The paper's leading article was headlined 'Thrilla in Rhyla', echoing the 'Thrilla in Manila' heavyweight title fight in 1975. ➤ See also PREZZA, THUMPER.

Two-Ton Tessie Tessie O'Shea (1917–95), British variety artist. An exuberant ukulele-playing performer, she earned her nickname *Two-Ton Tessie* from her size and her song 'Two-Ton Tessie from Tennessee'. In 1945 the RAF nicknamed a 22 000 lb bomb 'Ten-Ton Tessie' after her.

Tyburnia A residential district of London, north of Hyde Park (extending along the Bayswater Road from Marble Arch to Lancaster Gate and northwards). The 19th-century nickname *Tyburnia* alludes to its proximity to Tyburn, for nearly 600 years the site of public executions in London.

Tyne Tabard John de Baliol, titular king of Scotland (1249–1315). ➤ See TOOM *Tabard*.

Uu

Uccello   Paolo di Dono (*c*.1397–1475), Italian painter. According to Vasari, he was nicknamed *Uccello* (Italian for 'bird') because of his love of animals, especially birds. Not able to afford to keep any real ones, he surrounded himself with paintings of birds and other animals in his house. Uccello was based largely in Florence and is associated with the early use of perspective in painting. His surviving works include *The Rout of San Romano* and *The Hunt*, one of the earliest known paintings on canvas, noted for its atmosphere of fairy-tale romance.

The Unabomber   Theodore Kaczynski (b.1942). The *Unabomber* was a media nickname for a terrorist who carried out a series of bomb attacks in the US between 1978 and 1995 as part of an anarchist, anti-technology personal crusade. Because the attacks were made on academic institutions (and particularly scientists), the name Unabomber, a blend of *university* and *bomber*, was coined. Theodore Kaczynski, a former mathematics teacher at Berkeley University, was finally arrested and charged in 1996. In 1998 he was sentenced to four life terms of imprisonment.

Uncle Joe   Joseph Stalin (born Iosif Vissarionovich Dzhugashvili) (1879–1953), Soviet statesman, General Secretary of the Communist Party of the USSR 1922–53. *Uncle Joe* was a British wartime nickname for Stalin as the personification of Soviet Russia. The name is first recorded in a comment made by Winston Churchill to Franklin Roosevelt in 1943: 'The castigation we have both received from Uncle Joe...was naturally to be expected'. ➤ See also *The* MAN *of Steel*.

Uncle Miltie   Milton Berle (Mendel Berlinger) (1908–2002), US television comedian. ➤ See MR *Saturday Night*.

The Uncle of Europe   Edward VII (1841–1910), king of Great Britain and Ireland 1901–10. This designation was literally true. Edward was uncle to the German Kaiser, the Queen of Spain, and the Queen of Norway. In addition, his wife Queen Alexandra was aunt to the tsar of Russia, the king of Denmark, and the king of Greece. His mother Queen Victoria had been known as the GRANDMOTHER OF EUROPE. ➤ See also BERTIE, EDWARD *the Caresser*, EDWARD *the Peacemaker*, TUM-TUM.

Unconditional Surrender   Ulysses S(impson) Grant (1822–85), US Civil War general and 18th President of the US 1869–77. In February 1862 Grant besieged a Confederate garrison at Fort Donelson, whose commander General Simon B. Buckner wished to negotiate terms for a surrender. Grant replied: 'Sir: Yours of this date proposing Armistice and appointment of Commissioners, to settle terms of Capitulation is just received. No terms except unconditional and immediate surrender can be accepted. I propose to move immediately upon your works. I am sir, very respectfully, Your obt. svt. U. S. Grant, Brig. Gen.' The uncompromising phrase 'unconditional surrender' became closely associated with Grant and, given his initials, it was inevitable that he would become known as *Unconditional Surrender Grant.* ➤ See also *The* AMERICAN *Caesar, The* BUTCHER.

The Uncrowned King of Ireland   Charles Stewart Parnell (1846–91), Irish nationalist leader who, as MP for Cork, led the Irish Home Rule movement in Parliament. He was given the title the *Uncrowned King of Ireland*, a label first applied to Parnell by William Edward Forster in the house of Commons in 1883.

The Universal Doctor   St Albertus Magnus (*c.*1200–80). ➤ See DOCTOR *Universalis.*

The Unknown Prime Minister   Andrew Bonar Law (1858–1923), Canadian-born British Conservative statesman, Prime Minister 1922–23. Having succeeded Lloyd George, he died unexpectedly after only a year in office. He was buried in Westminster Abbey and his predecessor Herbert Asquith commented 'It is fitting that we should have buried the Unknown Prime Minister by the side of the Unknown Soldier.'

The Unready   Ethelred II (*c.*969–1016), king of England 978–1016. The epithet *Unready* has nothing to do with tardiness but is an alteration of *unredy* and means *redeless*, that is 'lacking good advice, without counsel'. Ethelred earned his nickname from his ill-advised policy of trying to buy off Danish raiders by paying Danegeld. In 1002 he ordered the massacre of the Danish settlers, which provoked the Danish king Sweyn I to invade England. The name Ethelred itself means 'noble counsel'.

Ursa Major   Samuel Johnson. The name (which is Latin for 'Great Bear') was given to him by James Boswell's father, Lord Auchinleck. In his *Journal of a Tour to the Hebrides* (1785) Boswell writes: 'My father's opinion of Dr Johnson may be conjectured from the name he afterwards gave him, which was *Ursa Major*. But it is not true, as has been reported, that it was in consequence of my saying that he was a *constellation* of genius and literature. It was a sly abrupt expression to one of his brethren on the bench of the Court of Session, in which Dr Johnson was then standing; but it was not said in his hearing' (6 November 1773). ➤ See also DICTIONARY *Johnson, The* GREAT *Cham of Literature.*

The Valentine State The US state of Arizona. The state was admitted into the Union on 14 February (St Valentine's Day) 1912, hence its nickname the *Valentine State*. Until Alaska was admitted in 1959, Arizona was also known as the *Baby State*. ➤ See also *The* APACHE *State, The* AZTEC *State, The* GRAND *Canyon State*.

The Vein-openers The 29th Foot, a regiment of the British army. Their nickname alludes to the 'Boston Massacre', an incident in Boston in 1770, prior to the American Revolution. A detachment of the 29th opened fire on a mob of anti-British rioters, killing four people and wounding several more. The regiment were subsequently dubbed the *Vein-openers* by the Americans.

Velvet Bruegel Jan Bruegel (1568–1623), Flemish artist, son of Pieter Bruegel the Elder. He painted flowers and other still-life subjects, landscapes, and mythological scenes in a highly-finished, detailed style which earned him the nickname *Velvet Bruegel*. ➤ See also HELL *Bruegel*, PEASANT *Bruegel*.

The Velvet Fog Mel Tormé (Melvin Howard Tormé) (1925–99), US singer with a much-admired smooth crooning style. He formed his own group the Mel-Tones in the 1940s, during which time he became known as the *Velvet Fog*, and in the second half of the decade he went solo. His autobiography was entitled *It Wasn't All Velvet*. ➤ See also *The* SINGER'S *Singer*.

The Venerable Bede St Bede (*c*.673–735), English monk, theologian, and historian. The epithet *Venerable* (that is, 'worthy to be revered') was first added to his name in the century following his death. ➤ See also *The* FATHER *of English History*.

The Venice of the North The city of Amsterdam, the Netherlands. Like Venice, the city is built on numerous islands separated by canals and connected by bridges, hence its nickname the *Venice of the North*. The epithet is also associated with Stockholm in Sweden. Other 'Venices' are the cities of Bangkok, Thailand (the *Venice of the East*) and Glasgow, Scotland (the *Venice of the West*). ➤ See also DIAMOND *City*, LITTLE *Venice*.

The Vicar of Hell Francis Bryan (d.1550), English courtier and translator. He was nicknamed the *Vicar of Hell* by Thomas Cromwell, shortly after Bryan had accepted a pension formerly in the possession of one of the men implicated in the fall of Bryan's cousin Anne Boleyn. It is likely to be Bryan to whom Milton refers in *Areopagitica* (1644): 'I name not him for posterity's sake, whom Henry VIII named in merriment his Vicar of Hell.' Some sources, however, identify this person as John Skelton (*c*.1460–1529), court poet to Henry VIII. Skelton had formerly been vicar of

Diss, in Norfolk, and it has been suggested that the king was punning on the name of Dis (or Pluto), the god of the underworld.

Vinegar Joe   Joseph W. Stilwell (1883–1946), US general. He acquired his army nickname *Vinegar Joe* when serving at the Infantry School, Fort Benning, Georgia (1929–33), because of his acid tongue. During the Second World War, Stilwell commanded Chiang Kai-shek's troops in Burma, when his caustic and irascible manner was evident in his dealings with other military leaders.

The Violet Corporal   Napoleon I (known as Napoleon; full name Napoleon Bonaparte) (1769–1821), emperor of France 1804–14 and 1815. Napoleon acquired the nickname the *Violet Corporal* (or *Corporal Violet*) when banished to Elba in 1814. He assured his supporters that he would return to France with the violets. This he did, returning to the Tuileries in Paris in March 1815, when the violets were in full bloom. ➤ See also BONEY, *The* CORSICAN *Ogre, The* LITTLE *Corporal, The* MAN *of Destiny.*

The Violet-Crowned City   Athens. ➤ See *The* CITY *of the Violet Crown.*

The Virgin Mary's Bodyguard   The 7th Dragoon Guards, a regiment of the British army. During the reign of George II the regiment was deployed to assist the army of Archduchess Maria Theresa of Austria, earning itself the facetious sobriquet the *Virgin Mary's Bodyguard.*

The Virgin Queen   Elizabeth I (1533–1603), daughter of Henry VIII, queen of England and Ireland 1558–1603. Elizabeth, who died unmarried and childless, was known as the *Virgin Queen.* The state of Virginia, the site of the first permanent European settlement in North America in 1607, takes its name from this epithet. ➤ See also GLORIANA, GOOD *Queen Bess,* ORIANA.

The Voice   Frank Sinatra (1915–98), US singer and film actor. This sobriquet, used to promote Sinatra, was coined in the 1940s either by the singer's press agent George Evans or by his agent Harry Kilby. He started to be billed under the title 'The Voice that Thrills Millions', and this was soon shortened to the *Voice.* It was the title of one his earliest albums (1945). ➤ See also BONES, *The* CHAIRMAN *of the Board,* OL' *Blue Eyes.*

The Voice of London   John (Merrick Mordaunt) Snagge (1904–96), British broadcaster, whose career as a BBC radio announcer began in 1928. During the Second World War, he became known as the *Voice of London,* authoritatively announcing such momentous events as the D-Day landings, VE Day, and VJ Day. He commentated on every Oxford-Cambridge Boat Race between 1931 and 1980.

The Volunteer State   The US state of Tennessee. Its official nickname the *Volunteer State* is an allusion to the large number of volunteers (some 30 000 men) contributed by Tennessee to the Mexican War of 1847. ➤ See also *The* HOG *and Hominy State, The* MONKEY *State.*

The Vulcan   John Redwood (b.1951), British Conservative politician, secretary of state for Wales 1993–95. In the mid 1990s, he began to be called the *Vulcan,* alluding to the race of aliens to which Mr Spock belongs in the *Star Trek* science fiction series.

Vulcans are noted for their logic, lack of emotion, and mental prowess, all characteristics that were thought to be shared by the politician.

The Vulture Emilio Butragueño (b.1963), Spanish footballer. He played for Real Madrid in the 1980s and 1990s and represented Spain 69 times, scoring 26 goals. His nickname *El Buitre* ('the Vulture' in Spanish) derived partly from the similarity between his surname and the Spanish word for the bird of prey and partly from his predatory poaching of goals around the penalty area.

Ww

Wacko Michael Jackson (b.1958), US pop singer and songwriter. ➤ See JACKO.

The Wake Hereward (11th century), semi-legendary Anglo-Saxon rebel leader, generally known as *Hereward the Wake*. A leader of Anglo-Saxon resistance to William I's new Norman regime, he is thought to have been responsible for an uprising centred on the Isle of Ely in 1070. The *Wake* apparently means 'the watchful one' and refers to his vigilance in defending Ely against the Normans.

Walking Stewart John Stewart (1749–1822), English traveller and explorer, whose journeys were largely carried out on foot. He travelled to Persia and Ethiopia, and came to Europe through the Arabian desert, walking through France and Spain in 1783. He also walked from Calais to Vienna in 1784 and in the US. De Quincey in his 'London Reminiscences' speaks of him as an interesting man but 'crazy beyond all reach of hellebore'.

The Walrus Craig Stadler (b.1953), US golfer, winner of the 1982 Masters. His thick, drooping moustache is thought to resemble the whiskers of a walrus, hence his nickname. He titled his autobiography *I am the Walrus*, after the Beatles song.

The Walrus of Love Barry (Eugene) White (1944–2003), US singer, composer, and producer. White's nickname the *Walrus of Love* derives from his large frame, his deep growl of a voice, and his singing of sensual love ballads such as 'You're the First, the Last, My Everything' (1974) and 'Can't Get Enough of Your Love, Babe' (1974). In 2002, marine scientists at Birmingham's National Sea Life Centre were reported to have played Barry White songs to their sharks in an effort to get them to mate.

The Warlike Bishop Henry Despencer (also known as Henry Spenser) (d.1406), English bishop of Norwich. ➤ See *The* FIGHTING *Bishop*.

The Warming Pan Baby James Francis Edward Stuart (1688–1766), the Old Pretender. Some disputed his claim to the throne on the grounds that he was an imposter. He became widely known as the *Warming Pan Baby* because of the story that as a baby he had been secretly smuggled into the bed of Mary of Modena, James II's second wife, in a warming pan after her own child was stillborn. ➤ See also *The* KING *over the Water, The* OLD *Pretender*.

The Warrior Queen Boudicca (d.AD 62), a queen of the Britons, ruler of the Iceni tribe in eastern England. Also known as Boadicea, she led her forces in revolt against the Romans and sacked Colchester, St Albans, and London before being defeated by the Roman governor Suetonius Paulinus. Boudicca, the *Warrior Queen*, came to personify native resistance to the Roman occupation.

The Wasp of Twickenham Alexander Pope (1688–1744), English poet and satirist, famous for his literary quarrels and caustic wit. ➤ See also *The* BARD *of Twickenham*.

The Water Poet John Taylor (1580–1653), English poet. He was apprenticed to a London waterman before being pressed into the navy. On his return to London he became a Thames waterman. He supplemented his income by rhyming, showing a talent for expressing himself in lively doggerel. He published in 1630 an edition of his collected works, *All the Workes of John Taylor, the Water Poet*. Alexander Pope mentions him in the *Dunciad*: 'Taylor, their better Charon, lends an oar,/(Once swan of Thames, though now he sings no more.)' Ben Jonson also refers to him as the *Sculler*.

The Wavy Navy The Royal Naval Volunteer Reserve. They were known as the *Wavy Navy* because of the wavy gold braid worn by officers on their sleeves prior to 1956.

The Weeping Philosopher Heraclitus of Ephesus (*c.*500 BC), Greek philosopher of the 5th century. He believed that all things in the universe are in a state of constant change and that the mind derives an illusory idea of permanence of the external world from the passing impressions of experience. His gloomy view of the fleeting character of life and of the folly of mankind led him to be called the *Weeping Philosopher*, in explicit contrast to Democritus, the LAUGHING PHILOSOPHER.

The Weeping Prophet Jeremiah (*c.*650–*c.*585 BC), Hebrew major prophet who foresaw the fall of Assyria, the conquest of his country by Egypt and Babylon, and the destruction of Jerusalem. The biblical *Lamentations* are traditionally ascribed to him.

Wee Willie Willie (William Henry) Keeler (1872–1923), US baseball player. ➤ See HIT *'em Where They Ain't*.

The Welsh Windbag Neil (Gordon) Kinnock (b.1942), British Labour politician, leader of the Labour Party 1983–92. Born in Wales, he was a passionate but sometimes verbose speaker, attracting the disparaging nickname the *Welsh Windbag*.

The Welsh Wizard[1] David Lloyd George (1863–1945), British Liberal statesman, Prime Minister 1916–22. He represented his Welsh constituency as an MP for 55 years. Lloyd George was known as the *Welsh Wizard* because of his masterly political skill and fiery oratory. John Maynard Keynes described him as, 'This extraordinary figure of our time, this syren, this goat-footed bard, this half-human visitor to our age from the hag-ridden magic and enchanted woods of Celtic antiquity'. ➤ See also *The* GOAT.

The Welsh Wizard[2] Billy (William Henry) Meredith (1874–1958), Welsh footballer. Meredith was an outstanding winger who during his long career played for both Manchester City and Manchester United and won 48 caps for Wales. He finally retired as a player at the age of 49.

W. G. W. G. Grace (1848–1915), English cricketer and doctor. ➤ See *The* GRAND *Old Man*[2].

The Whirlwind Jimmy White (b.1962), English snooker player. He has played in the final of the World Professional Championship six times but has been runner-up each time. White earned the nickname the *Whirlwind* from his flamboyant, rapid-fire style of play.

Whispering Bob   Bob Harris (b.1946), British broadcaster. He became known as *Whispering Bob* because of his quietly spoken and laid-back style presenting the BBC TV music programme *The Old Grey Whistle Test* in the 1970s.

Whispering Death   Michael Anthony Holding (b.1954), West Indian cricketer, an outstanding fast bowler. He was noted for his smooth, light-footed run-up, with which he could generate prodigious pace and fearsome bounce. His intimidating nickname *Whispering Death* stemmed from the fact that umpires used to claim that they could not hear him approaching behind them.

Whispering Grass   Shaw Taylor (b.1924), British television presenter. For nearly 30 years Taylor presented *Police Five* (1962–90), a weekly programme in which the police sought the public's help in solving crimes. At the end of the programme he would remind viewers to 'keep 'em peeled'. Criminals are said to have referred to him as *Whispering Grass*, the title of a popular song written by Fred and Doris Fisher. 'Grass' is a slang term for a police informer.

The White Feather   Fabrizio Ravanelli (b.1968), Italian footballer. His clubs have included Perugia, Juventus, Middlesbrough, and Marseille. During his time at Juventus he was known as the *White Feather* because of his prematurely grey hair.

White Lightning[1]   Alberto Juantorena (Danger) (b.1950), Cuban athlete. In 1976 the 6ft 2ins (1.90m), long-striding Juantorena won Olympic gold medals at both the 400m and the 800m. His all-white running strip led him to be known as *White Lightning*.

White Lightning[2]   Allan Anthony Donald (b.1966), South African cricketer, the only bowler to take more than 300 Test wickets for South Africa. The exceptional speed of his bowling and his blond hair has led to his nickname *White Lightning*.

The White Queen   Mary, Queen of Scots (known as Mary Stuart) (1542–87), daughter of James V, queen of Scotland 1542–67. She was known as *La Reine Blanche* (the *White Queen*) because of the traditional white mourning clothes she wore after the death of her first husband, Francis II of France (1544–60).

The White Shark   Greg (Gregory John) Norman (b.1955), Australian golfer. ➤ See *The* GREAT *White Shark*.

The Wickedest Man in the World   Aleister Crowley. ➤ See BEAST 666.

The Widow at Windsor   Victoria (1819–1901), queen of Great Britain and Ireland 1837–1901 and empress of India 1876–1901. After the death of her husband Albert, Prince Consort in 1861, Queen Victoria withdrew from public life. Thereafter wearing the black of mourning, she spent much of her time at Windsor Castle. The phrase the *Widow at Windsor* was used as the title of a poem by Rudyard Kipling (1890): ''Ave you 'eard o' the Widow at Windsor/With a hairy gold crown on 'er 'ead?' Victoria is buried next to her beloved Albert at Frogmore, in Windsor Park. ➤ See also *The* FAMINE *Queen, The* GRANDMOTHER *of Europe,* MRS *Brown.*

The Wild Geese   The Irish Jacobites who emigrated to the Continent after the defeat of James II, especially after the Treaty of Limerick. The name the *Wild Geese* is first found in a verse by Michael Joseph Barry (1817–89): 'The wild geese—the wild geese,—'tis long since they flew,/O'er the billowy ocean's bright bosom of blue' (*Spirit of the Nation*, 1845).

William the Silent   William I (1533–84), prince of the house of Orange, first stadtholder (chief magistrate) of the United Provinces of the Netherlands (1572–84). He led a nationalist revolt against Spanish rule from 1568. William gained the sobriquet *le Taciturne* (the *Silent*) from the discretion he showed in his dealings with the French court; he knew when to keep his own counsel.

The Windy City   The US city of Chicago, Illinois. While often taken as a literal reference to the breezes of Lake Michigan, Chicago's well-known nickname the *Windy City* is thought to have originally referred to the supposed bombastic verbosity of its citizens, especially its politicians. Recorded from the late 19th century, the sobriquet is thought to have been coined by the *New York Sun* newspaper editor Charles A. Dana. ➤ See also PHOENIX *City*.

Winnie   Winston (Leonard Spencer) Churchill (1874–1965), British Conservative statesman, Prime Minister 1940–45 and 1951–55. He was the inspirational leader of a coalition government during the Second World War. The familiar nickname *Winnie* reflects the great affection in which Churchill was held by the British people.

The Winter King   Frederick V (1596–1632), Elector Palatine of the Rhine. He occupied the throne of Bohemia 1619–20, for one winter only. In 1620 his army was defeated at White Mountain near Prague, and he was driven into exile.

The Winter Queen   Elizabeth Stuart (1596–1662), princess of Great Britain, married to Frederick, Elector Palatine of the Rhine. He was elected king of Bohemia in 1619 but driven out the following year, and they spent the rest of their lives in exile. ➤ See also *The* QUEEN *of Hearts*.

The Wisest Fool in Christendom   James I of England and VI of Scotland (1566–1625). A well-read scholar, James was dubbed by the Duc de Sully (1559–1641), at one time French envoy at the English court, 'the most learned fool in Christendom'. This was modified, either by Sully or by Henri IV of France (1553–1610), to the *Wisest Fool in Christendom*. ➤ See also *The* BRITISH *Solomon*.

Wislon   (James) Harold Wilson (1916–95), British Labour statesman, Prime Minister 1964–70 and 1974–76. Wilson was known to readers of the satirical magazine *Private Eye* as *Wislon*, a supposed (but recurrent) typographical error.

The Wizard of Menlo Park   Thomas Alva Edison (1847–1931), US inventor, who held more than a thousand patents for his inventions. Among these were the carbon microphone for telephones, the phonograph, and the carbon filament lamp. Edison also devised systems for generating and distributing electricity. He was known as the *Wizard of Menlo Park*, after the town in New Jersey where he lived and worked.

The Wizard of Oz   Ozzie (Osborne Earl) Smith (b.1954), US baseball player. One of the finest shortstops in the game, he played for the San Diego Padres and the St Louis Cardinals. His nickname the *Wizard of Oz* is derived from his first name and inspired by the character created by L. Frank Baum in his children's book *The Wonderful Wizard of Oz* (1900).

The Wizard of the Dribble   Stanley Matthews (1915–2000), English footballer. He played on the right wing for Stoke City and Blackpool and played for England 54 times in a career that lasted until he was 50. His outstanding performance for Blackpool in the 1953 FA Cup final led to the match becoming known as the 'Matthews Final'. Matthews, the *Wizard of the Dribble*, was famous for his outstanding ball control, dancing down the right wing as he evaded opposing players. He was the first European Footballer of the Year in 1956 and was the first English footballer to be knighted.

The Wizard of the North   Walter Scott (1771–1832), Scottish novelist and poet. ➤ See *The* GREAT *Magician*.

Wolfe's Own   The 47th Foot, a regiment of the British army. The regiment distinguished itself at the battle of Quebec in 1759 and, following the death of General Wolfe, it was the 47th's Commanding Officer Colonel Hale who delivered the news of the victory to London. The regiment subsequently wore a black mourning line in the officers' lace in memory of General Wolfe. ➤ See also *The* DEATH-OR-GLORY *Boys*.

The Wolverine State   The US state of Michigan, where wolverines are found. A wolverine is a heavily-built carnivorous mammal, related to the weasel and noted for its strength and ferocity. The term has been used as a nickname for a native or inhabitant of Michigan since at least the 1830s. ➤ See also *The* AUTO *State*, *The* GREAT *Lake State*.

The Wonderful Doctor   Roger Bacon. ➤ See *The* ADMIRABLE *Doctor*.

The Wonder of the World   Frederick II (1194–1250), Holy Roman Emperor (1220–50). ➤ See STUPOR *Mundi*.

Woodbine Willie   Geoffrey Studdert Kennedy (1883–1929), English priest and poet. As a chaplain during the First World War he was nicknamed *Woodbine Willie*, after the popular brand of cigarettes that he handed out to the soldiers in the trenches. Kennedy once described his ministry as taking 'a box of fags in your haversack and a great deal of love in your heart'.

Wor Jackie   Jackie (John) Milburn (1924–88), English footballer. A former pit apprentice, he joined Newcastle United in 1943, going on to make 354 league appearances for the club and scoring 179 goals. Milburn was known as *Wor Jackie* to the adoring Newcastle fans, 'Wor' being a North-East English form of 'Our'. There is a bronze statue of him in the city centre.

The World's Greatest Entertainer   Al Jolson (born Asa Yoelson) (1886–1950), Russian-born US singer, film actor, and comedian. The outstanding US entertainer of the 1920s and mid 1930s, he sang such hits as 'Swanee', 'Mammy', and 'Sonny Boy' in black make-up in imitation of black minstrel singers, often kneeling on one knee with his arms outstretched. Jolson starred in the first full-length talking film *The Jazz Singer* (1927), by which time he was already billing himself as the *World's Greatest Entertainer*.

The World's Sweetheart Mary Pickford (1893–1979), Canadian-born film actress.
➤ See AMERICA's *Sweetheart*.

Worzel Michael (Mackintosh) Foot (b.1913), British Labour politician. When he
was leader of the Labour Party (1980–83), Foot was given the nickname *Worzel*,
after Worzel Gummidge, a talking scarecrow with straw hair who is the central
character of a series of children's books by Barbara Euphan Todd (d.1976), later
televised. The nickname was first used in the satirical *Dear Bill* letters by Richard
Ingrams and John Wells, published in *Private Eye* magazine and purporting to
record the thoughts of Denis Thatcher during his wife's tenure as Prime Minister.
Foot's white hair and slightly dishevelled appearance were thought to make him
resemble the scarecrow.

Wottle the Throttle Dave Wottle (b.1950), US middle-distance runner. Wottle,
usually wearing a golf cap, used to hang back until the final stretch when with a burst
of speed he would snatch victory on the line. He won the 800m gold medal in the
1972 Olympics in the last few strides with just such a late run. This trade-mark
acceleration at the end of a race earned him the rhyming nickname *Wottle the
Throttle*.

Yy

The Yankee Clipper Joe DiMaggio (1914–99), US baseball player. He was first dubbed the *Yankee Clipper* around 1940, alluding both to his team the New York Yankees and to the speed with which he despatched the ball. The original Yankee Clipper was a type of US merchant ship built in the 19th century. ➤ See also JOLTIN' *Joe*.

Yardbird Charlie Parker. ➤ See BIRD.

Yellow Hair George Armstrong Custer (1839–76), US cavalry general. He was known by the American Indians as *Yellow Hair* or *Long Hair* because of his long, curly reddish-blond hair. His army nickname was *Ringlets*. Custer and his forces were defeated and killed by Sioux warriors on 25 June 1876 at Little Bighorn in Montana.

The Yellowhammer State The US state of Alabama. Its nickname the *Yellow-hammer State* refers to the yellowish tinge of the home-dyed grey uniforms worn by the Confederate soldiers during the Civil War. ➤ See also *The* COTTON *State, The* HEART *of Dixie*.

Yifter the Shifter Miruts Yifter (b.1938), Ethiopian long-distance runner. Yifter won the 5 000m and 10 000m gold medals at the Moscow Olympics in 1980. His admiring sobriquet *Yifter the Shifter* alluded to his ability to put on a sudden spurt in the last lap of a race.

Yogi Lawrence Peter Berra (b.1925), US baseball player. An outstanding catcher, he played for the New York Yankees from 1946 to 1965, later becoming the team's manager. His nickname *Yogi* Berra puns on the name of the US cartoon character Yogi Bear, created by William Hanna and Joseph Barbera.

The Yorkshire Ripper Peter (William) Sutcliffe (b.1946), British serial-killer. In the late 1970s he murdered 13 women in northern England and the Midlands before being captured in January 1981. The press dubbed Sutcliffe the *Yorkshire Ripper* because, like the 19th-century murderer Jack the Ripper, he mutilated his victims' bodies. ➤ See also JACK *the Ripper*.

You Beaut Country Australia. The phrase was originally coined by the Australian artist John Olsen (b.1928) in 1961 to describe the Australian landscape as depicted in his series of paintings 'Journey into You Beaut Country'. In Australian English the colloquial phrase *you beaut* is used to express admiration or praise. ➤ See also *The* LUCKY *Country*, OZ.

The Young Chevalier Charles Edward Stuart (1720–88). His father had assumed the title of Chevalier de St George, serving with the French army in the War of

Spanish Succession in the early years of his exile. ➤ See also BONNIE *Prince Charlie*, *The* KING *over the Water, The* YOUNG *Pretender.*

Young Hickory James K(nox) Polk (1795–1849), US Democratic statesman, 11th President of the US 1845–49. Polk's nomination as presidential candidate at the 1844 Democratic convention was engineered by his mentor Andrew Jackson, OLD HICKORY, leading to Polk being dubbed *Young Hickory.* ➤ See also *The* FIRST *Dark Horse,* OLD *Hickory.*

The Young Pretender Charles Edward Stuart (1720–88), the grandson of James II and elder son of James Edward Stuart (the OLD PRETENDER), on behalf of whose claim to the British throne he led the Jacobite uprising of 1745–46. Charles won the support of the Scottish Highlanders, with whom he invaded England and advanced as far as Derby. However he was driven back to Scotland by the Duke of Cumberland and defeated at the Battle of Culloden (1746). He escaped to the Isle of Skye with the help of Flora Macdonald, and hid for five months in the highlands with a price of £30 000 on his head. Eventually escaping to France, he later died in exile in Rome. A romantic figure, Charles was known as BONNIE PRINCE CHARLIE to his supporters and as the *Young Pretender* to the English, a name first recorded from 1745. A 'pretender' is one who lays claim to a throne or title. ➤ See also BONNIE *Prince Charlie, The* KING *over the Water, The* YOUNG *Chevalier.*

The Young Roscius William (Henry West) Betty (1791–1874), boy actor. He made his debut in Belfast in 1803, at the age of 11, appearing at Drury Lane to great acclaim the following year. William Pitt is said to have adjourned the House of Commons on one occasion so that members could see him performing as Hamlet. His final appearance as a boy actor was in 1808, at Bath. Betty was hailed as the *Young Roscius* (or the *Infant Roscius*), after Quintus Roscius Gallus (d.62 BC), the most celebrated of Roman comic actors, after whom many great actors were nicknamed. ➤ See also *The* ENGLISH *Roscius.*

Yvonne Princess Margaret (1930–2002), sister of Elizabeth II. *Yvonne* was the nickname used in the satirical magazine *Private Eye.*

Zz

Zizou Zinedine Zidane (b.1972), French footballer. Affectionately known as *Zizou*, he has played for such clubs as Bordeaux, Juventus, and Real Madrid. He was a key member of France's World Cup-winning team in 1998, heading two goals against Brazil in the final, and also helped France to victory in the European championship in 2000.

Appendix 1

Football club nicknames

Football club nicknames are diverse in origin and fall into various groups. Some simply, and rather unimaginatively, refer to the predominant colour of the team strip. So Birmingham City, Chelsea, and Manchester City, among others, are known as the *Blues*. Barnsley, Liverpool, and Nottingham Forest are the *Reds*. Burnley are the *Clarets* and Coventry City the *Sky Blues*. An assortment of birds and insects reflect other liveries. The black and white stripes worn by Newcastle United and Notts County earn both teams the nickname the Magpies, while red-shirted Cheltenham Town and Wrexham are the Robins. Watford are the *Hornets*, and both Barnet and Brentford the *Bees*.

Many clubs take their nickname directly from their full name. In some cases the team is popularly known simply as *City*, *United*, *Town*, *Rovers*, and so on. Other names of this type include the *Villans* (Aston Villa), the *Swans* (Swansea City), Spurs (Tottenham Hotspur), and *Wolves* (Wolverhampton Wanderers).

A few nicknames are inspired not by the name of the club, but by that of the stadium where the club play their home games. Fulham are the Cottagers because they play at Craven Cottage, while Halifax Town, who play at the Shay, are the *Shaymen*. Rotherham United play at Millmoor, hence their nickname the Merry Millers. Sheffield Wednesday's ground Hillsborough was originally known as Owlerton, from which the club became known as the Owls.

The nicknames of some clubs allude to some aspect of the club's history, particulary the circumstances in which it was founded. For example, West Ham United was formed in 1895 as the company team of the Thames Ironworks, hence their nickname the Hammers or, formerly, the *Irons*. Millwall are called the Lions because, as many of their early players were Scots, the club adopted the Scottish flag's lion rampant for its badge. Arsenal was formed by workers at the Royal Arsenal Armaments Factory in Woolwich in 1886, hence their nickname the Gunners. One of Bury's first chairmen once predicted that his team would give a rival team 'a good shaking', and so the Shakers they became. Similarly, when Peterborough United was formed in 1934, the fans were promised 'posh players for a posh new team'. They have been known as the Posh ever since. Darlington became the Quakers because their ground was originally owned by a prominent local Quaker John Beaumont Pease.

Many of the most colourful club nicknames derive from traditional local industries. Examples include the Blades (Sheffield United, steel and cutlery), the Hatters (Luton Town, millinery), the Cobblers (Northampton Town, shoe-making), the Potters (Stoke City, pottery), and the *Mariners* (Grimsby Town, fishing). Wycombe Wanderers owe their nickname the Chairboys to High Wycombe's tradition of furniture-making. Reading used to be known as the Biscuitmen because their ground was at one time owned by the biscuit manufacturer Huntley and Palmer.

Some nicknames spring from a local connection or association of some other kind. For example, Chesterfield take their nickname the SPIREITES from the crooked spire of St Mary's All Saints Church. Similarly, York City are known as the *Minstermen*, after the city's cathedral York Minster. Brighton and Hove Albion's seaside location is reflected in the nickname the *Seagulls*.

One or two clubs have an official nickname which is largely ignored by the fans. Few supporters refer to West Bromwich Albion as the THROSTLES, preferring to call their team the BAGGIES. Manchester City's official nickname is supposedly the *Citizens*, though the term is spurned by City's fans. Wimbledon have two nicknames: traditionally they are the *Dons*, but since the 1980s they have rejoiced in the rather less respectable sobriquet the *Crazy Gang*. Official nicknames have sometimes been intentionally discarded by clubs and replaced by new ones, usually in the hope of modernizing their image. So the *Pensioners* (Chelsea) became the *Blues*, the GLAZIERS (Crystal Palace) became the *Eagles*, and the BISCUITMEN (Reading) became the *Royals*.

Alphabetical list of football club nicknames

Those in small capitals are entries in the dictionary.

English League Clubs

ADDICKS (Charlton Athletic)
Albion (West Bromwich Albion)
BAGGIES (West Bromwich Albion)
Bantams (Bradford City)
Bees (Brentford)
BISCUITMEN (Reading)
BLACK CATS (Sunderland)
Black Watch (Everton, formerly)
BLADES (Sheffield United)
BLUEBIRDS (Cardiff City)
Blues (Birmingham City; Carlisle United; Chelsea; Chesterfield; Ipswich Town; Manchester City; Shrewsbury Town; Southend United; Wycombe Wanderers)
Boro (Middlesbrough)
CANARIES (Norwich City)
CHAIRBOYS (Wycombe Wanderers)
Cherries (Bournemouth)
Citizens (Manchester City)
Clarets (Burnley)
COBBLERS (Northampton Town)
Colliers (Barnsley)
COTTAGERS (Fulham)
County (Stockport County)
Crazy Gang (Wimbledon)
Cumbrians (Carlisle United)
Dale (Rochdale)

Diamonds (Rushden and Diamonds)
Dons (Wimbledon)
Eagles (Crystal Palace)
FOXES (Leicester City)
Gills (Gillingham)
GLAZIERS (Crystal Palace)
Grecians (Exeter City)
Gulls (Torquay United)
GUNNERS (Arsenal)
HAMMERS (West Ham United)
Harriers (Kidderminster Harriers)
HATTERS (Luton Town; Stockport County)
Hornets (Watford)
IRON (Scunthorpe United)
Latics (Oldham Athletic; Wigan Athletic)
Lilywhites (Preston North End)
LIONS (Millwall)
Mackems (Sunderland)
MAGPIES (Newcastle United; Notts County)
Mariners (Grimsby Town)
MERRY MILLERS (Rotherham United)
Minstermen (York City)
North End (Preston North End)
O's (Leyton Orient)
OWLS (Sheffield Wednesday)
Pensioners (Chelsea)
Pilgrims (Boston United, Plymouth Argyle)
Pirates (Bristol Rovers)

Pompey (Portsmouth)
Pool (Hartlepool United; Liverpool)
Posh (Peterborough United)
Potters (Stoke City)
Quakers (Darlington)
Railwaymen (Crewe Alexandra)
Rams (Derby County)
Rangers (Queens Park Rangers)
Red Devils (Manchester United)
Red Imps (Lincoln City)
Reds (Barnsley; Liverpool;
    Nottingham Forest)
Robins (Bristol City; Cheltenham Town;
    Swindon Town; Wrexham)
Rokermen (Sunderland, formerly)
Rovers (Blackburn Rovers;
    Tranmere Rovers)
Royalites (Burnley, formerly)
Royals (Reading)
R's (Queens Park Rangers)
Rubies (Cheltenham Town, formerly)
Saddlers (Walsall)
Saints (Southampton)
Salop (Shrewsbury Town)
Seagulls (Brighton and Hove Albion)
Seasiders (Blackpool)

Shakers (Bury)
Shrimpers (Southend United)
Silkmen (Macclesfield Town)
Sky Blues (Coventry City)
Spireites (Chesterfield)
Spots (Bolton Wanderers, formerly)
Spurs (Tottenham Hotspur)
Stags (Mansfield Town)
Swans (Swansea City)
Terriers (Huddersfield Town)
Throstles (West Bromwich Albion)
Tigers (Hull City)
Toffees (Everton)
Town (Ipswich Town; Shrewsbury Town)
Tractor boys (Ipswich Town)
Trotters (Bolton Wanderers)
Turfites (Burnley)
Tykes (Barnsley)
United (Leeds United)
U's (Cambridge United; Colchester United;
    Oxford United)
Valiants (Port Vale)
Villans (Aston Villa)
Wolves (Wolverhampton Wanderers)

Nationwide Conference Clubs

Bees (Barnet)
Blues (Chester City)
Boro (Farnborough Town; Nuneaton Borough;
    Scarborough; Stevenage Borough)
Brewers (Burton Albion)
Bucks (Telford United)
Cardinals (Woking)
City (Chester City)
Daggers (Dagenham & Redbridge)
Fleet (Gravesend & Northfleet)
Gate (Margate)

Glovers (Yeovil Town)
Poppies (Kettering Town)
Railwaymen (Leigh RMI)
Rovers (Doncaster Rovers; Forest Green
    Rovers)
Sandgrounders (Southport)
Shaymen (Halifax Town)
Shrimps (Morecambe)
United (Hereford United)
Vics (Northwich Victoria)
Whites (Dover Athletic)

Scottish League Clubs

Accies (Hamilton Academical)
Bairns (Falkirk)
Bankies (Clydebank)
Bhoys (Celtic)
Binos (Stirling Albion)
Black and Whites (Elgin City; Gretna)

Blue Brazil (Cowdenbeath)
Blues (Stranraer)
Blue Toon (Peterhead)
Borderers (Berwick Rangers)
Buddies (St Mirren)
Bully Wee (Clyde)

Caley Thistle (Inverness
   Caledonian Thistle)
City (Brechin City; Elgin City)
County (Ross County)
Dark Blues (Dundee)
Dee (Dundee)
Diamonds (Airdrieonians)
Dons (Aberdeen)
Doonhamers (Queen of the South)
Fifers (East Fife)
Gable Endies (Montrose)
Gers (Rangers)
Hearts (Heart of Midlothian)
Hibees (Hibernian)
Honest Men (Ayr United)
Jags (Partick Thistle)
Jambo's (Heart of Midlothian)
Killie (Kilmarnock)

Livvy Lions (Livingston)
Loons (Forfar Athletic)
Pars (Dunfermline Athletic)
Red Lichties (Arbroath)
Rovers (Raith Rovers)
Saints (St Johnstone)
Shire (East Sterlingshire)
Sons (Dumbarton)
Spiders (Queen's Park)
Staggies (Ross County)
Terrors (Dundee United)
Ton (Morton)
Warriors (Stenhousemuir)
Wasps (Alloa Athletic)
Waysiders (Airdrieonians)
Wee Rovers (Albion Rovers)
Well (Motherwell)

Appendix 2

British army regiments

The origins of regimental nicknames draw on a rich tradition and may be grouped into various categories.

Among the most proudly held nicknames are those that recall some celebrated episode in the regiment's history. For example, the 11th Foot became known as the BLOODY ELEVENTH in recognition of the heavy casualties sustained by the regiment in the Battle of Salamanca in 1812. Other nicknames won on the battlefield include the DELHI SPEARMEN (9th (Queen's) Royal Lancers), the DIEHARDS (57th Foot), the OLD STUBBORNS (Sherwood Foresters), and the SNAPPERS (15th Foot). The details of how each of these nicknames arose may be found at the relevant entry. Sometimes the name is associated not so much with a battle at which the regiment distinguished itself as with some colourful anecdote. The 50th Foot's nickname the DIRTY HALF-HUNDRED alludes to an incident at the Battle of Vimiero in 1808, when the men wiped their sweating brows with their black coat cuffs, transferring the black dye to their faces. Other stories account for the CHERRY-PICKERS (11th Hussars), PONTIUS PILATE'S BODYGUARD (1st Foot (later the Royal Scots)), SANKEY'S HORSE (39th Foot), and the SLASHERS (28th Foot). Celebrated commanding officers are remembered in such names as *Bingham's Dandies* (17th Lancers), *Bob's Own* (Irish Guards), the GREEN HOWARDS (19th Foot), the *Old Braggs* (28th Foot), and many others.

In some cases a nickname is simply an informal abbreviation (or acronym) of the regiment's full name. Among those listed below are the SKINS (5th Royal Inniskilling Dragoon Guards), the *Docs* (46th Foot (Duke of Cornwall's Light Infantry)), and the *Koylies* (King's Own Yorkshire Light Infantry). Nicknames that play on the regimental number are common in the British army. Obvious among these are the *Old Dozen* (12th Foot), the FIGHTING FIFTH (5th Foot), and *Two Fives* (55th Foot). Some names derive from the regimental number expressed in Roman numerals, such as the *Excellers* (40th Foot), based on the letters XL. Occasionally it is the shape of the numerals that inspires the nickname, as with the POT-HOOKS (77th Foot) and the *Ups and Downs* (69th Foot).

Nicknames often refer to the colour of part of the regimental uniform, in particular the colour of the facings, that is the collar, lapels, and cuffs on the jacket. Among those listed below are the BLACK WATCH (Royal Highland Regiment), the BRICKDUSTS (53rd Foot), the CHERRY-BREECHES (11th Hussars), the GREEN LINNETS (39th Foot), the *Lilywhites* (13th Hussars), the OXFORD BLUES (Royal Horse Guards), the SCARLET LANCERS (16th Lancers), and the SWEEPS (Rifle Brigade). The 2nd Foot, however, owe their nickname the TANGERINES to the fact that the regiment was raised in 1661 for service fighting Muslim forces in Tangier.

The regimental badge has sometimes inspired a nickname. The badge of the 17th Lancers depicts a death's head with the motto 'or glory', hence their nickname the

DEATH-OR-GLORY BOYS. Similarly, the DESERT RATS (7th Armoured Division) are so-called because of the jerboa that appears on the divisional badge. The 9th Foot became known as the HOLY BOYS when the figure of Britannia on their badge was repeatedly mistaken for the Virgin Mary during the Peninsular War.

Alphabetical list of regimental nicknames

Those in small capitals are entries in the dictionary.

Assaye Regiment (74th Foot)
Auxis (Auxiliary Division, recruited to fight Irish rebels)
Baker's Dozen (13th Hussars)
Barrell's Blues (4th Foot)
BAYS (2nd Dragoon Guard (Queen's Bays))
Belfast Regiment (35th Foot)
BENGAL TIGERS (17th Foot)
Bingham's Dandies (17th (Duke of Cambridge's Own) Lancers)
Birdcatchers (Royal Dragoons (1st Dragoons))
Black Cuffs (2nd Northamptonshire Regiment)
Black Horse (7th Dragoon Guards)
Black Knots (North Staffordshire Regiment)
BLACK WATCH (Royal Highland Regiment)
Blayney's Bloodhounds (87th Foot)
BLIND HALF-HUNDRED (50th Foot)
Bloodsuckers (Manchester Regiment)
BLOODY ELEVENTH (11th Hussars)
Blue Caps (VP branch of Royal Military Police)
Blue Horse (4th/7th Royal Dragoon Guards)
BLUES AND ROYALS (Royal Horse Guards and 1st Dragoons)
Bob's Own (Irish Guards)
Braggs (28th Foot (Gloucestershire Regiment))
Brickdusts (53rd Foot)
BUBBLY JOCKS (Royal Scots Greys)
Buckmaster's Light Infantry (3rd West India Regiment)
Buffs (3rd Foot (Royal East Kent Regiment))
Buttermilks (4th (Royal Irish) Dragoon Guards)
Carbs (3rd Carabineers, 6th Dragoon Guards (Carabineers))
Castle Reeves (55th Foot (Border Regimet))
Castor Oil Dragoons (Royal Army Medical Corps)
Chainy Tenth (10th Royal Hussars)
CHEESEMONGERS (1st Life Guards)
CHERRY-BREECHES (11th Hussars)

CHERRY-PICKERS (11th Hussars)
CHERUBIMS (11th Hussars)
Coldies (Coldstream Guards)
Crossbelts (8th (King's Royal Irish) Hussars)
Dambusters (617 Squadron of RAF)
DEATH-OR-GLORY-BOYS (17th Lancers)
DELHI SPEARMEN (9th (Queen's Royal) Lancers)
DESERT RATS (7th Armoured Division)
DEVIL'S OWN (88th Foot; Inns of Court Rifle Corps of Volunteers)
DIEHARDS (57th Foot)
DIRTY HALF-HUNDRED (50th Foot)
DIRTY SHIRTS (101st Foot)
Docs (46th Foot)
Drogheda Light Horse (18th (Queen Mary's Own) Hussars)
Duke of Wellington's Bodyguard (5th Foot)
Duke's (33rd Foot (Duke of Wellington's Regiment))
Dumpies (19th Hussars)
Earl of Mar's Grey-breeks (21st Foot, Royal Scots Fusiliers)
Elegant Extracts (105th Foot; Royal Fusiliers; 85th Foot)
Eliott's Tailors (15th (The King's) Hussars)
EMPEROR'S CHAMBERMAIDS (14th (King's) Hussars)
Ever Readies (Territorial Army Volunteer Reserve)
Ever-sworded 29th (29th Foot)
Excellers (40th Foot)
Faithful Durhams (68th Foot)
Farmer's Boys (Royal Berkshire Regiment)
FAUGH-A-BALAGHS (Royal Irish Fusiliers (87th Foot))
Few (RAF Fighter Command)
Fighting Fifteenth (15th (The King's) Hussars)
FIGHTING FIFTH (5th Foot)
Fighting Ninth (9th Foot)
Firms (Worcestershire Regiment)

1st Invalids (Welch Regiment)

1st Tangerines (Queen's Royal Regiment)

Fitch's Grenadiers (Royal Ulster Rifles)

Flamers (54th Foot (Dorset Regiment))

Fore and Aft (Gloucestershire Regiment)

Forty-Twas (42nd Foot (Black Watch))

Furst and Wurst (Royal Scots (1st Foot))

Fusil Jocks (Royal Highland Fusiliers)

Galloping Gunners (Royal Horse Artillery)

Galloping Third (3rd (King's Own) Hussars)

Gay Gordons (75th Foot (Gordon Highlanders))

Glasgow Greys (70th Foot (East Surrey Regiment))

Glesca Keelies (Highland Light Infantry)

Green Dragoons (13th Dragoons)

Green Horse (5th (Princess Charlotte of Wales's) Dragoon Guards)

GREEN HOWARDS (19th Foot)

GREEN LINNETS (39th Foot)

Grey Lancers (21st (Empress of India's) Lancers)

Greys (Royal Scots Greys)

Hampshire Tigers (Royal Hampshire Regiment)

HAVERCAKE LADS (33rd Foot (Duke of Wellington's Regiment))

Heavies/Heavy Gunners (Royal Garrison Artillery)

Hindustan Regiment (76th Foot)

HOLY BOYS (9th Foot (Royal Norfolk Regiment))

Horse Doctors (Royal Army Veterinary Corps)

HORSE MARINES (17th (Duke of Cambridge's Own) Lancers)

Howard's Green (South Wales Borderers)

Illustrious Garrison (Somerset Light Infantry)

IMMORTALS (76th Foot (Duke of Wellington's Regiment))

Ink Slingers (Royal Army Pay Corps)

Jaegers (King's Royal Rifle Corps)

Jocks (Scots Guards)

Jollies (Royal Marines)

Kiddies (Scots Guards)

KIRKE'S LAMBS (2nd Foot, Queen's Royal Regiment (West Surrey))

Kokky-Olly Birds (King's Own Scottish Borderers)

Kolis/Koylies (King's Own Yorkshire Light Infantry)

Kosbies (King's Own Scottish Borderers)

LACEDAEMONIANS (46th Foot (Duke of Cornwall's Light Infantry))

Lancashire Lads (Loyal Regiment (47th Foot))

Leather Hats (King's Regiment (8th Foot))

Light Bobs (Oxfordshire and Buckinghamshire Light Infantry)

Lilywhites (13th Hussars; East Lancashire Regiment)

Linseed Lancers (Royal Army Medical Corps)

Lions (King's Own Royal Regiment (4th Foot))

Micks (Irish Guards)

Minden Boys (Lancashire Fusiliers)

Moke Train (Royal Army Service Corps)

MOONRAKERS (62nd Foot (Wiltshire Regiment))

Mounted Micks (4th (Royal Irish) Dragoon Guards)

Mudlarks (Royal Engineers)

Mutton Lancers (2nd Foot, Queen's Royal Regiment (West Surrey))

Nanny-Goats (23rd Foot (Royal Welch Fusiliers))

Neptune's Bodyguard (Royal Marines)

Norfolk Howards (9th Foot (Royal Norfolk Regiment))

Nutcrackers (3rd Foot (Royal East Kent Regiment))

Old Agamemnons (Welch Regiment)

Old and Bold (Royal Northumberland Fusiliers; West Yorkshire Regiment)

Old Bold Fifth (5th Foot)

Old Braggs (28th Foot (Gloucestershire Regiment))

Old Brickdusts (53rd Foot (King's Shropshire Light Infantry))

Old Buffs (3rd Foot (Royal East Kent Regiment))

Old Canaries (3rd (Prince of Wales's) Dragoon Guards)

OLD CONTEMPTIBLES (British Expeditionary Force)

Old Dozen (12th Foot (Suffolk Regiment))

Old Eyes (Grenadier Guards)

OLD FIVE AND THREE PENNIES (53rd Foot (King's Shropshire Light Infantry))

OLD FOGS (Royal Irish Fusiliers (87th Foot))

OLD IMMORTALS (76th Foot (Duke of Wellington's Regiment))

Old Saucy Seventh (7th (Queen's Own) Hussars)

OLD STUBBORNS (Sherwood Foresters)

Orange Lilies (35th Foot)

OXFORD BLUES (Royal Horse Guards)

Paget's Irregular Horse (4th (Queen's Own) Hussars)

Peacemakers (Bedfordshire and Hertfordshire Regiment)

Perthshire Grey Breeks (90th Foot)

POACHERS (Royal Lincolnshire Regiment)

POMPADOURS (56th Foot)

PONTIUS PILATE'S BODYGUARD (Royal Scots)

POPSKI'S PRIVATE ARMY (Long-Range Desert Patrol)

POT-HOOKS (77th Foot)

Poultice Wallopers (Royal Army Medical Corps)

Pump and Tortoise (South Staffordshire Regiment)

QUEEN'S BAYS (2nd Dragoon Guards)

Quill Drivers (Royal Army Pay Corps)

Red Breasts (5th (Royal Irish) Lancers)

Red Caps (provost branch of Royal Military Police)

Red Devils (Special Air Service regiment of British Army)

Red Dragons (Royal Welch Fusiliers)

Red Feathers (46th Foot (Duke of Cornwall's Light Infantry))

Resurrectionists (3rd Foot (Royal East Kent Regiment))

Right of the Line (Royal Horse Artillery)

Rorys (91st Foot (Argyll and Sutherland Highlanders))

Ross-shire Buffs (78th Foot)

ROYALS (Royal Dragoons (1st Dragoons))

Royal Tigers (65th Foot (York and Lancaster Regiment))

RUSTY BUCKLES (2nd Dragoon Guards (Queen's Bays))

Sand Bags (Grenadier Guards)

SANKEY'S HORSE (39th Foot (Dorset Regiment))

Sappers (Royal Engineers)

Saucy Seventh (7th (Queen's Own) Hussars)

Saucy Sixth (6th Foot (Royal Warwickshire Fusiliers))

SCARLET LANCERS (16th (The Queen's) Lancers)

Sea Soldiers (Royal Marines)

Shiners (5th Foot (Northumberland Fusiliers))

Silent Service (submarine service)

Skillingers (6th (Inniskilling) Dragoons)

SKINS (5th Royal Inniskilling Dragoon Guards; 6th (Inniskilling) Dragoons; Royal Inniskilling Fusiliers)

Skull and Crossbones (17th (Duke of Cambridge's Own) Lancers)

SLASHERS (28th Foot (Gloucestershire Regiment))

SNAPPERS (15th Foot (East Yorkshire Regiment))

Springers (62nd Foot (Wiltshire Regiment))

Star of the Line (Worcestershire Regiment)

Steel Backs (1st Northamptonshire Regiment)

Strawboots (7th (Princess Royal's) Dragoon Guards)

Sugar Stick Brigade (Royal Army Ordnance Corps)

Supple Twelfth (12th (Prince of Wales's Royal) Lancers)

SWEEPS (Rifle Brigade)

Taffys (Welsh Guards)

TANGERINES (2nd Foot, Queen's Royal Regiment (West Surrey))

Terriers (Territorial Army)

Thin Red Line (93rd Foot (2nd Battalion (The Argyll and Sutherland Highlanders)))

Three Tens (30th Foot (East Lancashire Regiment))

Tichborne's Own (6th Dragoon Guards (Carabineers))

Tin Bellies (Life Guards)

TINS (Life Guards/Household Cavalry)

Trades Union (1st King's Dragoon Guards)

Twin Roses (York and Lancaster Regiment)

Two Fives (55th Foot (Border Regiment))

Two Fours (44th Foot (Essex regiment))

Two Tens (20th Foot (Lancashire Fusiliers))

Two Twos (22nd Foot (Cheshire Regiment))

Ups and Downs (69th Foot (Welch Regiment))

VEIN-OPENERS (29th Foot (Worcestershire Regiment))

VIRGIN MARY'S BODYGUARD (7th Dragoon Guards)

Warwickshire Lads (Royal Warwickshire Fusiliers)

WAVY NAVY (Royal Naval Volunteer Reserve)

Wild Macraes (72nd Foot (Seaforth Highlanders))

WOLFE'S OWN (47th Foot)

Xs (20th Hussars)

Young Buffs (31st Foot (East Surrey Regiment))

Young Eyes (7th (Queen's Own) Hussars)

Appendix 3

US states

All of the US States have an official nickname, and many have acquired several others since their founding. The stories behind many of the nicknames listed below may be found within the main text of the dictionary. The great majority of them derive either from some natural feature, animal, plant, or industry with which the state is associated (e.g. the GREAT LAKE STATE (Michigan), the COYOTE STATE (South Dakota), the MAGNOLIA STATE (Mississippi), the SILVER STATE (Nevada)) or from some allusion to the early days of the state's history (e.g. the CENTENNIAL STATE (Colorado), the CONSTITUTION STATE (Connecticut), the DARK AND BLOODY GROUND (Kentucky), the OLD COLONY (Massachusetts), the SOONER STATE (Oklahoma)).

Alphabetical list of US State nicknames

Those in small capitals are entries in the dictionary.

ALOHA STATE (Hawaii)
America's Dairyland (Wisconsin)
APACHE STATE (Arizona)
Artesian State (South Dakota)
AUTO STATE (Michigan)
AZTEC STATE (Arizona)
BADGER STATE (Wisconsin)
BATTLE-BORN STATE (Nevada)
BAYOU STATE (Mississippi)
BAY STATE (Massachusetts)
Bear State (Arkansas)
BEAVER STATE (Oregon)
Beef State (Nebraska)
BEEHIVE STATE (Utah)
Big Bend State (Tennessee)
Big Sky Country (Montana)
Blizzard State (South Dakota)
BLUEGRASS STATE (Kentucky)
BLUE HEN STATE (Delaware)
Bread and Butter State (Minnesota)
BUCKEYE STATE (Ohio)
BULLION STATE (Missouri)
Buzzard State (Georgia)
Camellia State (Alabama)
CENTENNIAL STATE (Colorado)

CHINOOK STATE (Washington)
COCKADE STATE (Maryland)
Colorful Colorado (Colorado)
CONSTITUTION STATE (Connecticut)
Copper State (Arizona)
CORNHUSKER STATE (Nebraska)
Corn State (Iowa)
COTTON STATE (Alabama)
Cowboy State (Wyoming)
COYOTE STATE (South Dakota)
CRACKER STATE (Georgia)
Creole State (Louisiana)
DARK AND BLOODY GROUND (Kentucky)
DIAMOND STATE (Delaware)
EMPIRE STATE (New York)
Empire State of the South (Georgia)
EQUALITY STATE (Wyoming)
Everglade State (Florida)
EVERGREEN STATE (Washington)
FIRST STATE (Delaware)
FLICKERTAIL STATE (North Dakota)
FOREIGNER STATE (New Jersey)
FREE STATE (Maryland)
GAMECOCK STATE (South Carolina)
GARDEN STATE (New Jersey)

GEM STATE (Idaho)
GOLDEN STATE (California)
GOOBER STATE (Georgia)
GOPHER STATE (Minnesota)
GRAND CANYON STATE (Arizona)
GRANITE STATE (New Hampshire)
GREAT LAKE STATE (Michigan)
Great Land (Alaska)
GREEN MOUNTAIN STATE (Vermont)
GUINEA PIG STATE (Arkansas)
HAWKEYE STATE (Iowa)
HEART OF DIXIE (Alabama)
HOG AND HOMINY STATE (Tennessee)
HOOSIER STATE (Indiana)
Hot Water State (Arkansas)
Iodine State (South Carolina)
Jayhawker State (Kansas)
JUMBO STATE (Texas)
KEYSTONE STATE (Pennsylvania)
LAND OF ENCHANTMENT (New Mexico)
LAND OF FLOWERS (Florida)
Land of Heart's Desire (New Mexico)
Land of Lincoln (Illinois)
Land of Opportunity (Arkansas)
Land of 10 000 Lakes (Minnesota)
Land of the Midnight Sun (Alaska)
LAND OF THE SAINTS (Utah)
Last Frontier (Alaska)
LITTLE RHODY (Rhode Island)
LONE STAR STATE (Texas)
MAGNOLIA STATE (Mississippi)
Mainland State (Alaska)
Modern Mother of Presidents (Ohio)
MONKEY STATE (Tennessee)
Mormon State (Utah)
MOSQUITO STATE (New Jersey)
MOTHER OF PRESIDENTS (Virginia)
MOTHER OF STATES (Virginia)
MOUNTAIN STATE (West Virginia)
Mount Rushmore State (South Dakota)
Natural State (Arkansas)
NAVEL OF THE NATION (Kansas)
NEW SWEDEN (Delaware)
NORTH STAR STATE (Minnesota)
NUTMEG STATE (Connecticut)
OCEAN STATE (Rhode Island)
OLD COLONY (Massachusetts)
OLD DOMINION (Virginia)

OLD LINE STATE (Maryland)
OLD NORTH STATE (North Carolina)
PALMETTO STATE (South Carolina)
PANHANDLE STATE (West Virginia; Idaho)
PEACE GARDEN STATE (North Dakota)
PEACH STATE (Georgia)
PELICAN STATE (Louisiana)
Peninsula State (Florida)
Pineapple State (Hawaii)
PINE TREE STATE (Maine)
Plantation State (Rhode Island)
PRAIRIE STATE (Illinois)
PUKE STATE (Missouri)
QUAKER STATE (Pennsylvania)
QUEEN STATE (Maryland)
Roughrider State (North Dakota)
SAGEBRUSH STATE (Nevada)
Salt of the Earth (Kansas)
SANDLAPPER STATE (South Carolina)
SHOW ME STATE (Missouri)
SILVER STATE (Nevada)
SIOUX STATE (North Dakota)
Small Wonder (Delaware)
SOONER STATE (Oklahoma)
Sportsman's Paradise (Louisiana)
Spud State (Idaho)
SQUATTER STATE (Kansas)
STUB-TOE STATE (Montana)
SUCKER STATE (Illinois)
Sugar State (Louisiana)
SUNFLOWER STATE (Kansas)
Sunset State (Oregon)
SUNSHINE STATE (Florida; South Dakota; New
    Mexico; California)
Switzerland of America (New Jersey)
TAR HEEL STATE (North Carolina)
TOOTHPICK STATE (Arkansas)
TREASURE STATE (Montana)
Tree Planters State (Indiana; Nebraska)
VALENTINE STATE (Arizona)
VOLUNTEER STATE (Tennessee)
Washoe (Nevada)
Wheat State (Kansas; Minnesota)
WOLVERINE STATE (Michigan)
Wonder State (Arkansas)
Yankee State (Ohio)
YELLOWHAMMER STATE (Alabama)

Appendix 4

United States army: US infantry divisions

America Division (23rd)
Battleaxe (65th)
Big Red One (1st)
Blackhawk (86th)
Black Panther (66th)
Blood and Fire (63rd)
Blue and Gray (29th)
Blue Devil (88th)
Blue Ridge (80th)
Buckeye (37th)
Buffalo (92nd)
Cactus (103rd)
Checkerboard (99th)
Cross of Lorraine (79th)
Custer (85th)
Cyclone (38th)
Deadeye (96th)
Dixie (31st)
Golden Acorn (87th)
Golden Lion (106th)
Hitler's Nemesis (9th)
Indianhead (2nd)
Iroquois (98th)
Ivy Division (4th)
Keystone (28th)

Lightning (78th)
Marne Division (3rd)
Mountaineers (10th)
Old Hickory (30th)
Onaway (76th)
Ozark (102nd)
Pathfinder (8th)
Railsplitters (84th)
Rainbow (42nd)
Red Arrow (32nd)
Red Bull (34th)
Red Diamond (5th)
Rolling W (89th)
Santa Fe (35th)
Statue of Liberty (77th)
Texas (36th)
Tough 'Ombres (90th)
Trailblazer (70th)
Trident (97th)
Tropic Lightning (25th)
Victory (24th)
Wildcat (81st)
Winged Victory (43rd)
Yankee (26th)

General Index

Hank Aaron
➤ Hammerin' Hank

John Adams
➤ The Colossus of Independence
➤ Old Sink or Swim

John Quincy Adams
➤ Old Man Eloquent

Konrad Adenauer
➤ Der Alte

Aeschylus
➤ The Father of Tragedy

James Aitken
➤ John the Painter

St Albertus Magnus
➤ Doctor Universalis
➤ The Universal Doctor

Alexander
➤ The Great

Alexander of Hales
➤ The Irrefragable Doctor

Alfred
➤ The Great

Muhammad Ali
➤ Gaseous Cassius
➤ The Greatest
➤ The Louisville Lip
➤ The Mouth

Ali Hassan al-Majid
➤ Chemical Ali

Ali Mohammed Saeed al-Sahaf
➤ Comical Ali

Idi Amin
➤ Big Daddy

Darren Anderton
➤ Sicknote

Paul Anka
➤ The Golden Boy

Anne
➤ Brandy Nan

➤ Mrs Bull
➤ Mrs Morley

St Thomas Aquinas
➤ The Angelic Doctor
➤ The Dumb Ox

Aristophanes
➤ The Father of Comedy

George Arliss
➤ The First Gentleman of the Screen

Henry Armstrong
➤ Homicide Hank
➤ Hurricane Hank

Louis Armstrong
➤ Dippermouth
➤ Pops
➤ Satchmo

W. W. Armstrong
➤ The Big Ship

Chester Alan Arthur
➤ The Dude President

Roger Ascham
➤ The Father of English Prose

Paddy Ashdown
➤ Paddy Pantsdown

Arthur Askey
➤ Big-Hearted Arthur

Herbert Henry Asquith
➤ Old Squiffy
➤ Squiffy

Ron Atkinson
➤ Big Ron

Attila the Hun
➤ The Scourge of God

Claude Auchinleck
➤ The Auk

Aurelius Antoninus
➤ Caracalla

Gene Autry
➤ The Singing Cowboy

Frankie Avalon
➤ The Golden Boy

Roger Bacon
➤ The Admirable Doctor
➤ Doctor Mirabilis
➤ The Wonderful Doctor

John Baconthorpe
➤ The Resolute Doctor

Robert Baden-Powell
➤ Bathing Towel

Max Baer
➤ The Livermore Larruper

Roberto Baggio
➤ The Divine Ponytail

Trevor Bailey
➤ Barnacle
➤ The Boil

Joan Bakewell
➤ The Thinking Man's Crumpet

Arthur Balfour
➤ Bloody Balfour

John de Baliol
➤ Toom Tabard
➤ Tyne Tabard

Klaus Barbie
➤ The Butcher of Lyons

P. T. Barnum
➤ The Prince of Showmen

John Barrymore
➤ The Great Profile

Bernard Barton
➤ The Quaker Poet

William James Basie
➤ Count

Basil II
➤ Basil the Bulgar-Slayer

Aubrey Beardsley
➤ Awfully Weirdly
➤ Daubaway Weirdsley

Lord Beaverbrook
➤ The Beaver

Franz Beckenbauer
➤ The Kaiser

Boris Becker
➤ Bonking Boris

William Beckford
➤ Fonthill Beckford

David Beckham
➤ Becks
➤ Goldenballs

Victoria Beckham
➤ Posh

St Bede
➤ The Father of English History
➤ The Venerable Bede

Harry Belafonte
➤ The King of (the) Calypso

Hilaire Belloc
➤ The Chesterbelloc

Tony Bennett
➤ The Singer's Singer

Nathaniel Bentley
➤ Dirty Dick

David Berkowitz
➤ Son of Sam

Milton Berle
➤ Mr Television
➤ The Thief of Badgags
➤ Uncle Miltie

Götz von Berlichingen
➤ Iron-hand

St Bernard of Clairvaux
➤ The Mellifluous Doctor

Sarah Bernhardt
➤ The Divine Sarah
➤ Sarah Heartburn

Lawrence Berra
➤ Yogi

Leon Berry
➤ Chu

George Best
➤ El Beatle

William Betty
➤ The Young Roscius

Ernest Bevin
➤ The Dockers' KC

Gilles de Bilde
➤ Bob de Bilde

Larry Bird
➤ Larry Legend

Otto von Bismarck
➤ The Iron Chancellor[1]

Tony Blair
➤ Bambi

Fanny Blankers-Koen
➤ The Flying Dutchwoman

Gebhard Leberecht von Blücher
➤ Marshal Forwards

Humphrey Bogart
➤ Bogie

Anne Boleyn
➤ Anne of the Thousand Days
➤ The Great Whore

Simón Bolívar
➤ The Liberator[2]

Joseph Bonanno
➤ Joe Bananas

Napoleon Bonaparte
➤ Boney
➤ The Corsican Ogre
➤ The Little Corporal
➤ The Man of Destiny
➤ The Violet Corporal

Napoleon Joseph Charles Paul Bonaparte
➤ Plon-Plon

Andrew Bonar Law
➤ The Unknown Prime Minister

St Bonaventura
➤ The Seraphic Doctor

Peter Bonetti
➤ The Cat

William Bonney
➤ Billy the Kid

Björn Borg
➤ The Iceberg[2]

Martin Bormann
➤ The Brown Eminence

James Boswell
➤ Bozzy

Ian Botham
➤ Beefy
➤ Guy the Gorilla

Sandro Botticelli
➤ Botticelli

Boudicca
➤ The Warrior Queen

Clara Bow
➤ The It Girl

Geoffrey Boycott
➤ Boycs
➤ Sir Geoffrey

Charles Boyer
➤ The Great Lover

Robert Boyle
➤ The Father of Chemistry

Lord Brabazon of Tara
➤ Brab

James Braddock
➤ The Cinderella Man

Donald Bradman
➤ The Don
➤ The Little Master

James Buchanan Brady
➤ Diamond Jim

Marlon Brando
➤ Buddy

Eric Bristow
➤ The Crafty Cockney

Gordon Brown
➤ The Iron Chancellor[2]

Lancelot Brown
➤ Capability Brown

Mordecai Brown
➤ Three-Fingered Brown

Jan Bruegel
➤ Velvet Bruegel

Pieter Bruegel the Elder
➤ Peasant Bruegel

Pieter Bruegel the Younger
➤ Hell Bruegel

George Bryan Brummell
➤ Beau Brummell

Ty Cobb
➤ The Georgia Peach

Richard Cobden
➤ The Apostle of Free Trade

William Frederick Cody
➤ Buffalo Bill

Michael Collins
➤ The Big Fellow

Stan Collymore
➤ Stan the Man

John Coltrane
➤ Trane

John Comyn
➤ The Red Comyn

Billy Connolly
➤ The Big Yin

Maureen Connolly
➤ Little Mo

Jimmy Connors
➤ Jimbo

Calvin Coolidge
➤ Silent Cal

Gerry Cooney
➤ The Great White Hope

Henry Cooper
➤ Our 'Enery

James J. Corbett
➤ Gentleman Jim

Gonzalo Fernández de Córdoba
➤ El Gran Capitán

William Cornwallis
➤ Billy Blue
➤ Blue Billy

Noël Coward
➤ The Master[4]

Joan Crawford
➤ The Clothes Horse

Marion Crawford
➤ Crawfie

Tom Cribb
➤ The Black Diamond

James Crichton
➤ The Admirable Crichton

Stafford Cripps
➤ Austerity Cripps

John Crome
➤ Old Crome

Oliver Cromwell
➤ The Almighty Nose
➤ Copper Nose
➤ Crum-Hell
➤ Ironsides
➤ King Oliver
➤ Nosey
➤ Old Noll
➤ Ruby Nose

Richard Cromwell
➤ King Dick
➤ Queen Dick
➤ Tumbledown Dick

Thomas Cromwell
➤ The Hammer of the Monks

Bing Crosby
➤ Der Bingle
➤ Old Groaner

Aleister Crowley
➤ Beast 666
➤ The Wickedest Man in the World

William, Duke of Cumberland
➤ The Bloody Butcher
➤ The Butcher

John Cunningham
➤ Cat's Eyes

George Armstrong Custer
➤ Long Hair
➤ Yellow Hair

Iva Ikuko Toguri D'Aquino
➤ Tokyo Rose

Freddie Davies
➤ Parrotface

William Ralph Dean
➤ Dixie

Democritus
➤ The Laughing Philosopher

Jack Dempsey
➤ The Manassa Mauler

Albert DeSalvo
➤ The Boston Strangler

Henry Despencer
➤ The Fighting Bishop
➤ The Warlike Bishop

Eamon de Valera
➤ The Chief[1]
➤ The Long Fellow[1]

Thomas E. Dewey
➤ The Man on the Wedding Cake

Diana, Princess of Wales
➤ Cheryl
➤ The People's Princess
➤ The Queen of Hearts

Emily Dickinson
➤ The Nun of Amherst

Marlene Dietrich
➤ Dutch[1]

John Dillinger
➤ Public Enemy No. 1

Joe DiMaggio
➤ Joltin' Joe
➤ The Yankee Clipper

Diogenes
➤ The Dog

Benjamin Disraeli
➤ Dizzy

Phyllis Dixey
➤ The One and Only

Tommy Docherty
➤ The Doc

Basil d'Oliveira
➤ Dolly

Engelbert Dollfuss
➤ The Pocket Dictator

Allan Donald
➤ White Lightning

Derek Dougan
➤ The Doog

Lord Alfred Douglas
➤ Bosie

Archibald Douglas
➤ Bell-the-Cat

James Douglas
➤ The Black Douglas

Stephen A. Douglas
➤ The Little Giant

William Douglas
➤ Old Q

Alan Freeman
➤ Fluff

John Charles Frémont
➤ The Pathfinder

Frankie Frisch
➤ The Fordham Flash

Mary Frith
➤ Moll Cutpurse

Elizabeth Fry
➤ The Female Howard

Clark Gable
➤ The King[1]
➤ The King of Hollywood

James A. Garfield
➤ The Dark Horse President

Joel Garner
➤ Big Bird

David Garrick
➤ The English Roscius

Paul Gascoigne
➤ Gazza

Lou Gehrig
➤ Biscuit Pants
➤ The Iron Horse

Geoffrey, Count of Anjou
➤ Plantagenet

George I
➤ The Turnip-Hoer

George III
➤ Farmer George

George IV
➤ Fum the Fourth

George V
➤ Grandpa England
➤ The Sailor King

George, Prince of Denmark
➤ Est-il Possible

George, Prince of Wales
➤ The Adonis of Fifty
➤ The Fat Adonis
➤ The First Gentleman in Europe
➤ Florizel
➤ The Prince of Whales
➤ Prinny

Althea Gibson
➤ Spider

Cass Gilbert
➤ The Father of the Skyscraper

Lester Nelson Gillis
➤ Baby Face Nelson

William Gladstone
➤ GOM
➤ The Grand Old Man[1]

Jackie Gleason
➤ Mr Saturday Night

Oliver Goldsmith
➤ Goldy

Benny Goodman
➤ The King of Swing

Lord Goodman
➤ Two Dinners

Mikhail Gorbachev
➤ Gorby

Charles George Gordon
➤ Chinese Gordon

George, Duke of Gordon
➤ The Cock of the North

John Gotti
➤ The Dapper Don
➤ The Teflon Don

Darren Gough
➤ Dazzler

Betty Grable
➤ The Girl with the Million Dollar Legs
➤ The Legs

W. G. Grace
➤ The Champion
➤ The Grand Old Man[2]
➤ W. G.

George Graham
➤ Stroller

Ulysses S. Grant
➤ The American Caesar
➤ The Butcher
➤ Unconditional Surrender

George Grenville
➤ The Gentle Shepherd

Wayne Gretzky
➤ The Great One

Lady Jane Grey
➤ Nine Days' Queen

D. W. Griffith
➤ The Master[2]

Florence Griffith-Joyner
➤ Flo-Jo

Andrei Gromyko
➤ Grim Grom

Hugh Richard Arthur Grosvenor
➤ Bend Or

Calouste Gulbenkian
➤ Mr Five-Per-Cent

Gustavus Adolphus
➤ The Lion of the North

Nell Gwyn
➤ Nell of Old Drury
➤ Sweet Nell

Marvin Hagler
➤ Marvelous Marvin

William Hague
➤ The Mekon

John Haighton
➤ The Merciless Doctor

Haile Selassie
➤ The Lion of Judah

William Gerald Hamilton
➤ Single-speech Hamilton

Tony Hancock
➤ The Lad ('Imself)

W. C. Handy
➤ The Father of the Blues

Keir Hardie
➤ Queer Hardie

Oliver Hardy
➤ Babe

Jean Harlow
➤ The Blonde Bombshell
➤ The Platinum Blonde

Harold I
➤ Harefoot

Harold II
➤ The Last of the Saxons

Arthur Harris
➤ Bomber Harris

Bob Harris
➤ Whispering Bob

Ron Harris
➤ Chopper

Benjamin Harrison
➤ Grandpa's Grandson

William Henry Harrison
➤ Log-Cabin Harrison
➤ Tippecanoe

Christopher Hatton
➤ The Dancing Chancellor

Coleman Hawkins
➤ Bean
➤ Hawk

Rutherford B. Hayes
➤ Dark Horse President
➤ Fraud

Rita Hayworth
➤ The Love Goddess

Seamus Heaney
➤ Famous Seamus

Thomas Hearns
➤ The Hit Man

Edward Heath
➤ The Grocer

Hugh Hefner
➤ Heff

Ernest Hemingway
➤ Papa

Fletcher Henderson
➤ Smack

John Henley
➤ Orator Henley

Henry I
➤ Beauclerc
➤ The Lion of Justice

Henry I of Germany
➤ The Fowler

Henry II
➤ Curtmantle

Henry V
➤ The English Alexander

Henry VI
➤ The Martyr King

Henry VIII
➤ Bluff King Hal

Heraclitus
➤ The Weeping Philosopher

Hereward
➤ The Wake

Herodotus
➤ The Father of History
➤ The Father of Lies

John Hervey
➤ Lord Fanny

Michael Heseltine
➤ Hezza
➤ Tarzan

Rudolf Hess
➤ The Prisoner of Spandau

Reinhard Heydrich
➤ The Hangman of Europe

Herbie Hide
➤ The Dancing Destroyer

Alex Higgins
➤ Hurricane

Stephen Higginson
➤ The Man of Ross

Earl Hines
➤ Fatha

Hippocrates
➤ The Father of Medicine

Alfred Hitchcock
➤ Hitch
➤ The Master of Suspense

Jack Hobbs
➤ The Master[3]

James Hogg
➤ The Ettrick Shepherd

Michael Holding
➤ Whispering Death

Billie Holiday
➤ Lady Day

Herbert Hoover
➤ The Chief[2]

Rogers Hornsby
➤ The Rajah

Harry Houdini
➤ The Handcuff King

John Howard
➤ Jockey of Norfolk

Geoffrey Howe
➤ Mogadon Man

Richard, Earl Howe
➤ Black Dick

George Hudson
➤ The Railway King

Emlyn Hughes
➤ Crazy Horse

Mark Hughes
➤ Sparky

Humphrey, Duke of Gloucester
➤ Good Duke Humphrey

Henry Hunt
➤ Orator Hunt

James Hunt
➤ Hunt the Shunt

Norman Hunter
➤ Bites Yer Legs

Barbara Hutton
➤ The Poor Little Rich Girl

Hypatia
➤ The Divine Pagan

Dolores Ibarruri
➤ La Pasionaria

Miguel Indurain
➤ Singing Indurain

William Ralph Inge
➤ The Gloomy Dean

Isabella of France
➤ The She-Wolf of France

Jack the Ripper
➤ Jack the Ripper

Andrew Jackson
➤ King Andrew the First
➤ Old Hickory
➤ Sir Veto

Joe Jackson
➤ Shoeless Joe

John Jackson
➤ The Emperor of Pugilism
➤ Gentleman Jackson

Donald Neilson
➤ The Black Panther[1]

Michel Ney
➤ The Bravest of the Brave
➤ Le Rougeaud

Jack Nicklaus
➤ The Golden Bear

Florence Nightingale
➤ The Lady of the Lamp

Richard Nixon
➤ Tricky Dick

Greg Norman
➤ The Great White Shark
➤ The White Shark

Jessye Norman
➤ Jessyenormous

Steven Norris
➤ Shagger Norris

Paavo Nurmi
➤ The Flying Finn

Annie Oakley
➤ Little Sure-Shot

Richard Oastler
➤ The Factory King

William of Occam
➤ The Invincible Doctor

Daniel O'Connell
➤ The Liberator[1]

Ernst Ocwirk
➤ Clockwork Ocwirk

Martin Offiah
➤ Chariots

Chris Old
➤ Chilly

Laurence Olivier
➤ Larry

Jacqueline Onassis
➤ Jackie O

Shaquille O'Neal
➤ Shaq

Julius Robert Oppenheimer
➤ The Father of the Atomic Bomb

Roy Orbison
➤ Big O

Tessie O'Shea
➤ Two-Ton Tessie

David Owen
➤ Dr Death[1]

Henry William Paget
➤ One-Leg Paget

Lord Palmerston
➤ Lord Cupid
➤ Pam

Silvana Pampanini
➤ The Anatomic Bomb

Charlie Parker
➤ Bird
➤ Yardbird

Matthew Parker
➤ Nosey Parker

Robert Leroy Parker
➤ Butch Cassidy

Charles Stewart Parnell
➤ The Uncrowned King of Ireland

John Parry
➤ The Blind Harper

George Patton
➤ Blood and Guts
➤ Two-Gun Patton

Jeremy Paxman
➤ Paxo

Walter Payton
➤ Sweetness

Stuart Pearce
➤ Psycho

Robert Peel
➤ Orange Peel
➤ The Runaway Spartan

Pelé
➤ The Black Pearl

Henry Percy
➤ Hotspur

Eva Perón
➤ Evita

Antoinette Perry
➤ Tony

William Perry
➤ The Refrigerator

John Pershing
➤ Black Jack[2]

Peter I of Russia
➤ The Great

Michele Pezza
➤ Fra Diavolo

Philip, Duke of Edinburgh
➤ Keith
➤ Phil the Greek

Mark Philippoussis
➤ The Scud

Ambrose Philips
➤ Namby-Pamby

Edith Piaf
➤ Little Sparrow

Mary Pickford
➤ America's Sweetheart
➤ The World's Sweetheart

Thomas Pitt
➤ Diamond Pitt

William Pitt the Elder
➤ The Great Commoner

William Pitt the Younger
➤ The Bottomless Pitt

James K. Polk
➤ The First Dark Horse
➤ Young Hickory

Jackson Pollock
➤ Jack the Dripper

Alexander Pope
➤ The Bard of Twickenham
➤ The Wasp of Twickenham

Dudley Pound
➤ Phoney Quid

John Prescott
➤ Prezza
➤ Thumper
➤ Two Jags

Elvis Presley
➤ Elvis the Pelvis
➤ The King[2]

J. B. Priestley
➤ Jolly Jack

Prince
➤ His Royal Badness

Mark Waugh
➤ Afghan

Steve Waugh
➤ Tugga

John Wayne
➤ Duke[2]

Daniel Webster
➤ Godlike Daniel

**Arthur Wellesley, Duke
of Wellington**
➤ The Achilles of England
➤ Conky
➤ The Iron Duke
➤ Old Conky
➤ Old Nosey

Thomas Wentworth
➤ Black Tom

Barry White
➤ The Walrus of Love

Jimmy White
➤ The Whirlwind

George Whitefield
➤ Dr Squintum

Paul Whiteman
➤ The King of Jazz
➤ Pops

**John Greenleaf
Whittier**
➤ The Quaker Poet

Ann Widdecombe
➤ Doris Karloff

Samuel Wilberforce
➤ Soapy Sam

Wilhelm II
➤ Kaiser Bill

Ray Wilkins
➤ The Crab

Ellen Wilkinson
➤ Red Ellen

Jess Willard
➤ The Great White Hope

David Willetts
➤ Two Brains

**William Frederick, Duke
of Gloucester**
➤ Silly Billy

William I
➤ The Bastard
➤ The Conqueror

William I of Orange
➤ William the Silent

William I of Scotland
➤ The Lion[1]

William II
➤ Rufus

William IV
➤ The Sailor King
➤ Silly Billy

William of Orange
➤ Dutch Billy
➤ The Great Deliverer
➤ King Billy

Esther Williams
➤ Hollywood's Mermaid

Marcia Williams
➤ Lady Forkbender

Ted Williams
➤ The Splendid Splinter
➤ Teddy Ballgame

Harold Wilson
➤ Wislon

Woodrow Wilson
➤ The Phrasemaker
➤ The Professor[1]

Henry Wood
➤ Old Timber

Alexander Woollcott
➤ The Butcher of
Broadway

Monty Woolley
➤ The Beard

Dave Wottle
➤ Wottle the Throttle

Harry Wragg
➤ The Head Waiter

St Francis Xavier
➤ The Apostle
of the Indies

Lev Yashin
➤ The Black Octopus

Jess Yates
➤ The Bishop

Miruts Yifter
➤ Yifter the Shifter

Lester Young
➤ The President
➤ Prez

Emil Zatopek
➤ The Iron Man

Zinedine Zidane
➤ Zizou

Thematic Index

Art

Baseball

Boxing

Football clubs

Literature

Military

Miscellaneous

....

Politics

Rulers and Royalty

Science and technology

Sport

See also **Baseball, Boxing, Cricket, Football, Tennis**

Television and radio

Tennis

Wild West

Oxford Paperback Reference

A Dictionary of Psychology
Andrew M. Colman

Over 10,500 authoritative entries make up the most wide-ranging
dictionary of psychology available.

'impressive ... certainly to be recommended'
Times Higher Educational Supplement

'Comprehensive, sound, readable, and up-to-date, this is probably the
best single-volume dictionary of its kind.'
Library Journal

A Dictionary of Economics
John Black

Fully up-to-date and jargon-free coverage of economics. Over 2,500
terms on all aspects of economic theory and practice.

A Dictionary of Law

An ideal source of legal terminology for systems based on English law.
Over 4,000 clear and concise entries.

'The entries are clearly drafted and succinctly written ... Precision for the
professional is combined with a layman's enlightenment.'
Times Literary Supplement

OXFORD